Ireland and Scotland in the Nineteenth Century

In this series

1 'Fearful Realities': New Perspectives on the Famine, edited by Chris Morash and Richard Hayes (1996).

2 Gender Perspectives in Nineteenth-Century Ireland: Public and Private Spheres, edited by Margaret Kelleher and James H. Murphy (1997).

3 Ideology and Ireland in the Nineteenth Century, edited by Tadhg Foley and Seán Ryder (1998).

4 Ireland in the Nineteenth Century: Regional Identity, edited by Leon Litvack and Glenn Hooper (2000).

5 Rebellion and Remembrance in Modern Ireland, edited by Laurence M. Geary (2001).

6 Ireland Abroad: Politics and Professions in the Nineteenth Century, edited by Oonagh Walsh (2003).

7 The Irish Revival Reappraised, edited by Betsy Taylor FitzSimon and James H. Murphy (2004).

8 Victoria's Ireland? Irishness and Britishness, 1837–1901, edited by Peter Gray.

9 Evangelicals and Catholics in Nineteenth-Century Ireland, edited by James H. Murphy (2005).

10 Ireland and Europe in the Nineteenth Century, edited by Leon Litvack and Colin Graham.

11 Land and Landscape in Nineteenth-Century Ireland, edited by Úna Ní Bhroiméil and Glenn Hooper.

12 Ireland and Scotland in the Nineteenth Century, edited by Frank Ferguson and James McConnel.

Ireland and Scotland in the Nineteenth Century

Frank Ferguson & James McConnel

EDITORS

FOUR COURTS PRESS

Set in 10 on 12.5 point Bembo for
FOUR COURTS PRESS LTD
7 Malpas Street, Dublin 8, Ireland
e-mail: info@fourcourtspress.ie
and in North America for
FOUR COURTS PRESS
c/o ISBS, 920 N.E. 58th Avenue, Suite 300, Portland, OR 97213.

A catalogue record for this title
is available from the British Library.

ISBN 978–1–84682–150–9

Printed in England
by Athenaeum Press, Gateshead, Tyne & Wear.

Contents

James McConnel & Frank Ferguson
Introduction   7

Kevin James
'In no degree inferior': Scotland and 'tourist development' in
late-Victorian Ireland   11

Clare M. Norcio
Societies and seminaries: technological exchange in Ulster agriculture   23

S. Karly Kehoe
Irish migrants and the recruitment of Catholic Sisters in Glasgow,
1847–1878   35

Andrew R. Holmes
Irish Presbyterian commemorations of their Scottish past, *c.*1830–1914   48

Frank Ferguson
'The third character': the articulation of Scottish identities in two
Irish writers   62

Patrick Maume
From Scotland's storied land: William McComb and Scots-Irish
Presbyterian identity   76

Peter Gray
Thomas Chalmers and Irish poverty   93

Matthew Potter
The urban local state in Scotland and Ireland to 1900: parallels and
contrasts   108

Susan Kelly
Tuberculosis cures used in Ireland, 1700–1950   119

Richard B. McCready
St Patrick's Day in Dundee, *c.*1850–1900: a contested Irish institution
in a Scottish context   134

Amy O'Reilly
'All Irishmen of good character': the Hibernian Society of Glasgow,
1792–1824   147

Máirtín Ó Catháin
Michael Collins and Scotland   160

Notes on contributors   177

Index   179

Introduction

JAMES McCONNEL & FRANK FERGUSON

Almost as soon as Sir Walter Scott set foot on the Glasgow–Belfast steamer in August 1825, he was plunged into the 'heart of the debatable land' by the actions of one of his fellow passengers. Having already loudly damned Popery, this Orange 'squireen' cajoled the other passengers into toasting the 'glorious memory' of, first, William of Orange, and then Oliver Cromwell. Given that the Orange Order had been proscribed only six months earlier (under the Unlawful Societies Act), Scott was one of several travellers who 'winced' at such a public demonstration of Irish loyalism and he managed to evade the second toast by a convenient fit of coughing.[1] Nor was this Scott's only encounter with militant Irish Protestantism during his 1825 tour: in Cork he met a 'savage old mine host of an Orange-man' who recounted the killing of 'papist dogs' at the so-called 'battle of Skibbereen' in 1823 as if it had been 'the natest thing the world'.[2]

Despite his romanticization of the '45, Scott was no Jacobite. In his twenties he had been bound over to keep the peace following a fistfight with anti-royalist Irish students and he was a committed supporter of the House of Hanover throughout his life.[3] And, like successive Hanoverian kings, he was publicly opposed to Catholic emancipation until the 1820s and privately remained convinced that another fifty years of vigorous penal legislation would have effectively 'extinguished' 'Popery' in Ireland.[4] Notwithstanding all this, he apparently found little in common with the ultra-loyalists he encountered on his tour of the island, regarding them instead as either socially disreputable or comically bloodthirsty.

Scott's experiences highlight not simply the nuances of Scottish and Irish loyalism; they also belie the cosy roseat glow of pan-Celticism which later coloured his reputation on both sides of the North Channel. Indeed, in the broader sense, they illustrate the fact that the relationship between the inhabitants of Ireland and Scotland could at times be fissile and fractious. While this book is not simply about varieties of Hiberno-Scottish tension, dissonance is one of the central themes to emerge from this collection. In this respect it echoes other recent explorations of the uneasy relationships between Scotland and Ireland in the nineteenth century.[5]

1 John Gibson Lockhart, *Memoirs of the life of Sir Walter Scott, Bart* (7 vols, Edinburgh & London, 1837), vi, 45–7. 2 H.J.C. Grierson, *The letters of Sir Walter Scott, 1825–1826* (12 vols, London, 1935), ix, 211. For the battle itself see *Morning Chronicle*, 8 July 1823. 3 David Hewitt, 'Scott, Sir Walter (1771–1832)', *Oxford dictionary of national biography*, Oxford University Press, Sept. 2004; online edn, Jan. 2008 [www.oxforddnb.com/view/article/24928, accessed 9 May 2008]. 4 John Gibson Lockhart, *Life of Sir Walter Scott, Bart* (Edinburgh, 1853), p. 201; idem, *Memoirs of the late Sir Walter Scott* (Edinburgh, 1845), p. 563. 5 David Duff & Catherine Jones (eds), *Scotland, Ireland, and the Romantic Aesthetic* (Cranbury, NJ, 2007).

The essays by Kevin James, Clare Norcio and Karly Kehoe, which open this collection, examine Irish-Scottish relationships which are characterized as much by jealousy, prejudice and alarm as cultural affinity or even Anglophobia. James' chapter explores how Victorian Irish tourist promoters both resented Scotland (patronized as it was by Scott's pen and Victoria's castles) and also saw it as a model to be emulated. His discussion casts new light on Dublin Castle's so-called 'killing home rule with kindness' strategy of the closing decades of the nineteenth century by shifting attention away from the traditional arenas of high politics and congested districts and instead placing greater emphasis on recognizably modern forms of economic activity. Constructive unionists sought to appropriate Irish tourism in defence of the Union since Irish commentators were persuaded that tourism had helped to pacify Scotland. Yet, as James shows, by marketing Ireland on the basis of its relative 'unspoiltness', promoters necessarily also drew attention to the island's limited progress since the Anglo-Irish Union.

Unflattering comparisons between the two countries are also considered in Clare Norcio's study of pre-Famine agricultural patterns in Ulster. Based on a close reading of the Ordnance Survey memoirs from the 1830s, she shows how the surveyors' observations and judgments of the modernity of Protestant farming techniques – relative to their Catholic neighbours – were often inflected, on the one hand, with racialized notions of the Scottish and Irish and on the other with a blindness to the imbalances of successive seventeenth-century land settlements.

Such perceptions were, as Karly Kehoe shows, by no means restricted to those who saw Scotland as a Protestant nation. Even within the Catholic church in Scotland there were deeply-held fears that the large numbers of Irish migrants might subvert its 'Scottish' character and jeopardize its project to be accepted as loyal, conservative and respectable. Kehoe examines how the church sought to cap the number of Irish-born nuns and restrict their promotion opportunities in order to arrest creeping Hibernicization.

It would be unfair to claim that the relationships of Scotland and Ireland were exclusively built on tension and disharmony. In the long history of migrations between the two landmasses the development of Presbyterianism in Ireland has been one of the most profound, if complicated, expressions of Scotland crossing the water. The nineteenth century in particular witnessed enormous changes within the family of Irish Presbyterian church government, organization and cultural expression and these developments (and their implications for Scotland) are charted in a series of essays in this collection.

Andrew Holmes' essay explores Irish Presbyterians' commemorations of their Scottish past from the period 1830 until 1914. His reasons for this are threefold. Irish Presbyterians' choices of events to memorialize distinguish key elements of their religious and ideological linkages to Scotland. It demonstrates also what Holmes argues are important features in the development of an Ulster-Scots identity within the

North of Ireland in the nineteenth century, a cultural construction that has found new popular expression in the present decade in Northern Ireland in the light of the Good Friday Agreement. Holmes' conclusion that this illustrates significant linkages and strong mutual dependence between the churches in the nineteenth century in Ireland and Scotland articulates the transnational sense that many Irish Presbyterians felt at this time.

The complex nature of the Ulster-Scottish cultural expression of northern Presbyterians is explored in Frank Ferguson's discussion of two Co. Antrim poets William Hamilton Drummond and Samuel Thomson. This seeks to complicate our understanding of Ulster poetry in the period after the United Irish rebellion and specifically the verse of writers who were implicated, if not involved, in the '98. Both poets adopt strategies of retreat from their radical personae of the 1790s that invokes a new dialogue with Scottish literature and culture. In Drummond's case his work functions as an intriguing development of Irish responses to James Macpherson's pillaging of medieval bardic verse in his Ossianic poetry. Drummond's *The Giant's Causeway* (1811) projects numerous negative characteristics associated with rebellion and violence onto Scotland's mythic heroes and seeks to write a new form of Irish patriotic epic. Samuel Thomson's articulation of his Irish and Scottish identity is explored through his use of Scot's vernacular language and verse forms. This verse, often denigrated as mere imitation of Burns, is in fact a carefully coded language that permits Thomson to manage his allegiances to Ireland and Britain and distance himself from previous radical incarnations. Both he and Drummond articulate a variety of responses to the concept of union and demonstrate the complicated nature of Ulster-Scottish identity in this period.

Patrick Maume's essay on William McComb recounts the literary career of one who was regarded by his peers as the 'laureate of Presbyterianism'. McComb's roles as a poet, compiler, bookseller and publisher in the service of orthodox Irish Presbyterianism make him one of the most important lay members of the denomination in the nineteenth century. Maume charts the significance of the Scottish Reformation on McComb's work and theology traced through a number of his publications. However, Maume offers an important caveat to the discussion on Irish Presbyterian linkages to Scotland. He argues that for all the significance that Scotland holds in the affections of Irish Presbyterians, their sense of worldwide mission and international alliance with other Presbyterian churches must be seen as a global phenomenon rather than merely part of a tie between two countries in the British archipelago.

The exploration of Irish Presbyterianism underscores this collection's determination to compare the nature of institutional structures (political, ecclesiastical and cultural) within the nation states of Ireland and Scotland. This is a theme that is developed by Peter Gray in his analysis of Thomas Chalmers' role in the debates surrounding poor law provision for Ireland. Chalmers, the leading Scottish Presbyterian evangelical clergyman of his generation, argued that a Scottish-style parochial system be adopted based on moralistic voluntarism in which poor relief was offered only to those incapable of providing for themselves. Despite gaining support in Ireland from a diverse swathe of opinion formers, for example Daniel O'Connell and Henry Cooke, an English system, driven by central government, was ultimately introduced. Gray's essay demonstrates that crucial differences existed between Ireland and Scotland in this period evidenced by state provision in welfare reform and attitudes regarding welfare and development.

In a broad analytical sweep from the medieval period to the present day, Matthew Potter examines the convergence and divergence of local government institutions within Scotland and Ireland. He perceives the nineteenth century as the period in which Scotland and Ireland began to differ most markedly in their system of local government. Unlike Scotland, where the work of government was devolved to a number of powerful local bodies, Ireland due to its very different political climate tended towards a highly centralized form of governance and service provision.

In a similar way to Potter, Susan Kelly approaches her comparison of Irish and Scottish TB folk cures over a longer time-frame. Although tuberculosis was endemic in both countries, Kelly explores how ordinary people in these two societies responded to the disease in the era before modern pharmaceutical intervention.

The final group of essays provide sidelights on three very different Irish experiences of Scotland. The well-known confrontations of Orange and Green are revisited in the less familiar context of mid-Victorian Dundee by Richard McCready. Dundee witnessed ethnic fractures not only within the Catholic community (along similar lines to those discussed in Kehoe's chapter), but also between Scottish Catholics and Irish nationalists in Scotland. McCready looks at how celebration of St Patrick's Day became highly politicized in the context of an urban landscape contested by a local Orange tradition which existing histories of the Order in Scotland have overlooked.

Commenting on Irish migrants and sectarian violence in the 1830s, one Scottish observer remarked that 'the well behaved of either sort always get out of the way'. Amy O'Reilly's essay explores the place of this 'better sort' within Glasgow's world of clubs, societies and fraternities and argues that there was, albeit briefly, a space in which Irish Protestants and Catholics co-operated. Unlike the Orange and Ribbon societies, the city's Hibernian Society stipulated only that prospective member should be 'Irish' – by birth, descent, residency or even association. By focusing on the mundane business of associational life, O'Reilly draws attention to an articulation of Irish-Scottish identity quieter than the bellicose Orange and Green demonstrations which competed with and ultimately outlived it.

Máirtín Ó Catháin's concluding essay deals neither with ethnic hostility nor fraternalism, but rather indifference. Michael Collins only visited Scotland once during his life and showed little interest in the 'Scottish Brigade' or in militant Scottish nationalists eager for an Irish piggyback. Intriguingly, while Ó Catháin examines the disputes between Collins and the Scottish IRA in great detail, he also hints that the relationship was soured by the former's Anglocentrism and the latter's Anglophobia.

'In no degree inferior': Scotland and 'tourist development' in late-Victorian Ireland

KEVIN JAMES

In the last decades of the nineteenth century, many state agencies and business groups championed tourism as an engine of Irish economic development. Railway companies, local and national tourist development bodies and the state, acting in collaboration and sometimes in competition with each other, aimed to create a modern mass-tourist infrastructure which would provide efficient transportation and comfortable accommodation to British and overseas visitors to Ireland. As they fashioned the public image of an enchanting 'Emerald Isle' offering dramatic landscapes and a legion of sporting pursuits, Scotland's achievements came under close scrutiny. Fashionable tourist destinations such as the Scottish Highlands appeared to some Irish observers as emblematic of Caledonia's rural prosperity and civil peace. Extensive and systematic comparisons of rural Scotland and Ireland as holiday sites were structured around putative similarities between their mountainous western landscapes, wind-swept islands and shimmering streams, and also around apparent contrasts between Scotland's highly-developed tourist sector and the shaky infrastructure and poor reputation that bedevilled Irish tourism. These assessments were underpinned by wider, often implicit comparative evaluations of political and social conditions, as well as economic 'progress', in the two countries. Exploring the positioning of Scotland within Irish tourist development discourses highlights its influence over Irish tourist programmes. It also situates the sector outside the Anglo-Irish and trans-Atlantic frameworks within which patterns of Irish cultural, social and political exchange are most frequently analyzed.

Tourism has become a central focus of historical research as scholars explore representations of national heritage, points of interaction between cultures and the development of a major sector in modern economies.[1] Although the historical development of the rural tourist sector in Ireland has only recently become a focus of scholarly inquiry,[2] extensive research on Scottish tourism offers valuable perspectives

1 John Urry, *The tourist gaze* (2nd edn, London, 2002); Brian Graham, G.J. Ashworth & J.E. Tunbridge, *A geography of heritage; power, culture & economy* (London, 2000); David T. Herbert (ed.), *Heritage, tourism and society* (London, 1995). 2 Irene Furlong, 'Frederick W. Crossley: Irish turn-of-the-century tourism pioneer', *Irish History: A Research Yearbook*, 2 (2003), pp

on another member country of the United Kingdom which historically played a key role in discussions of the Irish sector. Indeed, Scotland featured prominently as a comparator in contemporary evaluations of Ireland's prospects – evaluations which expressed contested views of the countries' conditions under the Union, and on the relationship between tourism, economic development and political peace.

Tourist development in Ireland was premised on 'opening' rural districts to tourists. Frequently subsumed under the wider rubric of 'constructive unionism',[3] opponents of home rule promoted it as a programme which would allow Ireland to develop its infrastructure, advance rural prosperity and attract tourists from Britain. In their advocacy of a range of initiatives, from the improvement of tourist accommodation to passenger steamer services, they made explicit reference to the Scottish Highlands, which had became a focus of extensive tourism in the nineteenth century.[4] There, rural landscapes, 'customs' and inhabitants were promoted as components of the national 'soul' by those who encouraged tourists to visit the district.[5] Tourists to Ireland were also promised glimpses into the 'last bastions' of a Celtic society that had not yet been diluted or reconstructed through processes of modernization. Rural Ireland, especially districts of the country's West, functioned for many

162–76; I. Furlong, 'Tourism and the Irish state in the 1950s', in Dermot Keogh, Finbarr O'Shea & Carmel Quinlan (eds), *The lost decade. Ireland in the 1950s* (Cork, 2004), pp 164–86; Glenn Hooper, *Travel writing and Ireland, 1760–1860: culture, history, politics* (Basingstoke, 2005); G. Hooper, 'The Isles/Ireland: the wilder shore', in Peter Hulme & Tim Youngs (eds), *The Cambridge companion to travel writing* (Cambridge, 2002), pp 174–90; G. Hooper (ed.), *The tourist's gaze: travellers to Ireland, 1800–2000* (Cork, 2001); Eric G.E. Zuelow, '"Ingredients for cooperation": Irish tourism in North-South relations, 1924–1998', *New Hibernia Review*, 10:1 (2006), 17–39; E. Zuelow, 'The tourism nexus: national identity and the meanings of tourism since the Irish Civil War', in Mark McCarthy (ed.), *Ireland's heritages: critical perspectives on memory and identity* (Aldershot, 2005), pp 189–204; E. Zuelow, 'Enshrining Ireland's nationalist history inside prison walls: the restoration of Kilmainham Jail', *Éire-Ireland*, 39:3&4 (2004), 180–201. **3** See Andrew Gailey, *Ireland and the death of kindness: the experience of constructive unionism, 1890–1905* (Cork, 1987). **4** Julie Rak, 'The improving eye: eighteenth-century picturesque travel and agricultural change in the Scottish Highlands', in Julie Candler Hayes & Timothy Erwin (eds), *Studies in Eighteenth-Century Culture*, 27 (Baltimore, 1998), 43–64; Christopher Smout, 'Tours in the Scottish Highlands from the eighteenth to the twentieth centuries', *Northern Scotland*, 5:2 (1983), 99–121; Alastair J. Durie, *Scotland for the holidays: a history of tourism in Scotland, 1780–1939* (East Linton, 2003); Katherine Haldane Grenier, *Tourism and identity in Scotland, 1770–1914: creating Caledonia* (Aldershot, 2005) and Katherine J. Haldane, '"No human foot comes here": Victorian tourists and the Isle of Skye', *Nineteenth Century Studies*, 10 (1996), 69–91. **5** Charles Withers, 'The historical creation of the Scottish Highlands', in Ian Donnachie & Christopher Whatley (eds), *The manufacture of Scottish history* (Edinburgh, 1992), pp 143–56; John R. Gold & Margaret M. Gold, *Imagining Scotland: tradition, representation and promotion in Scottish tourism since 1750* (Aldershot, 1995); R.W. Butler, 'Evolution of tourism in the Scottish Highlands', *Annals of Tourism Research*, 12:3 (1985), 371–91; Mairi MacArthur, '"Blasted heaths and hills of mist": the Highlands and Islands through travellers' eyes', *Scottish Affairs*, 3 (Spring 1993), 23–31.

late nineteenth- and early twentieth-century observers as a repository of this culture, and was the subject of intense political contest. In advocating the opening of the West to tourism, tourist development advocates pointed to the success of other smaller countries, such as Norway – until 1905 in a personal union of crowns with Sweden – and the independent state of Switzerland. Successful tourist sectors in these places were seen as harbingers for Ireland, whose scenery was regarded as no less appealing to the tourist. Norway's dramatic fjords were often compared with the landscapes of Ireland's western seaboard.[6] And Switzerland's hotels were identified as models for the Irish sector, the standards of which were judged to be inferior to those of the small Alpine state.[7] Indeed, as Switzerland became a favoured holiday destination, promoters of the Irish tourist sector elaborated a framework within which the attractions of Ireland could be highlighted to Britons through references to this fashionable, but distant, country.[8] As *The Times* reported in 1905:

> During a long course of years one of the perennial grievances of Ireland was the neglect by the British travelling public of the picturesque scenery of the sister island. The complaint was not without justification five-and-twenty or thirty years ago, and even at the present time thousands of English people who are more familiar with the Scottish Highlands and the Snowdon district of North Wales than with their own Lake Country have never crossed St George's Channel, or, at the best, have a very slight and casual acquaintance with Killarney and Connemara, far less intimate than that which they possess of Switzerland and the Tyrol. This has been due to a combination of causes, in which political disturbances, though these did not affect tourists to any appreciable degree, were a powerful factor. The inferior character of Irish hotels and inns of every class, except in a few well-known centres, was, perhaps, the greatest drawback in those days to travelling in Ireland, while the railway service did not keep pace with the improvement which had begun earlier in the cross-channel steamers.[9]

With landscapes that equalled the magnificent scenery of more popular destinations, and with the advantage of its proximity to Britain, Ireland's promoters believed that they could lure the British holiday-maker to the Emerald Isle. They were encouraged by people such as Morton P. Betts of Bristol, whose letter was reprinted in the pages of the *Irish Cyclist*:

6 See, for example, *Cook's Traveller's Gazette*, 22 Apr. 1911.   **7** See, for instance, [*The*] *I[rish] T[ourist]*, 4, 7 (Oct. 1897).   **8** For an excellent discussion of British tourists in Switzerland, see Laurent Tissot, 'How did the British conquer Switzerland? Guidebooks, railways, travel agencies, 1850–1914', *Journal of Transport History*, 16:1 (1995), 21–54 and *Naissance d'une industrie touristique: les Anglais et la Suisse au XIXᵉ siècle* (Lausanne, 2000). For a useful comparison of discourses of rural life in Ireland and Norway, see Ulrike Spring, 'Imagining the Irish and Norwegian peasantry around 1900: between representation and re-presentation', *Historisk Tidsskrift*, 80:1 (2001), 75–99.   **9** *The Times*, 14 Aug. 1905.

> Three friends are thinking of spending a short vacation with me in
> Switzerland this summer, but if you can kindly put me in the way of obtaining
> the necessary information as to route and approximate cost for a fortnight's
> tour or stay in the south of Ireland I shall certainly bring it before them.[10]

In the pages of many English, Scottish and Irish tourist periodicals prospective visitors queried the costs of travel and standards of tourist amenities in Ireland, asking if
they compared favourably with those found on the Continent and in Scotland, Wales
and England. The frequency with which Scotland was invoked in these discussions
was remarkable – as was the degree to which it was mobilized to market Ireland's
comparatively hidden charms. Allusions to Scotland's successful tourist sector had
particular value to advocates of the Union: to them, the stable, prosperous 'sister'
kingdom illustrated their aspirations for Ireland within the United Kingdom. Even
in marketing the attractions of Ireland, guidebooks built frameworks of trans-national
comparison within which tourists were invited to fix their gaze on complementary
sites in the sister kingdoms. Railway companies offered tours to Scottish and Irish
sites, encompassing the two countries in integrated travel itineraries such as six
'Combined Scotch and Irish' tours offered by Thomas Cook and Son in 1901, most
of which focused on the western coasts of both countries.[11] These tours also
contributed to an ongoing construction of rural Ireland in the popular tourist imagination through which the qualities of Irish landscapes, rural recreational pursuits and
tourist amenities were evaluated with reference to those in Scotland.

If Scotland's lucrative tourist trade inspired Ireland's tourist development champions,
it also positioned the Scottish Highlands as rural Ireland's key 'competitor'. Speaking
in Dublin in April 1895 to a meeting of parties interested in furthering Irish tourist
development, the lord lieutenant, Lord Houghton, proposed to 'institute a comparison which would be invidious to the sister kingdom of Scotland'.[12] Pointedly asking
'What advantage has Scotland as an attraction to travellers?', Houghton pithily cited
Scots' penchant for self-promotion, and enumerated other factors: the influence of
Sir Walter Scott; precedence over Ireland among 'those who like to follow the train
of fashion'; and proximity to lucrative tourist markets. Yet he asserted that a tour in
Ireland repaid the lengthier journey with landscapes rivalling those of the sister
kingdom: 'Ireland can show scenery which both in grandeur and of a softer beauty
can bear comparison to any in Scotland, and which is, in historical interest and association, in no degree inferior.'[13]

Despite Houghton's assertion, many comparative evaluations of the Scottish and
Irish tourist sectors offered unfavourable assessments of Ireland's infrastructure, and

10 *Irish Cyclist*, 25 Apr. 1900.   11 *Specimens of Cook's independent tours in England, Scotland and Ireland, season 1901* (London, c. 1901), pp 33–6.   12 *IT*, 2, 1 ('New Series', 1895).   13 *IT*, 2:1 ('New Series', 1895).

linked relatively modest levels of tourist traffic there to anxieties surrounding civil unrest. In Houghton's view, the standard of tourist amenities in Scotland served as a barometer of relative under-development in the Irish sector. It also signalled possibilities for Irish prosperity under carefully-stewarded tourist development programmes. He wrote in 1895 that:

> It is to be hoped that before many years have passed, hotels of various grades, but approaching in each case the best Swiss or Scottish standard, may be found at all places in Ireland to which tourists are for any reason likely to resort. That this is not yet the case may frankly be owned.[14]

In his analysis, Scotland's tourist traffic offered a benchmark for evaluating the lamentable level of visitors to Ireland. But it also suggested to Houghton that the Irish sector could flourish: he believed that Irish landscapes and recreational attractions were at least as appealing as those to be found across the Irish Sea. Gerald Balfour, the Irish chief secretary, endorsed such a comparison in an 1896 speech to the Irish Tourist Association, a body featuring leading landed figures, political leaders such as Horace Plunkett, and individuals connected with tourist businesses in Ireland:

> If they compared Ireland with Scotland they must admit that the development of the tourist traffic in Ireland fell far short of that in the sister country. It was hard to say what was the reason. As a Scotchman he might be allowed to say that it appeared to him that Ireland was at least as attractive as Scotland to the tourist, so far as the advantages conferred by nature were concerned.[15]

Of the much-maligned Irish climate, another putative hindrance to the industry's development, Lord Houghton asserted that 'it is only necessary to say that in the matter of rainfall it does not compare unfavourably with that of western Scotland. As in the Scottish Highlands, the moister atmosphere clothes the landscape and the ocean-plain with a kind of pearly light, a mysteriousness of distance, not to be found in harsher and dryer latitudes.'[16] The weather on the West coast, the leading trade periodical, the *Irish Tourist*, also insisted, was neither as tempestuous as snowstorms in the Alps, nor as dense as the mists of the Scottish Highlands, which turned them into 'a delusion and a snare'.[17] From this perspective, Scotland's landscapes and climate served as a foil for extolling Ireland's comparative attractions. Such favourable assessments featured in many commentaries, including remarks by the noted Scottish writer Alexander Innes Shand in his 1884 'Letters from the West of Ireland', published as a series in *The Times* and later as a book.[18] Sometimes regions such as the Donegal

14 The piece, 'Ireland unvisited', by Lord Houghton, by now the former lord lieutenant, appeared in the July 1895 edition of the *National Review* and was reprinted in *Littell's Living Age*, 206:2668 (24 Aug. 1895), 496–503. This quotation appears on p. 498 of the reprint. **15** *IT*, 3:3 ('New Series', 1896). **16** Houghton, 'Ireland', p. 499. **17** *IT*, 10:5 (Aug. 1903). **18** Alexander Innes Shand, *Letters from the west of Ireland* (Edinburgh, 1885).

Highlands – whose very appellation evoked the better-known Highlands of Scotland – were characterized as diminutive versions of those found in Caledonia. The *Irish Times*'s 1888 publication *Tours in Ireland* advised that tourists beholding the scenery from Carrick to Ardara in Donegal might imagine themselves 'transported' to a Scottish Highland moor.[19] But *The Scotsman* asserted that the Scottish Highlands offered a much more dramatic landscape. 'As compared with the Highlands of Scotland,' it advised readers in 1880, 'the Highlands of Donegal will probably be regarded by most lovers of the picturesque as in many respects inferior.' They lacked the Scottish district's 'richness in the scenery, owing partly no doubt to the absence of woods and copses, which diversify the grandeur of our Scottish landscapes', and also lacked the 'impression of awful loneliness that is to be experienced in many mountain fastnesses of Scotland'.[20] Though a tourist in Donegal might not encounter unrivalled landscapes, the newspaper reassured its readers that he could find other things to 'interest him', including the 'novelties of the life and manners brought under his notice'. But in other evaluations of Ireland's charms, the newspaper judged that Irish landscapes were more scenic than those found in many Scottish districts: it described Slieve League in Co. Donegal, Achill Head in Co. Mayo and the 'Twelve Pins' in Co. Galway in 1892 as 'as fair as anything in Ross-shire or Sutherlandshire, in Scotland; while the historical interest of Innisboffin, and still more of Aran, is greater than that of any spot on the western Scottish coast, except Iona'.[21] In addition to these scenic delights, the tourist in Ireland could roam unrestricted through rural terrain and enjoy sport that was unconstrained by heavy regulation or ruinous commercialization.

Lord Houghton asserted that 'In the region of sport, a comparison with Scotland naturally suggests itself – a comparison which, for the purpose of this article, Ireland need not hesitate to face.'[22] He argued that Ireland had virgin terrain which offered tourists of modest means an opportunity to engage in sports which they could not enjoy in Scotland. In Ireland, he wrote, a day of shooting in the West might be enjoyed with only 'a letter or two of introduction'. Houghton also rhapsodized about the Emerald Isle's attractions for the angler, asserting that 'the Irish tourist will find himself distinctly more favoured than the Scottish'. While Ireland offered 'more numerous and varied' opportunities for the angler, Houghton nevertheless cautioned that 'As the country becomes better known, the balance will doubtless be corrected.'[23] In this analysis, Ireland's 'undiscovered' charms included unregulated sport, and terrain which had not been fully commercialized. Houghton stressed this point in 1895:

> And what seems to me a very important point, that for those who like to leave the beaten tracks of the road, and also for sporting, there is considerably

---

19 *'Irish Times' tours in Ireland: a descriptive handbook for tourists* (Dublin, 1888), p. 78. **20** *The Scotsman*, 3 July 1880. **21** *The Scotsman*, 9 July 1892. **22** Houghton, 'Ireland', p. 500. **23** Ibid., p. 500.

more freedom than can be found, so far as I know, in any part of Scotland; and I believe that if a similar comparison were instituted with Norway (which has of late years become so favourite a resort for tourists), Ireland would by no means suffer in any such comparison.[24]

Relatively uncontrolled angling in Irish salmon streams also attracted favourable comment, and did not escape the notice of the Scottish press, which reported in 1892 that the Fishery Board for Scotland had dispatched the Inspector of Salmon Fisheries to report on the elaborate salmon ladders erected in Ballisodare, Co. Sligo.[25] Other observers offered equally positive assessments of the sportsman's prospects in Ireland, the writer Alexander Innes Shand suggesting that an informant who 'knows Scotland well' had remarked on the unrivalled quality of shooting grounds near Buncrana, Co. Donegal.[26] To proponents of Irish tourism, the Emerald Isle's rural districts offered open fields, and Irish holiday spots provided unfettered and unmediated access to sportsmen, regardless of their means. The *Irish Tourist* also welcomed the assessment of Grant Govan, who advised the *Weekly Irish Times* that "'you have quite as good a country as Scotland from a sportsman's point of view'".[27] the *Irish Tourist* enthused that 'This is good, coming as it does, from a Scotchman, and from one having such a wide experience and practical knowledge in sporting matters.'[28] In 1895 the period-ical repeated a familiar refrain in asserting that shooting in Ireland cost 'much less' than in both Scotland and England.[29] At the same time, it noted that one of Scotland's advantages lay in its careful stewardship of game, which was in Caledonia 'a national business, just as it ought to be here in Ireland'.[30] Yet, inverting a familiar critique of the primitive and 'under-developed' character of the Irish sector, it under-scored the special appeal of rural districts, depicting the absence of commercial sporting tourism as an advantage to tourists in the Emerald Isle.

Commentaries on the prospects for Irish tourist development which represented Scotland as a country offering similar landscapes and comparable (if more expensive) rural recreations were also part of broader analyses of the comparative economic and civil condition of the two countries. While the absence of extensive tourist traffic led some observers to extol Ireland's charms as a sporting-ground, to others it was an index of its chronic under-development. This, in turn, reflected the instability and poverty which plagued the sister kingdom.

Most observers agreed that tourism was a foundation for rural Scotland's pros-perity, though they debated why Ireland had not matched it in popularity. The poet-laureate Alfred Austin, writing in *Blackwood's Magazine*, decried the condition of the Irish Mail as he boarded his train for Holyhead, observing that the Scottish Mail

24 *IT,* 2:1 ('New Series', 1895). **25** *The Scotsman,* 8 Aug. 1891. **26** *The Times,* 26 Aug. 1884. **27** Quoted in *IT,* 1:2 (July 1894). **28** Ibid. **29** *IT,* 2:4 ('New Series', 1895). **30** Ibid.

was given precedence in leaving the platform, 'as though it will always be soon enough to get to Ireland'. He also contrasted the condition of the carriages:

> The Scotch Mail consisted of every conceivable kind of railway carriage, each a model of sumptuous, almost ostentatious, comfort; and the occupants gave like indications of opulent ease. Footmen, valets, and ladies'-maids moved to and fro with dignified obsequiousness, instructing porters solicitous to please as to the disposal of gun-cases, fishing-rods, and dressing-bags. Pointers, retrievers, and lapdogs were the object of the most sedulous attention; and the young men of Messrs Smith & Co.'s bookstall carried none but the smartest editions and the sixpenny Society papers to the carriage windows.[31]

Austin decried the fact that as the Scottish train 'glided away' from Euston Station the platform book-stall was closed, leaving those boarding the much humbler Irish train without amenities afforded travellers to Scotland. T.W. Russell, parliamentary secretary to the Local Government Board, also condemned the 'English' railway companies' lack of attention to Ireland, and suggested that until they 'gave the traveller to Ireland equal facilities with the traveller to Scotland the latter country would have the advantage'.[32] In these assessments, Ireland's relative poverty was presented as an obstacle to the development of a high-quality tourist infrastructure. As long as railways, tourists and the British state privileged Scotland, the charms of rural Ireland would continue to be unknown to tourists.

The relatively simple, and at times rough, reputation of Ireland's hotels and inns was also regarded as a hindrance to improving Ireland's image. Yet Alexander Innes Shand saw them as part of the West's appeal as *terra incognita*. He described Scotland's premier Highland tourist accommodations as 'three or four great hotels, each and all of them overflowing with their supercilious landlords spoiled by prosperity'.[33] In Shand's estimation, Ireland's relatively rustic accommodations were emblematic of a less crassly commercialized sector than in Scotland. The condition of Irish accommodations had long served as a proxy for discussions of the 'primitive' features of the Irish tourist sector generally. Marie O'Dowda, writing in the *Irish Tourist*, insisted that though to *voyageurs*, 'our little island, by comparison, holds its place as unrivalled amid the countries and scenes of the entire globe', the charms of Scotland were nonetheless more accessible to the tourist who sought comfort as well as fine scenery:

> Some few years since, when returning to Ireland, we were forced to notice the lack of tourist accommodation, as well as the indifference shown with regard to regulating and suggesting their movements, routes, &c.
>
> We had remarked that while in Scotland, although quite foreign to the country, we were enabled to see its most interesting features within the

31 These pieces were reprinted in Alfred Austin, *Spring and autumn in Ireland* (Edinburgh, 1900), pp 49–50. **32** *IT*, 3:3 ('New Series', 1896). **33** *The Times*, 26 Aug. 1884.

compass of a very short time, because at each spot our arrival was anticipated by the general system which prevailed partout, and boats, cars, guides, &c., were provided previously, to effect our transport from place to place.[34]

A related assessment of Ireland's historically poor reputation as a tourist destination stressed that it lacked an articulate champion of its landscapes and people – a figure such as Sir Walter Scott, who could popularize rural space and carve a distinctive cultural identity in the wider British imagination. A 'travelling correspondent' for *The Scotsman* rhapsodized in 1894 about the Emerald Isle's potential as tourist-ground, extolling the charms of Wicklow, the grandeur of Killarney and the Giant's Causeway and the majesty of 'the wilds [*sic*] heights of Connemara and Donegal, as yet a *terra incognita* to the stranger-tourist'.[35] Asking, as many others did, why the scenery attracted relatively few tourists, he lamented that 'there never has been that rush of visitors from abroad which has done so much to enhance the fame of Scottish scenery, and to add to the prosperity of Scotland in her utmost borders'.[36] But then, Scotland's 'utmost borders' had Scott as their patron – the '"Divine Poet"' credited with discovering 'Loch Katrine and the Trossachs, Benvenue, and Ben Aan'.[37] This sentiment was shared by Shand, who lamented in his fourth 'Letter from the West of Ireland' that the Irish people had not benefited from a 'mighty magician to bring gold out of the rocks by the wand of the enchanter. It is curious to speculate as to what might have happened had Walter Scott been born an Irishman.'[38] He also asked why the Irish scenery he lauded in *The Times* had escaped the notice of so many artists who found inspiration in Scotland: 'We have any quantity of Scotch highland landscapes at the Academy, *à la* Graham and Maculloch, but seldom or never a scene from the West of Ireland.'[39] Lord Houghton also lamented that Ireland did not, like Scotland, enjoy 'the advantage of the magic name of Sir Walter Scott',[40] and Gerald Balfour explicitly identified the need for the Irish Tourist Association to assume Scott's mantle in Ireland:

> As regards advertisement, the Association had already done a good deal. Scotland had had her praises sung by a great writer. He wished Ireland, too, could have her Walter Scott. Till such a man arose, however, they must be content to resort to humbler methods.[41]

From this perspective Ireland was seen as lacking neither the attractions nor prospects for increased tourism; it suffered in comparison with Scotland because it lacked an eloquent tribune to enshrine it within the consciousness of the wider world. It was also a unionist rejoinder to those who allied the nascent Irish Literary Revival to political nationalism. To ardent defenders of the Union, Scott, the arch-

34 *IT*, 7:3 (July 1900). 35 *The Scotsman*, 11 Sept. 1894. 36 Ibid. 37 Ibid. 38 *The Times*, 2 Sept. 1884. 39 *The Times*, 8 Sept. 1884. 40 *IT*, 2:1 ('New Series', 1895). 41 *IT*, 3:3 ('New Series', 1896).

Tory unionist, offered an ideal example of a writer who had devised distinctive images of Scotland, without questioning the merits of its political incorporation within the United Kingdom. Scotland's experience illustrated how programmes of economic and cultural development might be intertwined to fix the landscapes of Ireland's West within the national and international imagination, without challenging the tenets of political Union. This agenda was adopted by groups such as the Irish Tourist Association, founded in the mid-1890s by leading landed figures, politicians and businessmen to promote the sector's development, and by a related body, Tourist Development (Ireland) Co., Ltd. In noting recent improvements in the tourist infrastructure, Marie O'Dowda heaped praise on the Association for promoting standards of tourist amenities in Ireland which approached those of the sister kingdom – a salutary development which, she contended, would bring much more prosperity to Ireland 'than futile efforts to obtain Home Rule'.[42]

O'Dowda was by no means the only commentator to incorporate evaluations of Irish tourism within discussions of Ireland's turbulent politics, critiques of political nationalism and favourable allusions to relatively settled conditions in Scotland. Although many assessments of tourists' personal security in Ireland concluded that the countryside was safe for travel, they nevertheless highlighted a feature of rural Ireland's popular reputation that placed contrasts with Scotland in sharp relief. In 'Ireland unvisited', Lord Houghton enumerated concerns that deterred tourists from visiting Ireland, particularly, he lamented, 'the much-abused "South and West"' which some people held to be a risk to visit, 'like Somaliland, or the Solomon Islands'.[43] *The Scotsman*'s correspondent also expressed regret that Ireland had to contend with 'civil strife and political agitation' which, the writer asserted from personal knowledge, had 'contributed very largely to the tardy progress of touring in the country', especially among female travellers.[44] Yet through tourist development the piece identified prospects for advancing tourism and undermining political nationalism by demonstrating the fruits of Union. Indeed, it expressed the desire that:

> ... all Scotsmen, and especially Scottish advocates for Home Rule to Ireland, will next year give tangible proof of their heartfelt interest in Ireland's welfare by making a tour in the country, or by settling down for some weeks in one of her health-giving resorts. Let them examine its beautiful scenery, enjoy its sporting golf links, and make the acquaintance of its witty, good-natured, and kind-hearted peasantry, and they will thus do more to promote the lasting good of Ireland than if they were to breakfast agitators all the year round and applaud to the echo their tawdry rhetoric and their mistaken patriotism.[45]

This forthright denunciation of home rule expressed an important dimension of tourist development discourses that was more implicitly offered by energetic tourism

42 *IT*, 7:3 (July 1900).   43 Houghton, 'Ireland', p. 497.   44 *The Scotsman*, 11 Sept. 1894.
45 Ibid.

proponents such as F.W. Crossley in the pages of the *Irish Tourist*. In their estimation, the development of a programme of tourist improvement illustrated the merits of Ireland's full political integration within the United Kingdom, intensifying human flows between the 'sister islands' and strengthening the economic and political foundations of the Union. Scotland was the exemplar of such salutary achievements.

Despite assessments of the relatively backward condition of rural Ireland, the primitive position of its tourist amenities and the unsettled character of its politics, comparisons of tourist facilities on either side of the Irish Sea did not always find inferior institutions in Ireland. Indeed, programmatic efforts to improve the sector in Ireland under the aegis of the Irish Tourist Association and the Tourist Development (Ireland) Co. won plaudits from across the Irish Sea.[46] The formation of the body provided an impetus for the Scottish tourist industry to reflect on means of improvement, too. As *The Scotsman* noted in 1896:

> While men of all parties in Ireland are thus devoting time and money to attract tourists to that country 'without expecting any return for the same, except good to Ireland,' movements of a similar kind have been started in several districts of Scotland, to secure, if possible, greater patronage from summer visitors. Popular as the Highlands have long been with tourists from the South, the new manager of the Highland Railway is persuaded that there are many people in England who have hitherto been prevented from coming so far North by the costliness of a brief stay in the Highlands.[47]

There was an undertone of anxiety in these remarks on the potential impact of Ireland's tourist improvement programme. The *Sunday Times* also mischievously intimated this in comments on the formation of the Irish Tourist Association:

> The movement is one worthy of support. For beauty of natural scenery the 'Emerald Isle' runs close even 'Caledonia stern and wilde,' [sic] and we have heard travelled Scots declare their doubts whether their own 'land of the Mountain and the Flood' or the Sister Country took the palm.[48]

To defenders of the Union, Scotland offered evidence that a small country could reap the rewards of political integration with England and prosper from its tourist traffic. Promoters of a royal residence in Ireland also pointed to the success of the royal presence in Scotland; indeed, the *Irish Tourist* insisted that efforts to establish an

---

46 For a review of tourist development bodies in Ireland, see D.J. Wilson, 'The tourist movement in Ireland', *Journal of the Statistical and Social Inquiry Society of Ireland*, 11, part 81 (1900–1), 56–63. **47** *The Scotsman*, 10 Apr. 1896. **48** Quoted in *IT*, 3:3 ('New Series', 1896).

official royal residence would see Ireland surpass Scotland as a tourist destination.[49] The annual meeting of the Hotel and Restaurant Proprietors' Association in Dublin in 1897 endorsed this position, insisting that Ireland had the potential to become more 'fashionable' than Scotland, owing partly to its wider variety of scenery.[50] Those who believed that economic development through tourism would cement sentimental bonds between people in Britain and Ireland, direct British leisure tourist expenditure to the sister country, increase Ireland's prosperity and secure its economic and political development within the Union, found in Scotland a bastion of civil peace and prosperity.

Underpinning many of these comparative assessments of Irish and Scottish tourism were broader cultural, political and even racial evaluations, which intertwined discussions of the undiluted and undisciplined character of Irish 'Celtic' culture with assertions that unsettled politics retarded the progress of commerce and industry. Alfred Austin, rhapsodizing about a journey in Ireland, declared:

> My parting exhortation, therefore, naturally is – 'Go to Ireland, and go often.' It is a delightful country to travel in. Doubtless the Irish have their faults; I suppose we all have. Ireland never had, like England, like most of Scotland, like France, like Germany, like Spain, the advantage of Roman civilisation and Roman discipline, by which their inhabitants are still influenced far more than they dream of.[51]

Scotland was central to many of these evaluations of Ireland's nascent tourist development programme. In them, the sister kingdom served variously as a mirror and a foil. While their physical landscapes and salmon streams were often identified as equals, discourses on terrain, hotels and tourist routes were central to broader evaluations of the Scottish and Irish economies, their political and civil conditions and the relative place of their 'utmost borders' in the national and international imagination. To proponents of the Union, Scotland, through its tribune, Sir Walter Scott, and carefully-stewarded development of its tourist sector, had fixed these borders firmly, without challenging the political boundaries of the state within which it was incorporated. Their positioning of Scotland within discussions of Ireland as a tourist destination reveals the complex relationship between cultural appraisal and political ideology in the construction of the United Kingdom's western and northern holiday-grounds.

49 *IT*, 1:4 ('Special Horse Show Number', 1894). James Loughlin notes that Victoria's enthusiasm for Ireland was much more tempered than for Scotland, where the royal imprint under her reign was deep. See James Loughlin, 'Allegiance and illusion: Queen Victoria's Irish visit of 1849', *History*, 87:288 (2002), 491–513. **50** *IT*, 4:1 (May 1897). **51** Austin, *Spring and autumn*, p. 45.

Societies and seminaries: technological exchange in Ulster agriculture

CLARE M. NORCIO

This chapter offers a fresh perspective on pre-Famine Ulster agricultural patterns. Traditional explanations of agricultural differences across the province have relied on cultural differences between Scots settlers and Irish natives. But this explanation cannot satisfactorily accommodate similar agricultural patterns and techniques in areas of mixed population. Relying on the information collected in the Ordnance Survey memoirs,[1] this chapter offers a new explanation: environmental conditions, rather than settlement patterns, had more of an effect on agricultural techniques. The exchange of agricultural technology and knowledge was both formal and informal, creating a web of knowledge across the countryside. Formal methods of exchange, especially farming associations and farm schools, reinforce the notion of Scots as agents of modernization in Ulster, but cannot account for regional differences in agricultural techniques. Informal methods of exchange, such as observation and neighbourly conversations, indicate that local environmental conditions had a tremendous influence on farming. For elite farmers and those who participated in farming societies, technology was viewed as inherently good; they aimed to change the environment to suit the technology. But this was not always possible, and small farmers especially were more likely to adapt technology to suit their environments. The progress and improvement technology could bring were not practicable everywhere.

As ordnance surveyor Thomas Fagan made his way across Co. Antrim in the winter of 1838–39, he heard a story in the parish of Culfeightrin that he recorded in his notes:

1 The Ordnance Survey was conducted 1824–42, mapping Ireland at six inches to the mile. According to initial proposals, the survey would include both maps and memoirs which would document at the parish level the natural resources, agricultural productivity and social mores of Irish life. Officers, guided by a thirty-seven page pamphlet, were to keep journals detailing natural features and history, such as climate, botany, and zoology; ancient and modern topography, including mills, ruins, and general scenery; the social economy, including obstructions to improvements, schools, habits, religion, and emigration; and the productive economy, including manufacturing, fairs, grazing, fishing, and planting. Due to the ambitious nature of the project, in addition to severe budgetary constraints, however, the memoir project was abandoned with data collected for only a fraction of the country's thirty-two counties. Those which were completed – Londonderry, Antrim, Down, Armagh, Tyrone, Donegal, Fermanagh, Cavan, and Monaghan – are all in Ulster. See J.H. Andrews, *A paper landscape: the Ordnance Survey in nineteenth-century Ireland* (Oxford, 1975), p. 147.

In Barnish and holding of Alexander Hunter, and immediately adjoining the
road leading from Ballycastle to Cushendall [*sic*], there stands an ancient house
said to have been the residence of 3 giantesses, who, for a series of time, were
in the habit of killing and devouring such persons as they caught traveling an
ancient line of road passing that way between Cushendall and Ballycastle.
However, these cannibals were at length killed by 3 Scottish chieftains who,
after landing some part about Cushenden, heard concerning the dangerous
characters they had to meet with in the above old road, but the Highland
dirks put a speedy end to the long-dreaded and destructive females above
mentioned.[2]

Leaving aside the gender implications, this story is freighted with significance. Most
important, perhaps, is the implication that Scotsmen had to free Irishmen from what
kept them hostage. The giantesses were bloated, cannibalistic creatures destroying the
countryside from within. The enterprising and fearless Scottish chiefs handily
dispatched them, leaving the countryside free to recover and prosper.

The arrival of the Scots marked a new beginning for Ireland according to
observers. Ordnance surveyors certainly considered the plantation to have been an
important and improving chapter in Irish history, as the Scots brought Protestantism
(even if they were Dissenters) and agricultural techniques more familiar to English
farmers. Though there was considerable archeological evidence of earlier inhabitants,
surveyors often began their historical accounts with the plantation, as if that were the
true starting point of Ulster history.[3] There are repeated references to the 'earliest
improvements' of an area being the arrival of Scottish settlers in the sixteenth and
seventeenth centuries. As one surveyor of the plantation in Antrim put it, 'The great
event which may undoubtedly be regarded as the earliest and almost sole cause of
improvement in the habits, morals and general character of the people of this country
was its colonization by the Scots in the early part of the 17th century.'[4] A survey
officer in Londonderry cautiously allowed ('it is not improbable') that pre-plantation
politics were stable enough to allow settled agriculture and the high culture that
accompanied it to prosper, but decided that the Scots ultimately played the decisive
role, and their arrival 'fix[ed] the epoch from which may be more confidently dated

2 Angelique Day, Patrick McWilliams & Lisa English (eds), *The Ordnance Survey memoirs of
Ireland: vol. 24: parishes of county Antrim IX, 183–2, 1835, 1838–9* (Belfast & Dublin, 1990), p. 50.
3 On the plantation see Nicholas Canny, *Making Ireland British 1580–1650* (Oxford and New
York, 2001), pp 187–300 for an exhaustive discussion of plantation in Ulster. In the memoirs,
however, the term 'plantation' serves as a shorthand for the Scottish settlement of Ulster in
general, whether formal or informal. 4 Angelique Day, Patrick McWilliams & Lisa
English (eds), *The Ordnance Survey memoirs of Ireland: vol. 29: parishes of county Antrim XI, 1832–
3, 1835–9, Antrim town and Ballyclare* (Belfast & Dublin, 1990), p. 23. Angelique Day, Patrick
McWilliams & Lisa English (eds), *The Ordnance Survey memoirs of Ireland: vol. 2: parishes of
county Antrim (i), 1838–9* (Belfast & Dublin, 1990). For similar statements, see Day et al. (eds),
The Ordnance Survey memoirs of Ireland: vol. 2, p. 5, 20.

a steady improvement'.[5] Scots brought with them Protestantism (Presbyterianism, in particular), temperance and a moral sobriety the surveyors found pleasing. They noted with approval that Ulster Scots were more likely to have few amusements other than Bible societies or temperance meetings, while the Irish were more likely to amuse themselves with drinking or dancing.

This chapter will focus on one area in which Scots were credited with tremendous progress: agriculture. When the ordnance surveyors described the Irish countryside, their primary focus was the condition of farming. They wanted to determine the capacity and potential of Irish agriculture, and they measured this productivity in specific ways: fences, drains, green crops, the extent of the survival of traditional land allotment patterns such as clachans and rundale.[6] They found that, on the whole, agricultural techniques differed between the descendants of Scots settlers and Irish natives. By and large, Ulster Scots had better quality fences, constructed of stone rather than hedges or earth, allowing farmers to keep grazing animals out of their fields and protect the maturing grain crops. Sheep and cattle could be grain-fed in barns, rather than migrating from mountain to meadow every year in search of food. Keeping livestock sheltered in barns allowed the farmers to collect manure, providing them with a steady and reliable source of fertilizer. Scottish farmers also tended to use iron (Scotch) ploughs, which were heavier than the traditional Irish wooden ploughs and could create deeper furrows for seeds. A farmer using an iron plough could seed his field more quickly, and create more regular (and visually pleasing) rows. Ulster Scots' farmers also tended to add green crops (such as turnips or clover) to their rotations, thus preserving soil fertility and providing winter feed for their livestock. All of these improved techniques were enabled by the size and shape of their farms: large, square fields were infinitely easier to plough and maintain. All of these techniques combined to create a thoroughly more modern method of husbandry than what many of the Irish practiced; Irish farmers continued to maintain small, poorly fenced plots of land, in which crops and grazing animals often co-existed.

Traditional explanations for these varying farming practices have emphasized cultural difference between the Scots and the Irish. The Irish, argued nineteenth-

5 Angelique Day, Patrick McWilliams & Lisa English (eds), *The Ordnance Survey memoirs of Ireland: vol. 33: parishes of county Londonderry XII, 1829–30, 1832, 1834–36, Coleraine and Mouth of the Bann* (Belfast & Dublin, 1990), p. 35. 6 Green crops were most common where farms were large enough to enable farmers to keep a field out of production for a season (though the turnips or clover which he planted were usually fed to livestock). Surveyors mentioned green cropping most often in describing farming in Antrim and Londonderry, especially in areas where there was a model farm or a branch of a farming society. See Day et al. (eds), *The Ordnance Survey memoirs of Ireland: vol. 21*, p. 60; Day et al. (eds), *The Ordnance Survey memoirs of Ireland: vol. 29*, pp 72–3; Angelique Day, Patrick McWilliams & Lisa English (eds), *The Ordnance Survey memoirs of Ireland: vol. 28: parishes of county Londonderry IX, 1832–8, West Londonderry* (Belfast & Dublin, 1995), pp 55–7; Day et al. (eds), *The Ordnance Survey memoirs of Ireland: vol. 33*, p. 104.

century critics, were inherently afraid of change; they were conservative with a 'high leisure preference' (that is, lazy).[7] These differences, however, cannot explain why farming methods overlapped in some areas of Ulster but not in others. Techniques had common characteristics in areas of mixed populations on all types of land, from the most fertile to the boggiest and rockiest. Looking to the environment, rather than the population, explains this: land quality had a direct influence on the type of farming employed.

Farming societies reinforced the techniques associated with Ulster Scots' farmers. The first farming society in Ireland was established by a group of English gentry in 1731 as the Dublin Society to teach English standards of farming in Ireland. The Society began ploughing trials the next year, and began awarding prizes for them in 1741. Forty years later, it opened a museum in Dublin to showcase the latest farming implements. The earliest local societies were in Antrim, Kildare and Louth, but they faltered because of limited resources.[8] Regional societies had better success. The Northwest of Ireland Agricultural Society was established in 1821 for Counties Londonderry, Tyrone and Donegal. It emphasized improving 'fisheries, manufactures, agriculture, and cattle breeding' in western Ulster, and published a short-lived magazine in 1823–5.[9]

Historians of farming societies in the United States and Australia have argued that they were indispensable in both colonizing and nation-building enterprises. Farming societies in Australia provided English settlers with a pool of knowledge about farming conditions, reasonable expectations of the extent of agricultural production, and information as to how to overcome difficulties in transforming the colony into a new England.[10] American farming societies were trying both to restore their landscape to a state of natural fertility and create national self-sufficiency. Both impulses are also evident in the goals and polices of Irish agricultural societies. Theorists and reformers, such as Joseph Elkington, James Smith and Josiah Parkes, wanted to remake Irish agriculture in the model of English and lowland Scottish farming.[11] It was an attempt to make Ireland less obviously different from the rest of the United Kingdom. Some historians of empire have argued that this is an example of 'internal colonialism', an attempt to civilize the 'Celtic fringe'.[12] At the same time, however, many of the men behind the impetus to change Irish agriculture were Irish landlords who wanted to commercialize agricultural production to create, in conjunction with improved manufacturing, a self-sufficient industrializing nation. Furthermore, a religious overtone permeated the discussion of agricultural improvement in the United States and Ireland. According to the leaders of farming societies in the northeastern

---

7 Jonathan Bell & Mervyn Watson, *Irish farming: implements and techniques* (Edinburgh, 1986), pp 1–2. **8** Ibid., pp 5–8. Bell and Watson do not specify who the gentlemen were. **9** Ashmur Bond, 'The North-West Agricultural Society', in William P. Coyne (ed.), *Ireland: industrial and agricultural* (Dublin, 1902), p. 213. **10** Michael White, 'Agricultural societies in colonial Western Australia 1831–70', *History of Education*, 29 (2000). **11** Bell & Watson, *Irish farming*, pp 17–19. **12** Michael Hechter, *Internal colonialism: the Celtic fringe in British national development, 1536–1966* (Berkeley and Los Angeles, 1975).

United States, industrious farmers could redeem humanity from the 'curse of Adam' by completely subduing nature.[13]

Before the Famine, farming societies in Ireland achieved some success in their efforts to modernize Irish agriculture. When surveyors arrived in the Grange of Doagh, in Co. Antrim, in 1839, they learned Doagh had had a farming society since 1818. There, the surveyors found that

> the system of farming is generally advanced and modern. With the more extensive farmers it is quite Scottish and of an improved and systematic style, potatoes being almost invariably planted by the plough, the farming implements, gates, homesteads and fences being of an improved description, and the cultivation of green crops being now pretty general.[14]

Other branches of the Northwest Farming Society and the North East of Ireland Farming Society dotted the countryside in the twenty years preceding the Famine. The branches were especially prominent in Londonderry and Antrim, though Monaghan had been home to a branch as well (it closed before 1830 due to internal disagreements).[15] They held yearly ploughing matches, judging both speed and technique, livestock shows, and published minutes or journals to disseminate the methods of modern scientific agriculture as far as they could. Surveyors felt that the Northwest Farming Society had been so successful in expounding the virtues of composts and manures in Co. Londonderry that 'it is unnecessary to recapitulate what is already so well known'.[16]

Model farms also reinforced the preferences among the gentry for Scottish methods of agriculture. In the parish of Drumachose in Co. Londonderry, for example, 'the land stewards are almost always procured from Scotland' because of their perceived technical superiority.[17] There remained, however, in the minds of the British surveyors, a definite hierarchy of agricultural productivity in the British Isles. Scottish farmers in Scotland were considerably more productive than Ulster Scots farmers, who, in turn, were more advanced than the peasantry in the south of Ireland.[18]

Surveyors offered several explanations for these differences. One officer in

13 Charles W. Turner, 'Virginia state agricultural societies, 1811–1860', *Agricultural History*, 38 (1964), 167; Donald B. Marti, 'In praise of farming: an aspect of the movement for agricultural improvement in the northeast, 1815–1840', *New York History*, 41 (1970), 355–7, 370. 14 Day et al. (eds), *The Ordnance Survey memoirs of Ireland: vol. 29*, p. 75. 15 Ibid.; Angelique Day, Patrick McWilliams & Lisa English (eds), *The Ordnance Survey memoirs of Ireland: vol. 9: parishes of county Londonderry II, 1833–1835* (Belfast & Dublin, 1990); Angelique Day, Patrick McWilliams & Lisa English (eds), *The Ordnance Survey memoirs of Ireland: vol. 40: counties of south Ulster, 1834–8, Cavan, Leitrim, Louth, Monaghan, and Sligo* (Belfast & Dublin, 1990), p. 108; Ashmur Bond, 'The North-West Agricultural Society', in William P. Coyne (ed.), *Ireland: industrial and agricultural* (Dublin, 1902), p. 213. 16 Day et al. (eds), *The Ordnance Survey memoirs of Ireland: vol. 9*, p. 99. 17 Ibid., p. 88. 18 Ibid., p. 109

Londonderry fell back on racial differences between the Irish and the Scots.[19] Dismissing the Ulster Scots' own long history in, and attachment to, Ireland, he declared that the Irish had an overly romantic attachment to the soil, and this hampered their development. The Scots were entirely more practical. Here, again, the idea of plantation was seen as crucial to Irish history, 'Indeed to him [a Scot], Erin's ancient story possesses little interest: nay his most triumphant historical recollections are connected with her degradation and her downfall. To Scotland he yet looks as his mother country, and with her name associates everything distinguished in intellect, valuable in science and venerable in religion.'[20] The Irish romanticization of their landscape competed with, and hampered, the Scottish commodification of it. The Irish, according to surveyors, were preoccupied with useless reminiscences, and too caught up in the past to make good use of the present. Scots settlers and their descendents were unencumbered by a romantic attachment to Irish land and its past, and so could use science to develop the land into a revenue-producing resource.

The scientific approach inherent in the Scottish outlook is quite important. Scotland was at the forefront of the professionalization of agriculture at the end of the eighteenth century. Until then, Ireland and Scotland had been in a relatively similar state. Poor soil, mountains and a cool, damp climate combined to make agriculture difficult for small farmers. Professionalization of agriculture depended on several factors. New techniques had to have been developed; green cropping, the use of an iron plough, and better drain construction were the techniques which English and Scottish farmers would introduce to Ireland. English farmers actually led this process, but lowland Scots farmers adopted many of the new ideas wholesale, creating a dramatic and concentrated rise in the productivity of Scottish agriculture. For these techniques to constitute a new profession of agricultural husbandry, however, they

19 Race, as a scientific theory, was increasingly prominent during the early nineteenth century. In this period, racial characteristics were thought to be fixed and immutable, and races exhibited differing levels of 'intellectual and moral capacities'. See Hanna Franziska Augstein (ed.), *Race: the origins of an idea, 1760–1850* (Bristol, 1996), p. x. The five races categorized in the eighteenth century had expanded into countless races in the nineteenth. By the 1810s, theorists catalogued three European races: the Celts, the Germans (which included Englishmen and lowland Scots), and the Slavonic. See William Lawrence, 'On the causes of the varieties of the human species', in Augstein (ed.), *Race*, pp 109–10. John Gibson Lockart categorized five European races in 1831: Celts, Teutons (including Saxons), Sclavonic, Laplanders and Finns, and Greeks and Romans. He based these categorizations on direct observation, historical records, and linguistic similarities. He documented the presence of two of the races in the British Isles: Celts in Wales, Ireland and the Scottish Highlands, and Saxons in lowland Scotland and England. See John Gibson Lockart, 'The German origin of the Latin language and the Roman people', in Augstein (ed.), *Race*, pp 141–7. Thus, by the time the Ordnance Survey memoirs were written, the notion that the Irish were a race separate from, and inferior to, the English and lowland Scots was gaining widespread acceptance.   20 Angelique Day, Patrick McWilliams & Lisa English (eds), *The Ordnance Survey memoirs of Ireland: vol. 11: parishes of county Londonderry III, 1831–5* (Belfast & Dublin, 1990), p. 123.

had to be standardized and justified scientifically. This important process occurred in Scottish universities, especially the University of Edinburgh; they were among the best in Europe, and contained excellent chemistry departments, which became the scientific foundation of the new professional agriculture. The first chair of agriculture in the British Isles was established in 1790 at the University of Edinburgh.[21]

One of the most interesting outgrowths of this drive for the professionalization of agriculture was the establishment of farm schools. Such schools developed, with varying levels of success, throughout the nineteenth century.[22] One such was the Templemoyle Agricultural Society in Co. Londonderry. The seminary was built in 1826 in Faughanvale, financed in part by private subscriptions and in part by a grant from the Grocers' Company.[23] It was affiliated with the North West of Ireland Agricultural Society, who:

> considered that the improvement of agriculture would be much advanced by the permanent founding of a school in which the sons of farmers could be instructed in the scientific and practical knowledge of farming pursuits, receiving also at the same time a good English education.[24]

Boys were admitted regardless of religious persuasion (the student body was almost equally divided between Protestants and Catholics, with Presbyterians greatly outnumbering Anglicans). The ultimate goal of the seminary was to equalize knowledge and rents; agricultural reformers felt rents were too high, not based on soil

21 Stewart Richards, 'Agricultural science in higher education: problems of identity in Britain's first chair of agiculture, Edinburgh 1790–*c*.1831', *Agricultural History Review,* 33 (1985), 59–60. **22** La Charmoise was built in the French countryside in 1850 to modernize French farming methods. Though elite farmers and scientists believed it was successful and useful, parents were unwilling to send their sons for education: 'there was ... a real and prolonged opportunity cost to parents in terms of the withdrawal from their farm of their son's labour for four years just at the time when he was beginning to contribute substantially to work on the farm.' See Alan R. H. Baker, 'Farm schools in nineteenth-century France and the case of La Charmoise, 1847–1865', *Agricultural History Review,* 44 (1996), 54–5. Reformers in Meiji Japan in the 1860s established an agricultural college to westernize their farming methods in an ultimately successful attempt to modernize and compete on western terms. See Hiroko Willcock, 'Traditional learning, western thought, and the Sapporo Agricultural College: a case study of acculturation in early Meiji Japan', *Modern Asian Studies,* 34 (2000). There were also farm schools in the northeastern United States, but they lacked the component of liberal education common to the other schools; farming education in the US was designed not to create 'gentlemen farmers' but farmers who were educated 'to help a particular class fulfill its assigned role.' See Marti, 'In praise of farming: an aspect of the movement for agricultural improvement in the northeast, 1815–1840', *New York History,* 41 (1970), 361. **23** The Grocers' Company was one of the London merchants' societies commissioned during the plantation of Ulster. See Canny, *Making Ireland British 1580–1650,* pp 199–223. **24** Angelique Day, Patrick McWilliams & Lisa English (eds), *The ordnance survey memoirs of Ireland: vol. 36: parishes of county Londonderry XIV, 1833–4, 1836, 1838, Faughanvale* (Belfast & Dublin, 1990), p. 39.

quality, but based on the ignorance of small farmers. If they could be made more knowledgeable (that is, more scientific and efficient) they could be productive enough to pay higher rents. The curriculum was divided between a liberal English education, described in the memoirs as including 'spelling, reading, English grammar, writing, arithmetic, geography, bookkeeping as it applicable to farming accounts, *Euclid's elements*, algebra, trigonometry ... and land surveying', and a grounding in agricultural techniques, to enable graduates to become gentlemen farmers or to manage large farms.[25] The masters were to be men of impeccable moral character and renown in their fields. The agriculture master provided 'evening lectures on the theory and practice of agriculture, illustrated by their daily practice.'[26] He taught his charges how to use a plough, construct a drain, manage livestock, and rotate crops. Like the land stewards in other parts of the county, this man was a Scot, hired for his superior agricultural knowledge. The Ordnance Survey memoirs provide a list of twenty-seven questions which students were expected to be able to answer upon graduation. A selection of them indicates that the questions were quite technical, and students were expected to have a mastery of all aspects of modern farming:

> Question One: When a tenant or steward enters upon a farm of land all in disorder and irregular, what should first be done to get it into a regular rotation of crops as soon as possible?

> Question Ten: What common plough is most approved of by head farmer and what rules are to be applied to ascertain when the sole shoe, mould-board, coulter and sock are set in a proper manner; also what length should the chain be from the muzzle to the foot-tree, so as to allow the plough to work in an easy manner; and what is the proper length for a foot-tree and swing-tree for a plough?[27]

Though the seminary was struggling financially when the surveyors observed it in the 1830s, it remained self-supporting until the mid-nineteenth century. It affiliated with the National Board of Education in 1850, after the Famine reduced its pool of potential students and funding opportunities. The National Board of Education closed the seminary permanently in 1860. Between its foundation in 1826 and when it ceased independent operations in 1850, the seminary educated 800 students from Ireland, England and Scotland.[28]

The activities of farming societies and seminaries might lead one to believe that the exchange of knowledge about agriculture went in one direction, that Scots taught, and presumably improved, the Irish. But, in fact, the situation was more complicated than that. Settlement patterns are crucial to understanding the extent and directions of technological exchange. In places where Scots had displaced the

25 Ibid., p. 41. 26 Ibid. 27 Ibid., pp 26–27. 28 Sir Patrick Keenan, 'Agricultural education in Ireland', in Coyne (ed.), *Ireland: industrial and agricultural* (Dublin, 1902), p. 137; Bell & Watson, *Irish farming*, p. 10.

Irish during and after the seventeenth-century plantation, there were obvious differences in farming techniques. In places where Scots were integrated into Irish areas, differences were much less common. This is evidenced as well in the comments surveyors made about the cultural integration of the Scottish and Irish in Ulster, even within the same county. In some places in Antrim, for example, surveyors documented communities that were distinctly Scottish, with stark differences between them and the Irish. The surveyor delineated the differences thoroughly: 'In their habits considerable difference exists, the Scottish being rather industrious and peaceable and well-disposed, and more neat in their system of farming, and still retaining much of the custom and dialect of their forefathers; while the others [i.e., native Irish] are careless, turbulent and quarrelsome, slovenly in their persons, and not very civil or obliging.'[29] In another part of Antrim, however, a surveyor quotes Lady Morgan's sentiment that the Ulster Scots inhabit a cultural no-man's land between Irishness and Scottishness. He agrees with her, that Ulster Scots are Irish by their residence, Scottish by their ethnicity and religion, but 'by their character and actions they are neither one nor the other'. The chief virtues of each (Irish hospitality and Scottish literacy) had been obscured by greed.[30] The English surveyors explained this by falling back on race and class explanations: the Scots in traditionally Irish areas were poor because they had gone native. In Antrim, for example, Nicholas Crommelin received a grant in 1824 to colonize a remote part of the country. The majority of the population was Protestant (one third Presbyterian, one third Anglican, one third Catholic). Ten years later, when surveyors came through, Crommelin still had not succeeded in turning a profit. The people were poor and lazy, he said, and impeded his progress. Surveyors described the area as 'mountainous and wild' and 'cold and sterile'.[31]

The surveyors hit on the crucial point as an afterthought. The Scots, more often than not, settled in more fertile areas, so of course they appeared to be better, more prosperous farmers. The techniques of mixed populations in fertile areas were indistinguishable from each other, as were the techniques of mixed populations in marginal lands. Farmers in the mountains, regardless of their religious affinity, used spades and old Irish cars rather than iron ploughs and horse carts because that was the best way to till the soil.[32] In the parish of Magilligan, in Co. Londonderry, for

29 Angelique Day, Patrick McWilliams & Lisa English (eds), *The Ordnance Survey memoirs of Ireland: vol. 19: parishes of county Antrim VI, 1830, 1833, 1835–8* (Belfast & Dublin, 1990), p. 6; another similar comment, though not as inflammatory, can be found in Day et al. (eds), *The Ordnance Survey memoirs of Ireland: vol. 2*, p. 2. **30** Angelique Day, Patrick McWilliams & Lisa English (eds), *The ordnance survey memoirs of Ireland: vol. 8: parishes of country Antrim II, 1832–8* (Belfast & Dublin, 1990), p. 15. **31** Angelique Day, Patrick McWilliams, & Lisa English (eds), *The Ordnance Survey memoirs of Ireland: vol. 13: parishes of county Antrim IV, 1830–8* (Belfast & Dublin, 1990), pp 78–82. **32** Ibid., p. 26, 112; Angelique Day, Patrick McWilliams & Lisa English (eds), *The Ordnance Survey memoirs of Ireland: vol. 32: parishes of county Antrim Xii, 1832–3, 1835–40, Ballynure and district* (Belfast & Dublin, 1990), pp 98–125; Angelique Day, Patrick McWilliams & Lisa English (eds), *The Ordnance Survey memoirs of*

example, the population was overwhelmingly Protestant, with equal numbers of English Anglicans and Scots Presbyterians. The farming methods were recognizably Irish, with no enclosures and land farmed in conacre. Old methods persisted because the soil was poor and the area isolated.[33] It is not impossible that Irish techniques survived in areas the Irish no longer inhabited. Thus, though it puzzled surveyors, in Layd, Co. Antrim, old Irish-language stories of Finn and Ossian were very, very popular, though the Irish themselves had been displaced long ago.[34]

The observations of the Ordnance Survey officers echoed the criticisms of early nineteenth-century Irish agriculture: crop rotations were infrequent, the fields were weedy, the land was exhausted due to over-cropping, and agricultural implements were inadequate. Farming practices in pre-famine Ulster, however, were rational and efficient given the available resources. Cultivation ridges (called 'lazy beds' where potatoes were grown), for example, were roundly criticized by both theorists of improved agriculture and the surveyors, but they functioned superbly for poor farmers. The shape of the ridges depended on the crops grown on them, the soil type and the climate. Critics claimed that the alternating strips of ridges and furrows left nearly one-third of the field uncultivated and therefore wasted. Farmers continued to use ridges, however, because they facilitated drainage, and only abandoned them when drainage technology was more affordable and effective. Alternating ridges and furrows each year preserved soil fertility, and spade, rather than plough, cultivation could break up clay subsoil more effectively. Spade cultivation was incredibly labour intensive, but labour in Ireland was cheap and plentiful.[35]

Mechanization could be profitable in the long run, but it was prohibitively expensive in the short term. Most Ulster farms were small, bolstered by the linen industry, and farmers, especially in marginal areas, could grow only for subsistence. Their caution towards new technology was justifiable, since much of it was unproven and expensive, and required large initial outlays with uncertain returns.[36] Drainage technology, for example, changed rapidly over the course of a few years. Early nineteenth-century experts, such as the Scotsman James Smith, recommended their programmes be followed rigidly for the best results. Smith, in particular, did not account for soil type or the slope of the hill, and farmers refused to implement his recommendations. Within a few years, new experts were taking into account environmental variations when designing their drainage schemes, and farmers found this flexibility more workable.[37]

Mervyn Watson, a historian of Irish ploughs and ploughing techniques, has argued that agriculture should not be separated from socio-economic or environmental conditions. When agricultural reformers tried to implement improved

Ireland: vol. 37: parishes of county Antrim XIV, 1832, 1839–40, Carrickfergus (Belfast & Dublin, 1990), p. 64; Angelique Day, Patrick McWilliams & Lisa English (eds), *The Ordnance Survey memoirs of Ireland: vol. 4: parishes of county Fermanagh I, 1834–5* (Belfast & Dublin, 1990), pp 15, 21. **33** Day et al. (eds), *The ordnance survey memoirs of Ireland: vol. 11*, p. 107, 115, 140. **34** Day et al. (eds), *The Ordnance Survey memoirs of Ireland: vol. 13*, p. 3. **35** Bell & Watson, *Irish farming*, pp 24–7. **36** Ibid., pp 229–32. **37** Ibid., pp 19–20.

techniques in unimproved or unimprovable (for example, mountains) local conditions, they failed. Mountain farmers with steep, rocky, marginal land, and who were
too poor to afford draught animals, simply could not use a heavy Scottish plough.[38]
Examining the situation environmentally, the persistence of spade agriculture and
old-fashioned techniques, and the Scotch adoption of them, makes sense.

Irish farms did not look like British or lowland Scottish farms, and Irish farming
methods seemed impracticable to British observers. On a superficial level, Irish
farming seemed old-fashioned, too conservative and inefficient. The examples of
modern agricultural husbandry the surveyors recorded were attributed directly to an
improving Scottish influence. The British were predisposed to equate Scottishness
with agricultural advancement, perhaps influenced by nineteenth-century Scottish
contributions to modern, scientific, professional agriculture. British assessments of
the contributions of Scots to Irish agriculture were reinforced by settlement patterns
of plantation, especially in Co. Antrim, where the Scots Presbyterians continued to
occupy the most fertile land while the Irish occupied the margins. This schema was
complicated by integrated populations in well-managed and productive areas, though
the English attributed Irish Catholic wealth to the superior moral force of the Scots.
But this falls apart entirely when the Scots and Irish shared marginal land. In these
instances, surveyors cobbled together an explanation that the Scots were poorly
educated, poorly catechized, and poorly managed by absentee landlords.

The structure of Ulster farming and agricultural techniques makes much more
sense if we look at the Ulster environment. Agriculture is a product of a social and
economic system dependent upon the ecological landscape. Where the environment
cannot support a new and improved technique, the technique will fail, regardless of
the race or religion of the person employing it. Scots who farmed marginal land used
the methods that were best suited to their environment, just as the Irish in more
fertile areas adopted the new methods that their environment could support.

The Ordnance Survey memoirs provide unique insight to the question of the
role of the natural environment in Ulster agriculture. Their stated aim was to document agriculture and society in Ireland, and they do so extensively in Ulster. They
contain a wealth of information about farming practices and agricultural technology
that is invaluable in analysing the extent and productivity of agriculture in the
northern counties of Ireland. In addition, however, the memoirs are a reflection of
administrative attitudes toward Ulster and its inhabitants. Discussions of agricultural
techniques are inextricably tied to received wisdom about race and culture, and their
influence on farming practices. Embedded within these discussions, however, is
another, if largely unacknowledged, explanation of varied agricultural practices across
Ulster: the constraints of the environment acted as a check on the spread of modern,
scientific agriculture. Not every corner of Ulster could support the new methods,
and this is documented in the memoirs as well. It is important not to reduce this to

---

38 Mervyn Watson, 'Common Irish plough types and tillage techniques,' *Tools and Tillage,* 5
(1985).

environmental determinism in an effort to emphasize the importance of ecology in Ulster history. People across Ulster could, and did, manipulate their environment to suit their needs. But it is important to ask how and why people farmed as they did, and the environment is a key but neglected part of that answer.

Irish migrants and the recruitment of Catholic Sisters in Glasgow, 1847–1878[1]

S. KARLY KEHOE

There is not an Irishman who owns an acre of land in Scotland, this unsettled exclusiveness gives offence to the country and causes the Irish to be unfavourably looked upon … The people of Scotland are prejudiced against Catholicity to a degree unequalled in any other country … Now this antipathy to our holy faith is much intensified here in the western district because it is seen to be professed by congregations almost exclusively belonging to a race which is regarded with distrust if not aversion.[2]

The opinion offered by John Gray, a man conspicuously positioned as the 'Scottish' vicar-apostolic of the Western District, alongside James Lynch, his 'Irish' coadjutor, reveals something of Catholicism's precarious position in the west of Scotland. Increased levels of Irish migration between 1800 and mid-century had forced a reappraisal of the Roman church and sparked widespread anti-Catholic and anti-Irish sentiment. Whilst these were a serious concern, the perceived 'vulgarity' of Irish Catholicism served to further divide the migrants from the native-born population, who projected feelings of intense contempt and distrust towards the newcomers. In Scotland, Catholicism's aristocratic ties and the conservative character it had adopted since the Reformation had enabled its survival on the fringes of society, but the influx of Irish and the perception that many harboured subversive religio-political agendas caused many to regard the migrants with a wary eye. It was believed by a number of Scots Catholics that the Irish would undermine any possibility of Catholicism being accepted as part of Scottish society and its adherents being welcomed as loyal British subjects. In Glasgow, where the Irish congregated in their greatest numbers, the Scottish clergy, particularly the Banffshire-born cohort of bishops (Andrew Scott, John Murdoch, Alexander Smith and John Gray), invested tremendous energy in attempting to minimize Irish influence over Catholic identity in Scotland. Their main concern was the establishment of a religious-run system of Catholic education that would work to transform the city's Catholic population into respectable and loyal citizens, whilst simultaneously sublimating Irish Catholic culture.

1 The author would like to express her thanks to Graeme Morton, Carmen Mangion, David Stewart, Paul Jenkins and Dara Price for their comments on earlier drafts of this chapter.   2 John Gray, *Report on the state of religion in the Western District,* 1866, G[lasgow] A[rchdiocese] A[rchives], WD12/43.

Women religious, specifically sisters from active communities that concentrated on teaching,[3] were to become a central component to this initiative since their religious status, expanding membership and practical training gave them a decided advantage over lay teachers. And in spite of the turbulent relationships that often existed between priests and sisters, Catholic education in Glasgow was very much a cooperative effort. This chapter focuses on two specific communities, the Franciscan Sisters of the Immaculate Conception, founded by two French nuns, and the Sisters of Mercy, whose foundation stemmed from Limerick. Sisters were a fundamental element in the complex, though not entirely successful, campaign to integrate the Irish migrants with Scottish Catholic culture in Glasgow. As the first to provide any 'systematic education' in the city,[4] their role as educators afforded them considerable spiritual authority that extended well beyond their classrooms. The degree to which Sisters influenced Catholic education, identity and culture can be seen through the spread of devotional activities since it corresponded with the expansion of the religious communities and with the increase in the number of schools. The construction of an 'appropriate' convent or community ethos is an important theme to consider because the work women religious undertook with infants, girls and young women placed them in a unique position to shape the social and religious culture of future generations. It was believed that Sisters who were steeped in a decidedly Scottish tradition would ensure the transmission and adoption of a Scottish Catholic culture. Not only is this a useful starting point for further investigation, but it offers the opportunity to consider the importance of ethnicity within religious communities. Archival material that includes annal entries, personal correspondence, reports and unofficial statements reveals that although the number of Irish-born Sisters was high in both communities, they usually remained subordinate to their Scottish or English counterparts and rarely occupied key positions such as superior or novice mistress during the foundations' formative years.

Much of the scholarship written about women religious comes from Ireland, North America and England,[5] very little comes from Scotland. Francis J. O'Hagan has

3 The term 'active' refers to sisters who undertake various works of charity outside of their convent whereas a 'contemplative' order pertains to nuns who remain enclosed.   4 Bernard Aspinwall, 'The formation of the Catholic community in the West of Scotland: some preliminary outlines', *Innes Review*, 33 (1982), 46–8.   5 Some of the major studies are: Mary Peckham Magray, *The transforming power of the nuns: women, religion and cultural changes in Ireland, 1750–1900* (New York, 1998); Mary C. Sullivan, *Catherine McAuley and the tradition of mercy* (Blackrock, Co. Dublin, 1995); Susan O'Brien, 'French nuns in nineteenth-century England', *Past and Present*, 154 (1997), 142–80; Barbara Walsh, *Roman Catholic nuns in England and Wales, 1800–1937* (Dublin, 2002); Jo Ann Kay McNamara, *Sisters in arms: Catholic nuns through two millennia* (Cambridge, 1996); Carol K. Coburn & Martha Smith, *Spirited lives: how nuns shaped Catholic culture and American life, 1838–1920* (Chapel Hill, 1999); Marta Danylewycz, *Taking the veil: an alternative to marriage, motherhood and spinsterhood in Quebec, 1840–1920* (Toronto, 1987).

produced two books on Glasgow's male and female teaching communities,[6] but neither include much archival material from the convents themselves and his most recent work places too much emphasis on educational theory. Conversely, John Watts' monograph on the Franciscan Sisters of the Immaculate Conception is rich with archival material; so, despite being a general history of the congregation in Scotland, its meticulously researched content makes it a valuable resource.[7] Nevertheless, despite these works, the study of women religious in Scotland remains localized to the west whilst centres like Dundee and Edinburgh in the east, and those Catholic regions in the north-east and south-west remain unexamined.[8] While this chapter is also Glasgow-centred, by considering women religious as agents of Catholic cultural transformation, it represents an important departure from the existing scholarship and is a useful first step in the construction of a comparative study with Edinburgh, where the recruitment of women religious also occurred in response to Irish migration.

In this context, the work of two scholars who consider the Irish and Catholicism in Scotland becomes invaluable: Martin Mitchell's ground-breaking book on Irish political activity in the west of Scotland examines the tension that existed between some of the migrants and church authorities, whilst Bernard Aspinwall's writing on the relationship between Catholicism and British identity stresses the inherent need that Scots Catholics had to take part in the Scottish nation as 'loyal' citizens.[9] Together, they highlight the complexities in a relationship charged with ethnic and religious tension at a time when the emergence of ultramontanism threatened the hegemony of the old recusant families. In Ireland, where studies about women religious are more abundant, Mary Peckham Magray's *The Transforming Power of the Nuns* is a highly influential study proposing that between 1750 and 1900 Sisters and nuns transformed Ireland's Catholics into a 'wealthy, well-educated, ambitious, socially disciplined and notoriously devout' population that challenged the hegemony of the Protestant Ascendancy.[10] Whilst her assertions provide support for a similar argument about Glasgow, there is a fundamental difference: despite rapid population growth

6 Francis J. O'Hagan, *The contribution of the religious orders to education in Glasgow during the period 1847–1918* (Lampeter, 2006); *Change, challenge and achievement: a study of the development of Catholic education in Glasgow in the nineteenth and twentieth centuries* (Glasgow, 1996). 7 John Watts, *A canticle of love: the story of the Franciscan Sisters of the Immaculate Conception* (Edinburgh, 2006). 8 Other works include Martha Skinnider, 'Catholic elementary education in Glasgow, 1818–1918', in James Scotland (ed.), *History of Scottish education* (London, 1969), pp 13–25 and S. Karly Kehoe, 'Special daughters of Rome: Glasgow and its Roman Catholic Sisters, 1847–1913' (PhD, University of Glasgow, 2004) and 'Nursing the mission: the Franciscan Sisters of the Immaculate Conception and the Sisters of Mercy in Glasgow, 1847–1866', *Innes Review*, 56 (2005), 46–60. 9 Martin J. Mitchell, *The Irish in the west of Scotland: trade unions, strikes and political movements* (Edinburgh, 1998). Bernard Aspinwall, 'Catholic devotion in Victorian Scotland', Manuscript of paper delivered in May 2003 at the University of Aberdeen. Also, 'Varieties of modern Scottish Catholic conservatism', in Sheridan Gilley (ed.), *Victorian churches and churchmen* (Woodbridge, Suffolk, 2005), pp 110–38. 10 Magray, *The transforming power,* p. 87.

and legislative reforms, Catholics in Scotland were never in a position to realistically challenge Presbyterian hegemony, despite exaggerated fears over the so-called 'Catholic creep'.

Mary Hickman's work is equally important since she rightly insists on the need for an alternate historiography for the Irish in nineteenth-century Britain that accounts for their subjection to 'active strateg[ies] of incorporation', particularly those pursued by the Catholic church.[11] She identifies Catholic education as one such strategy since it had the best chance of enabling authorities in England and Scotland to realise their ambition of 'produc[ing] good Catholics [as well as] … a body of loyal, respectable working-class English and Scottish Catholics of limited social mobility'.[12] Carmen Mangion's piece on the professional identity of Sisters echoes this point and emphasizes that in England, the education of working-class children was the 'prime objective' of the newly re-established hierarchy after 1850.[13] In Scotland, which remained a mission until its Catholic hierarchy was restored in 1878, church organization and the establishment of a Catholic education system was logistically complicated due to the shortage of resources, but it was diligently pursued as part of the wider Scottish Catholic desire for acceptance as loyal citizens because like England, loyalty to the state was a contentious issue that divided the native-born population and the Irish migrants.[14]

According to the Census, Glasgow's population in 1801 was 77,385, but only roughly 500 or 600 were Catholic, and whilst the majority of these would have been Scots, a number were Irish (an exact breakdown cannot be provided because records were not kept). By 1851, the tail end of the Famine, Glasgow's population had jumped to 329,097 including some 59,801 Irish. Two decades later in 1871 the Irish-born represented 14.32 per cent of the city's 477,732 inhabitants and of these it is usually assumed that roughly three quarters were Catholic.[15] As Martin Mitchell's investigation of Irish political activity in the west of Scotland emphasizes, the tension between the Irish migrants who were politically active and the Scottish Catholic clergy, particularly Bishops Andrew Scott and John Murdoch, had been a factor in slow church development since the early 1820s.[16] Issues such as the establishment of the Glasgow Catholic

11 Mary J. Hickman, 'Alternative historiographies of the Irish in Britain: a critique of the segregation/assimilation model', in Roger Swift & Sheridan Gilley (eds), The Irish in Victorian Britain (Dublin, 1999), p. 241. 12 Ibid., p. 249. 13 Carmen Mangion, '"Good teacher" or "good religious"? The professional identity of Catholic women religious in nineteenth-century England and Wales', Women's History Review, 14:2 (2005), 229. 14 Mary J. Hickman, 'Incorporating and denationalizing the Irish in England: the role of the Catholic church', in Patrick O'Sullivan (ed.), The Irish Worldwide: history, identity. Volume 5: religion and identity (London, 1996), p. 202. 15 Charles Withers, 'The demographic history of the city, 1831–1911', in W. Hamish Fraser & Irene Maver (eds), Glasgow: volume II (Manchester, 1996), pp 142 and 148–9. Graham Walker, 'The Protestant Irish in Scotland', in T.M. Devine (ed.), Irish immigrants and Scottish society (Edinburgh, 1991), pp 49–50. 16 Mitchell, The Irish.

Association in 1823, the Catholic Emancipation Act in 1829 and the Repeal movement of the 1840s made the Scottish clergy fearful of the repercussions such political activities would create for the image of Catholicism in the west of Scotland, and the risk this posed to the financial support that had been received from prominent Protestants.[17] In response, the bishops launched aggressive campaigns aimed at both Irish clerics and laymen, but the blanket bans on participation in political movements, verbal insults, and the transfer of 'disobedient' priests to remote parishes proved largely ineffective.[18] Education thus became a vital stimulus for a culture of devotion and an important recourse for the integration of the Irish with Scottish society, where perceptions of Irish racial, cultural and religious inferiority abounded.[19]

Whilst causing alarm in some Protestant circles, the presence of Sisters and nuns generally tended to enhance external opinions about the progress of the Catholic community and this was not simply because of the extensive social welfare services Sisters provided, but also because of their ability to reshape people's devotional attitudes. In 1850, for example, a report on a reception ceremony for the Franciscan Sisters in the *Glasgow Herald* stated that 'Our fathers would have looked upon the making of nuns in this city with perfect horror and we do not like it yet ... [but] no one is entitled to disturb them in the exercise of their religion so long as these are orderly and peaceful.[20] Devotional activities in the west of Scotland included sodalities, processions, winter concerts and choirs, and in his pioneering study of the Irish in Scotland, James Handley made a point of mentioning the organizational abilities of sisters and emphasized that with service, their authority grew to the point that 'their word was law in many a household'.[21] Sodalities in particular have been identified as important elements in the development of religious culture, and the Sodality of the Immaculate Heart of Mary and that of the Children of Mary in Ireland, for example, had a tremendous influence on transforming the 'devotional attitudes' of young women and, as a result, their family and friends.[22] Sodality membership could often result in vocations, as was the case with the Dublin Sisters of Charity and their Children of Mary where 370 of the first 1,675 members chose the religious life in Ireland and abroad.[23] Both the Children of Mary and the Immaculate Heart of Mary existed in Glasgow, the former being under the direction of the Mercies as early as 1858.[24] Unfortunately, apart from the *Catholic Directory for Scotland*, which is littered

---

17 Ibid., p. 118. **18** Ibid. **19** Colin Kidd discusses this in 'Sentiment, race and revival: Scottish identities in the Aftermath of Enlightenment', in Laurence Brockliss & David Eastwood (eds), *A union of multiple identities: the British Isles, c. 1750–1850* (Manchester, 1997). The broadsides, or the 'tabloids of their day' are useful indicators and some anecdotal references include: *The monkey barber. An account of the wonderful monkey of Glasgow*, c. 1825; *Edinburgh Irish festival; or the popish showman. An account of the procession and progress of Dan, king of the Beggars*, in Edinburgh, c. 1835; *Paddy on the railway*, c. 1860–1880. See the National Library of Scotland's *Word on the Street*. http://www.nls.uk/broadsides/, accessed 9 May 2008. **20** *Glasgow Herald*, 12 Apr. 1850. **21** James Handley, *The Irish in modern Scotland* (Cork, 1947), pp 226–7. **22** Magray, *The transforming power*, p. 100. **23** Ibid., p. 105. **24** S[cottish] C[atholic] D[irectory], particularly editions after 1858.

with errors and omissions, mid-century documentation about sodalities in Glasgow is sparse since the *Observer*, the city's official Catholic paper, only began publication in 1885 and the dissident *Free Press*, which ran between 1823 and 1834, and again between 1851 and 1867,[25] carried little information about devotional activities. What does exist, however, provides enough of a picture to show that devotional activities, directed by male and female religious, were on the rise from the 1850s.

Apart from these types of organizations, the sister-run schools, which included convent, parish and Sunday schools, were perhaps the most effective way for women religious to exert their influence and transform the religiosity of new generations of Catholic children. When the first Sisters arrived in Glasgow, there were but a handful of Catholic schools and only four missions: St Andrew's (1816); St Mary's (1842); St John's (1846); St A. Liguori's (later St Alphonsus') (1846). Twenty years later, the growth was impressive with an additional four new missions: St Joseph's (1850); St Patrick's (1850); St Mungo's (1850); St Vincent de Paul's (1859). Seven of the eight missions had day and Sunday schools, four are listed as having had evening schools and there were also three convent boarding schools, run by the Franciscan Sisters and Sisters of Mercy, the Jesuits' St Aloysius' College and an academy run by the Marist Brothers.[26] By the time the Scottish Catholic hierarchy was restored in 1878, there were fourteen parishes (a mission officially became a parish after restoration) and all of which had day schools with the vast majority offering primary schools for girls, boys and infants. Around this time, the estimated number of school-age children in Glasgow was approximately 18,578 and, although there was only accommodation for 12,360, it represents the fruits of a collective effort. Overall, by 1880, the Franciscan Sisters and the Sisters of Mercy were responsible for sixteen of the twenty-seven schools for infants and girls in the city, but it must also be recognized that the majority of the lay female teachers working in the other schools would have received their own education from the sisters.[27] The construction of new schools corresponded with the expansion of the religious communities, particularly the Franciscan Sisters of the Immaculate Conception. Although having been located at Charlotte Street since 1847, the community had grown enough by 1861 to merit the opening of another house in Abercromby Street, and this was in addition to its other houses already established in Inverness and Aberdeen. Their status as a pontifical institute enabled them to work in a number of missions simultaneously; so, although they had only two Glasgow addresses, their presence was felt across the city.[28] The Mercies, a diocesan community, remained comparatively small, but they too made a considerable impact on the young Catholic women of Glasgow.

Since Catholic education was regarded as a way to curb 'urban working class' problems such as poverty, intemperance and apostasy,[29] the recruitment of teaching

25 John K. M'Dowall, *The people's history of Glasgow: an encyclopedic record of the city from the prehistoric period to the present day* (Republished ed., Wakefield, 1970), p. 51. 26 CDS, 1848 and 1868. 27 *Detailed Statistics of Each School*, 1878–1879 and 1880–1881, Education Reports, GAA, ED7. The Franciscan Sisters were present in 13 parishes whilst the Sisters of Mercy were active in three. 28 Watts, *A canticle*, Appendix Two, p. 258. 29 McNamara,

Sisters, into whose religious communities specific cultural values would be instilled, represented an important first step in the process of cultural transformation. In 1847, the Franciscan Sisters of the Immaculate Conception were the first religious to arrive in Glasgow and the second to return to Scotland since the Reformation.[30] Two years later, the Sisters of Mercy arrived and like the Franciscans they had been recruited by Fr Peter Forbes, an enterprising priest from Glasgow's St Mary's Parish, Abercromby Street. Like most women religious in the mid-nineteenth century, these sisters responded to sporadic crises, undertaking nursing work during epidemics and the administration of poor relief during periods of extreme impoverishment, but their rules show that education was a primary focus. For example, the *Rule* of the Franciscan Sisters states that they were primarily a teaching community whose Sisters 'devote themselves chiefly to impart a sound Christian education to young girls ... [and] to form their hearts of virtue',[31] whilst that of the Mercies stressed 'a most serious application to the instruction of poor girls, visitation of the sick and protection of distressed women of good character'.[32]

Although Forbes had asked the Sisters of Mercy to come to Glasgow before the Franciscan Sisters (they were unable to do so), it is important to view this request as one of necessity rather than a willingness to welcome Irish Catholic culture. On a practical level, it made sense to recruit from Ireland and France, where Sisters and nuns were far more numerous than in either England or Scotland. In Scotland there were just fourteen Ursulines based in Edinburgh and the vast majority of England's thirteen orders and congregations were contemplative (enclosed) with active sisters (unenclosed) numbering somewhere in the region of sixty. Eight congregations established themselves in England between 1841 and 1849, with the majority being in and around London, but just two arrived in Scotland over the same period.[33] In Ireland the number of women religious increased from just 120 in 1800 to roughly 1,500 by 1850,[34] whereas in France roughly 200,000 women joined over 400 congre-

---

Sisters in arms, p. 621.   **30** The first were the Ursulines of Jesus who arrived in Edinburgh from France in 1834. Charles Smith, *Historic south Edinburgh* (Edinburgh, 2000), p. 49. Agnes Trail, *Revival of conventual life in Scotland: history of St Margaret's convent, Edinburgh, the first religious house founded in Scotland since the so-called reformation; and the autobiography of the first religious sisters Agnes Xavier Trail* (Edinburgh, 1886) pp 20–1.   **31** Box marked 'Copies of Early Constitution', #031.30, F[ranciscan] S[isters of the] I[mmaculate] C[onception] A[rchives]. This object was retained when the *Rule and Constitutions* were revised in 1853. **32** *Rules and constitutions of the religious called the sisters of mercy, part Ist, Glasgow 1849, shelfbooks*, S[isters of] M[ercy] C[onvent] A[rchives], Glasgow.   **33** Carmen Mangion, unpublished statistics (2007). The first simple-vowed congregations were the Faithful Companions of Jesus, London (1830), Institute of the Blessed Virgin Mary, York (1836) and the Sisters of Mercy, London (1839). Walsh, *Roman Catholic nuns*, pp 165, 170–1. *Census of the population in Scotland, 1841*, Convent, St Margaret's, S[cottish] C[atholic] A[rchives], MC/3/7/11. Seven were listed as being foreign, one was from England and five were Scottish, though none of the Scots were from Edinburgh. They ranged in age from 20 to 35. Two servants, one from England and one from Edinburgh were also listed, but they were likely lay sisters. **34** Magray, *The transforming power*, pp 8 and 26.

gations between 1800 and 1880 – a phenomenal trend considered to be a powerful attempt to 're-Christianise French culture and society'.[35]

Although the Scottish mission had important links with England, Ireland and the Continent, based on aristocratic ties, kin networks, migration and through the numerous Scots seminaries located in France, Spain, Italy and Belgium, the mission was distinct and somewhat detached, and this was due as much to geography as to custom and 'Scottish clannishness'.[36] Sisters north of the border were more isolated than their counterparts elsewhere and this would have increased their susceptibility to clerical interference. Convincing women religious to come to Scotland was only the first step in establishing them as part of its religious landscape; the manipulation of a religious community's ethnicity was the second. It was at this stage that conflict often erupted, either between the religious community and male clerics or amongst Sisters themselves. The manipulation of a community's ethnic identity was a common feature of religious life and there are numerous illustrative examples of this from England, France and North America. Ethnic tension was widespread within religious communities, and although Sisters were expected to move beyond this, it is clear that nationalisms and cultural biases were rarely left behind in 'the world'.[37] In England, for example, it is recalled that the election of an English superior to a French community sparked distress amongst the French sisters who did not welcome the 'infus[ion of] … an Anglo-Saxon spirit'.[38] In Scotland, the French culture of the Franciscan foundresses Adelaide Vaast, who was struck down by cholera in 1849, and Veronica Cordier, also proved to be occasional obstacles, but it was the Sisters of Irish birth who posed a more immediate concern to the city's leading clerics. As the number of Irish entrants grew, which is not surprising given the fact that Glasgow housed one of the densest Irish populations in Britain, second only to Liverpool, there were increasing fears that Irish-born Sisters would assume positions of authority within the convents.[39] In the first seven years of the Franciscan Sisters' existence, and before their first branch house was opened in Inverness, there were fifteen Irish entrants and ten Scots, though surnames and place of birth (Glasgow) indicate that at least three were of Irish descent.[40] The circumstances were somewhat different for the Sisters of Mercy who were an Irish congregation and whose Glasgow establishment had been started by five Irish sisters from Limerick: Mother M. Elizabeth (Anne) Moore, the Limerick superior who returned after the initial foundation

35 O'Brien, 'French Nuns', 144.   36 In 1926, the archbishop of Glasgow cited this as one of his reasons for supporting the canonization and beatification cause of Edinburgh's Margaret Sinclair. D. Mackintosh to Fr T. Agius, 1 Dec. 1926, SCA. HC13/2/1.   37 This theme is dealt with in McNamara's *Sisters in arms*, pp 265–99.   38 O'Brien, 'French nuns', pp 156 and 164.   39 Irene Maver, *Glasgow* (Edinburgh, 2005), pp 84. Roger Swift, 'The historiography of the Irish in nineteenth-century Britain', in Roger Swift (ed.), *Volume 2: The Irish in new communities* (Leicester, 1992), p. 57.   40 Kehoe, 'Special daughters', Database 1.

arrangements were taken care of, Sr M. Catherine (Anne) McNamara, who became the first superior, Sr M. Clare (Mary) McNamara, Sr M. Joseph (Margaret) Butler and Sr M. Clare (Helen) Kerrin. During their first twenty years, twenty-one women were professed: eight of Irish birth, nine of Scottish birth and four from England.[41]

As mentioned above, convent leadership was a significant concern for the Scots clergy and was thus subjected to considerable scrutiny, intervention and manipulation. Although Sisters had a significant degree of autonomy, it is important to remember that they were not autonomous and that priests and bishops often used their positions as ecclesiastical advisors or superiors to implement changes. In some cases, if they exerted too much pressure, entire communities of Sisters would simply pack-up and relocate to a parish where the priest was more accommodating, but in Glasgow, where individual Sisters did leave under such circumstances, the foundations were never completely abandoned. Much of the tension surrounded two of the most important positions within a convent: the superior or prioress and the mistress of the novices. Superiors were elected by professed sisters and aside from managing a convent's practical affairs they shaped religious identity and set an example for the rest of the community. Superiors were to 'govern with advantage to the community' and were responsible for the selection of Sisters for key posts such as sub-prioress or assistant superior, bursar and novice mistress.[42] The latter was a tremendously influential office whose bearer took responsibility for shaping the religious identity of the new entrants. Both the Franciscan Sisters and Mercy community experienced the close surveillance of these positions by their male superiors and almost as soon as they arrived, the Mercies in particular encountered problems. While gender was an important factor and certainly influenced relations between the clergy and the women religious, much of the tension centred around the ethnicity of the founding Sisters and the control exerted by Mercy Superiors in Limerick and Liverpool. In a statement about the community's troubled state of affairs in the early 1850s, Alexander Smith observed that Murdoch's 'national feelings' made his relationship with the Sisters particularly difficult.[43]

In 1850 a serious dispute erupted over Sister Mary Bernard (Margaret) Garden, a young Aberdeenshire woman whom Murdoch had placed in the Mercy Liverpool novitiate so that she could eventually head the Glasgow foundation. Her transfer from the Mercy community in Liverpool to Dublin and then Limerick during the pervious year had sent a strong message to Murdoch about the authority structure within female communities, but his failure to respect this soured relations with the mother superiors, whose membership in a growing international religious congregation afforded them significant collective support. What transpired resulted in Murdoch being forced to travel to Limerick to retrieve the Scottish Sister himself to carry out his ultimate goal of 'phasing out' the original Irish sisters with the installa-

41 Ibid., Database 2.   **42** John Nicholas Murphy, *Terra incognita or the convents of the United Kingdom* (London, 1873), pp 702–4.   **43** Alexander Smith, *Statement of the convent of mercy* (1857), Mercy International Centre Archives, Dublin.

tion of a Scottish superior. Understanding this to be the case, and having deep suspicions of his 'anti-Irish feelings', the superior in Glasgow, following orders from Moore in Limerick, had begun to gradually remove the original Irish Sisters.[44] The following year, the community fractured along ethnic lines. The transfer back to Limerick of the two remaining Irish Sisters sparked an angry exchange between Peter Forbes, who was anxious for work to be accomplished in his parish, and Sr M. Catherine McNamara, the mother superior, that resulted in the egregious exodus of seven Sisters (three professed and four novices).[45] Just two young professed Sisters remained in Glasgow, among them was Garden who was immediately appointed superior by Murdoch, and five novices and postulants; all but one were Scottish.[46] Ultimately, the Scottish clergy believed they had been wronged by the Mercy superiors who had a poor understanding of the position of Catholicism in Scotland:

> I think those who opposed MMB's coming to Glasgow were quite in the wrong … They might have thought that she was not ripe to become superior. In this I and you too would have joined them … It was I understand necessity … But to seek to prevent a Scotch woman from giving & her own poor country women who stood so much in need of religious instruction … was I think unreasonable and contrary to all due order.[47]

For her part, Garden also exhibited a desire for Scottish, as opposed to Irish, sisters when, in a letter to Smith asking him to send along young women who might be inclined for the religious life, she added, 'we could get as many sisters as we wished from Ireland, but we want persons from this country, if possible.'[48] Her term as superior lasted just one year, her health having broken down on account of the stress of the situation, and aside from an interim superior who arrived from Liverpool to save the fledgling community, there were just three superiors between 1854 and 1871 and all were Scots considered capable of instilling a Scottish identity within the community that could then be transmitted through their schools and other social welfare activities. It was only in 1871 that an Irish superior was elected, but this was three years after Charles Eyre, an Englishman, assumed the position of bishop in an effort to alleviate once and for all the tension between the Irish and Scottish Catholics.[49]

What the above discussion illustrates is that the Glasgow clergy made a direct link between the presence of a Scottish-born superior and the survival of a Catholic identity in Glasgow that was distinctively Scottish. A candid comment from James Kyle, bishop of Scotland's Northern District, is particularly revealing and serves to empha-

44 Ibid.   45 Kehoe, 'Special daughters', p. 62.   46 Names of Sisters who entered in Glasgow, SMCA, Glasgow.   47 Bishop Kyle to Bishop Murdoch, 3 May 1852, SCA, OL2/83/5.   48 Sr M. Bernard Garden to Alexander Smith, 2 Oct. 1851, SCA. BL6/615/1. 49 Names of sisters who entered in Glasgow, held in green plastic binder marked 'Brief History of Glasgow Foundation' and 'Hand-written Account of Foundation', SMCA, Glasgow. Bernard Aspinwall, 'Anyone for Glasgow: The Strange Nomination of the Rt. Rev. Charles Eyre in 1868', Recusant History, 23 (1997), 589–601.

size the importance placed upon creating a Scottish Catholic identity, '[had Garden not returned to Scotland] the Glasgow establishment would never have been, or would have been liable to instant annihilation as the frat of those who know nothing of [the] circumstances.'⁵⁰ Such examples of the deliberate exclusion of Irish women from positions of authority also exist with the Franciscan Sisters, but seem rather to have been the result of Bishop Smith's interventions as opposed to Murdoch's. It was often the case in missions that difficulties surfaced when continental nuns tried to preserve the older traditions, and whilst it is clear that Cordier's French ways did not suit everyone, the congregation's pontifical status provided a stronger buffer against clerical interference, but even with this status their vow of obedience often meant that they were forced to conform to the wishes of the bishop, into whose mission they had been invited.⁵¹ Upon arriving in Scotland, the Franciscan Sisters officially broke from their old congregation and formed a new one, but they retained the rule from Tourcoing until 1853 when one more suited to their needs in Glasgow, and co-written by Smith, was finally approved by Rome. When the new rule was being constructed, a conflict arose between Cordier and Smith, and although the details of this dispute remain obscured, the rule Rome approved provided their ecclesiastical superior (who at this point was Smith) with considerable authority as evidenced by the following excerpt:

> The religious convinced that their bishop or any of his deputies to them is the representative of God, and that whatever commands they receive from him are issued in the name and with the sanction of his Divine Master, will submit with alacrity to whatever orders or direction he may be pleased to communicate to them.⁵²

Smith exercised his position as ecclesiastical superior with great assiduousness over a number of important decisions including the community's elections. In 1854, during the first general chapter, Cordier was officially elected prioress and had selected Sr M. Angela (Hannah) McSwinney, a native of Co. Cork, as sub-prioress and novice mistress, but Smith vetoed this choice in favour of Sr M. Aloysius (Barbie) McIntosh, a Jamaican-born woman of Scottish-Catholic parentage. Smith's appointment of McIntosh split the community and after three years of tension, Cordier resigned and, went with three other sisters to found another congregation in Jamaica.⁵³ When

---

50 Bishop Kyle to Bishop Murdoch, 3 May 1852, SCA. OL2/83/5. 51 A pontifical institute has a superior general and a mother house and its cardinal protector is appointed by Rome to 'decide in any case of difficulty'. A diocesan community is independent of other communities and has the local bishop at its ultimate authority. However, in both cases, the local bishop preserves all diocesan rights. SCA. MC1/4. General Council, St Margaret's Convent. 52 *Rule of the community of the third order of St Francis, Glasgow, as revised and modified by the sacred congregation of bishops and regulars at Rome and approved by his holiness, Pius IX A.D. 1853.* Ch.2.1.1.1, FSICA. 53 *Obituary list,* FSICA. In 1862 Cordier returned to Tourcoing in poor health, but survived until 13 November 1913. The interesting Scoto-

Cordier resigned her position, the community elected McSwinney prioress and,w although Smith did not approve of this choice, her status as one of the foundation's first entrants and as a Sister who had acquired considerable experience under Cordier, would provide the Sisters with much-needed stability at a difficult time. Aware of the potential damaging impact the foundress' resignation could have upon the community and of the protest already being exercised by the Sisters who elected McSwinney, Smith accepted her as superior, and she held the post from 1856 to 1860 and again from 1866 to 1869. The presence of an Irish prioress, however, was clearly displeasing and despite his earlier criticisms of Murdoch's anti-Irish opinions, Smith complained:

> The Franciscans – don't please me at all. There is nothing very far amiss – but the prioress is intensely Irish – Irish in her feelings & prejudices, associations, want to order, want of cleanliness – manifesting her sympathies – this in respect to priests, nuns & people and children.[54]

Interestingly, the number of Irish women rejected by the community before McSwinney assumed control was ten (two were French, one was Scottish and seven were Irish), whereas during her leadership no Irish women were dismissed. In addition, it is also worth mentioning that when her second term as prioress came to an end in 1869, all of the succeeding prioresses until 1908 were Scots of old Catholic stock.[55]

Although the majority of the women who joined the Franciscan Sisters were from Scotland (mainly Glasgow and the north east) over 40 per cent were Irish-born and yet this high percentage did not translate into a comparable number of Irish sisters assuming positions of authority. In the Mercy community, Scottish sisters, mainly from Kirkcudbrightshire in the south west and from Glasgow, predominated in a community that had been founded by Irish sisters from an Irish congregation. Just nine of the forty-two Sisters of Mercy (less than 25 per cent) were Irish, a stark contrast to the Franciscan Sisters.[56] This difference must tie in with the clergy's concerted efforts to contain the influence of the Irish sisters in the Mercy community during the early years of the foundation. It also goes some way towards showing that whilst the Franciscan foundresses were also ethnically distinct, their culture was perceived as less threatening and less subversive than the Irishness of the Sisters of Mercy since it was only when Irish Sisters were proposed for the positions of sub-prioress and novice mistress in the Franciscan community that the clergy ordered changes.

In spite of the challenges outlined above, some 194 women joined the Glasgow novitiate of the Franciscan Sisters of the Immaculate Conception between 1847 and 1913 before being scattered across Scotland to serve in one of the congregation's thirteen communities.[57] Between 1849 and 1907, forty-two women became Sisters of Mercy in Glasgow, but the overall impact of both groups is put into even greater perspective when it is learned that these were just two of the eight female congregations who were active in the city at this time and engaged in work ranging from education, nursing and poor relief to running homes for the disabled, the elderly and the orphaned. In contrast, the number of priests belonging to religious orders was 55 in 1878, growing to 94 by the outbreak of the First World War.[58] These numbers highlight the potential women religious had to influence the masses, and although it has been noted that in 1849 Smith feared Glasgow was 'not yet prepared for the good sisters',[59] just seven years later, he was writing of their indispensability.[60]

Empire and the age of industry had given Scotland the recognition it had long desired and as ideas about nationhood and identity began to emerge and take shape, the Scots Catholics struggled to claim their place in a nation that had defined itself by what it was not – Catholic. Like their counterparts elsewhere, the Scottish Catholic clergy were working to keep both their institution and culture afloat,[61] but unlike Ireland and England, there were fundamental population, cultural and religious differences at play that made Scotland's experience unique. The desire to foster a decidedly Scottish identity within these two congregations of women religious must be seen as a consequence of the deeper notions about identity and citizenship that were confronting the Catholic community in Scotland as a whole. The clash of the Irish and Scottish Catholic cultures saw the Scots adopt an offensive stance and successfully retain the most powerful positions within the mission church for themselves, and it has been shown that notwithstanding the agency of the Sisters, their ethnicity remained a key concern. Their daily contact with 'the people' at a range of levels meant that they were more accessible than the clergy; their religiosity was what would shape that of their pupils, patients and the poor who relied upon them for help. The deliberate exclusion of Irish-born Sisters from the key posts within the religious communities is thus indicative of the broader need to have the Sisters impart a decidedly Scottish influence over the Catholic population, whose exposure to the religious culture of the Sisters would, at a young age or during a period of vulnerability, plant the seeds for a more devout and, ideally, Scottish Catholic community.

---

57 For a full list see Watts, *Canticle*, Appendix Two, pp 258.   **58** Mark Dilworth, 'Religious orders in Scotland, 1878–1978', *Innes Review*, 29 (1978), 103-7.   **59** Quoted in Aspinwall, *Catholic devotion*, Footnote 81 in unpublished version.   **60** Smith to T.W. Allies on the subject of education by religious – with account of progress, 28 Oct. 1856, SCA, OL2/86/10.   **61** Magray, *The transforming power*, p. 3.

Irish Presbyterian commemorations of their Scottish past, c.1830–1914

ANDREW R. HOLMES

The vocabulary of 'memory', 'forgetting', 'commemoration' and 'identity' has become ever-present in recent historical scholarship. Historians are now much more aware of how national identity has been 'imagined' or 'narrated' by particular groups, and how this process involves remembering certain historical events and personalities through acts of commemoration.[1] Certainly there is a complex relationship between the historical material available and the use of it for contemporary political and cultural ends. This complexity has fuelled much of the current debate between those who would wish to emphasize the invention of national traditions in the second half of the nineteenth century and those who adopt an ethno–symbolic approach and examine the re-working of pre-existing materials for contemporary needs.[2] Memory, it seems, has 'a history of its own', and a study of the assembling and articulation of past experiences by various groups tells us much about what they believed was important to their identity at any given period of time.[3]

Remembering is a central component of the identity of not only nations and individuals but also of Christian denominations. Christianity is a supremely historical religion in which the recollection of the redemptive acts of God in history define the content of true belief.[4] Throughout the Old Testament the Children of Israel were implored by prophets, poets and kings to remember that God had delivered them from Egypt and brought them to the Promised Land of Canaan. In the New Testament, redemption occurred through the earthly life, death and resurrection of Jesus the Christ, his sacrifice on the cross regularly commemorated through the sacrament of communion. Despite the historical claims and essence of Christianity, very little attention has been devoted to how Christians, specifically in the United Kingdom and Ireland, remembered and commemorated their denominational past.[5] This is particularly inexplicable in an Irish context where 'collective groups have ...

---

1 J.R. Gillis (ed.), *Commemoration: the politics of national identity* (Princeton, 1994); Patrick Hutton, 'Recent scholarship on memory and history', *History Teacher*, 33 (2000), 533–48; Jay Winter & Emmanuel Sivan (eds), *War and remembrance in the twentieth century* (Cambridge, 1999). 2 See the readings collected by John Hutchinson & A.D. Smith in *Nationalism* (Oxford, 1994). 3 The phrase is from I.R. McBride, 'Memory and national identity in modern Ireland', in I.R. McBride (ed.), *History and memory in modern Ireland* (Cambridge, 2001), p. 6. 4 R.E. Frykenberg, *History and belief: the foundations of historical understanding* (Grand Rapids, MI, 1996), pp 191–241. 5 R.N. Swanson (ed.), *The church retrospective*, Studies in Church History, 33 (Woodbridge, 1997).

expressed their values and assumptions through their representations of the past' and where religion is entwined in a variety of ways with political allegiances.[6]

This essay seeks to address this lack of scholarly attention for the largest and culturally most important Protestant denomination in the north of Ireland, the Presbyterian church. In particular, it examines how and why Presbyterians in Ireland commemorated their Scottish origins and character in the period between c.1830 and 1914. The principal commemorations were organized for the Scottish Second Reformation of 1639 (1839), the formation of the first presbytery in Ireland by Scottish chaplains in 1642 (1842), the beginnings of the Scottish Reformation in 1560 (1860), the death of John Knox in 1572 (1872), his birth in 1505 (1905), and the coming of the first Presbyterian minister to Ireland from Scotland in 1613 (1913). By examining the content of these commemorations this essay develops three broader themes. First, it uncovers some important religious and ideological linkages between Presbyterians in Scotland and Ireland during this period and the sense of mutual dependence they shared. Second, scholars have noted the growing importance of a distinctive Ulster or Ulster-Scots identity during the home rule crises between 1885 and 1914 that built upon the prosperity of Belfast, provincial confidence, and various technical advances. This was given classic expression on Ulster Day, 28 September 1912, when around 450,000 men and women pledged themselves to oppose home rule by signing documents directly modelled upon the Scottish Solemn League and Covenant of 1643.[7] This essay sketches in some of the pre-history of the emergence of an Ulster-Scots identity by showing how a provincial identity was already in place and was related to the Presbyterian understanding of the Scottish character of their religion and their central role in the evolving history of both the northern province and the British state.

Finally, the Irish Presbyterian commemoration of their Scottish past expressed central components of their religious, cultural and political identity in the nineteenth century. By drawing attention to these themes, this chapter offers a corrective to existing scholarship that has focused on the origins of Irish republicanism within Presbyterianism in the late eighteenth century while their nineteenth-century successors have been either dismissed as evangelical reactionaries or treated as a homogenous denominational label rather than as a group containing a variety of conflicting political and theological groupings.[8] By considering how Irish

---

6 McBride, 'Memory and national identity in modern Ireland', p. 3.   7 James Loughlin, 'Imagining "Ulster": the north of Ireland and British national identity, 1880–1921', in S.J. Connolly (ed.), *Kingdoms united? Great Britain and Ireland since 1500: integration and diversity* (Dublin, 1999), pp 109–22; Graham Walker, *A history of the Ulster Unionist party: protest, pragmatism and pessimism* (Manchester, 2004), pp 32–6.   8 I.R. McBride, *Scripture politics: Ulster Presbyterians and Irish radicalism in the late eighteenth century* (Oxford, 1998). For the nineteenth century see J.R.B. McMinn, 'Presbyterianism and politics in Ulster, 1871–1906', *Studia Hibernica*, 21 (1981), 127–46; B.M. Walker, *Ulster politics: the formative years, 1868–1886* (Belfast, 1989); Paul Bew & Frank Wright, 'The agrarian opposition in Ulster politics, 1848–87', in Samuel Clark & J.S. Donnelly, Jr. (eds), *Irish peasant: violence & political unrest, 1780–1914* (Manchester and Madison, WI, 1983), pp 192–229.

Presbyterians understood their sense of Scottishness through commemoration, this essay begins to sketch some of the key theological and political priorities of Presbyterians in Ireland. It shows how these were articulated in response to specific developments such as the reformation of Presbyterian church life in the first decades of the century, the emergence of Puseyism within Anglicanism, the re-organization of the Roman Catholic church in Ireland, and the growing demand for Irish home rule. In particular, five interconnected principles or themes will be illustrated. First, Presbyterians were convinced that Presbyterianism contained the essential doctrines of the Christian faith, reflected best the biblical model of church government (especially that found in the New Testament), and had been vindicated by the spread of the denomination across the globe. Second, the truth of Presbyterianism was contrasted with the erroneous character and principles of Anglicanism and Catholicism. Indeed, the re-articulation of their Scottish past reinforced the traditional anti-Erastian, anti-episcopal and anti-Catholic principles of politically-liberal Presbyterians in particular. Third, it was claimed that the scriptural character of Presbyterianism embodied and propagated freedom from political and spiritual tyranny and oppression. Presbyterians in both Ireland and Scotland during this period asserted that British civil and religious liberty was established by John Knox in the sixteenth century, developed by the Covenanters in the seventeenth, and confirmed by William III, portrayed as a staunch Calvinist, at the Glorious Revolution. Fourth, the influence of Presbyterianism in Scotland and Ulster had led to the economic and moral improvement of those areas and their elevation to global prominence. Evidently, true Presbyterian religion made nations great. Finally, Presbyterianism not only made Ulster and Scotland great, but it was firmly believed that it could also transform the spiritual and social lives of those living in the south of Ireland and overseas. Consequently, nineteenth-century Presbyterians were active in the Protestant missionary movement, bringing the Gospel, and much else besides, to the four corners of the globe.[9]

Presbyterianism came to Ireland with the arrival of Scottish settlers to Ulster in the early years of the seventeenth century. Over the following century they consolidated a separate ecclesiastical and political identity in the northeastern counties of Ireland through the establishment of congregations, presbyteries and the General Synod of Ulster in 1690. Though the majority of Presbyterians would remain committed to the doctrines and structures of seventeenth-century Presbyterianism, the influence of moderate theological opinion in both Scotland and Ulster in the eighteenth century led to the deterioration of relations between the Synod of Ulster and the Church of Scotland, which culminated in the termination of ministerial communion in 1818.[10]

9 A.R. Holmes, 'The shaping of Irish Presbyterian attitudes to mission, 1790–1840', *Journal of Ecclesiastical History*, 57 (2006), 711–37. For a broader discussion see Andrew Porter, *Religion versus empire? British Protestant missionaries and overseas expansion, 1700–1914* (Manchester, 2004).

In reaction to the influence of this moderate theological outlook, and encouraged by various economic and cultural developments, Presbyterianism in Ulster and Scotland underwent a far-reaching process of religious reform and revival during the first half of the nineteenth century that sharpened Presbyterian denominational identity and self-confidence.[11] In Scotland, the process of reform contributed to the worsening of relations between the state and the evangelical party within the Established Church of Scotland, led by Thomas Chalmers, over the spiritual independence of the church. The dispute reached a decisive climax in the Disruption of 1843 when over 450 minsters and around two-thirds of the lay members of the Established Church finally withdrew to form the Free Church of Scotland. In Ulster, the movement for reform within Presbyterianism had its roots firmly within the Presbyterian theological tradition and had a profound impact upon church life, leading to the expulsion of a number of Arian and non-subscribing ministers from the Synod of Ulster in 1829, the formation of the present-day General Assembly of the Presbyterian Church in Ireland in 1840, and the outbreak of the 1859 revival. The Presbyterian evangelicals who spearheaded this reformation in the 1820s and 1830s saw their task as one of revival and recovery; they wanted to return their church to the Reformed theology and spiritual experience of the Scottish founders of Irish Presbyterianism in the early seventeenth century and to the doctrinal standards of the Westminster Assembly.[12] For them, Scottishness was intimately related to correct church government, theological orthodoxy and missionary activism.

Two important aspects of this shared process of reform are worth noting. First, two-way connections were made by Irish Presbyterians with Reformed churches in Scotland, continental Europe, the British colonies, and the United States.[13] This allowed Presbyterians to transcend their specific location and to participate in a self-conscious denominational network that provided a common front against the formidable social, political and theological threats of the day. These links were developed and strengthened over the course of the nineteenth century, culminating in the formation of the Alliance of the Reformed Churches Holding the Presbyterian System in 1876, a self-styled union of Presbyterians against 'infidelity and saceradotalism'.[14]

The second aspect to note is that the reformation of church life in this period was facilitated by the re-appropriation by both Scottish and Irish Presbyterians of their common Scottish Presbyterian heritage, which they employed to explain their campaign for orthodoxy and to provide a model of conscientious churchmanship. In other words, there was a symbiotic relationship between their contemporary needs

10 Robert Allen, *James Seaton Reid: a centenary biography* (Belfast, 1951), pp 91–3.   11 A.R. Holmes, *The shaping of Ulster Presbyterian belief and practice, 1770 to 1840* (Oxford, 2006); S.J. Brown, *The national churches of England, Ireland, and Scotland 1801–46* (Oxford, 2001).   12 For an overview of the concept of revival within Presbyterianism see, A.R. Holmes, 'The experience and understanding of religious revival in Ulster Presbyterianism, c. 1800 to 1930', *Irish Historical Studies*, 34 (2005), 361–85.   13 *Minutes of the General Synod of Ulster* (Belfast, 1830), 35; (1832), 38–41; (1835), 86–9; (1837), 41–2; (1839), 47–8, 61–6; (1840), 63–6.   14 M[inutes of the] G[eneral] A[ssembly of the Presbyterian Church in Ireland], v (1876), 102.

and what they choose to remember from their collective past. In Scotland, Thomas McCrie, a minister of the conservative Original Secession Church, reminded Presbyterians, especially in the Established Church, of the personality and principles of their forefathers through his biographies of John Knox (1811) and Andrew Melville (1819). Along with James Hogg and others, McCrie also defended the character of the Covenanters from the unfavourable description of them by Sir Walter Scott in *Old Morality* (1816).[15] In Ireland, James Seaton Reid in his magisterial three-volume *History of the Presbyterian Church in Ireland*, volume one of which was published in 1834, vindicated the evangelical party within the Synod of Ulster and demonstrated how Presbyterianism had made Ulster prosper.[16] More importantly, both Reid and the Scottish historians argued that by protesting against the spiritual absolutism and political tyranny of Catholicism and Stuart Erastian Episcopalianism, the Scottish Reformers of the sixteenth century and the Covenanters of the seventeenth were not only upholding scriptural Presbyterianism and promoting a revival of religion but were also the true originators of British civil and religious liberty.[17] Reid especially contrasted Scottish and Ulster Scots support for civil and religious liberty in the 1630s and 1640s with popish tyranny and prelatical persecution, pointing out that the Solemn League and Covenant of 1643 not only laid the foundations for the moral and economic prosperity of Ulster but also 'ascertained and united the friends of civil and religious liberty, and inspired them with fresh confidence in the arduous struggle in which they were engaged'.[18]

This renewed sense of denominational pride had implications for the relationships between Presbyterians in Ireland and the Anglican and Catholic churches who were also undergoing a similar process of internal reform and religious revitalization.[19] In the decades before 1870 in particular, Presbyterians interpreted developments within these churches through the lens of biblical prophecy, discerning the perfidious influence of the papal 'man of sin' in such developments as the rise of O'Connellite nationalism, the re-organization of the Catholic church under Cardinal Cullen, and the rise of Puseyism within the Anglican established churches in England and Ireland that prioritized ritual over evangelical doctrine.[20] The eschatological

15 Sherman Isbell, 'McCrie, Thomas', in N.M. de S. Cameron (org. ed.), *Dictionary of Scottish church history and theology* (Edinburgh, 1993), pp 506–7; Beth Dickson, 'Sir Walter Scott and the limits of toleration', *Scottish Literary Journal*, 18:2 (Nov. 1991), 46–62; D.M. Murray, 'Martyrs or madmen? The Covenanters, Sir Walter Scott and Dr Thomas McCrie', *Innes Review*, 43 (1992), 166–75; R.S. Rait, 'Walter Scott and Thomas McCrie', in H.J.C. Grierson (ed.), *Sir Walter Scott to-day: some retrospective essays and studies* (Edinburgh, 1932), pp 1–37. 16 Allen, *James Seaton Reid*. 17 Neil Forsyth, 'Presbyterian historians and the Scottish invention of British liberty', *Records of the Scottish Church History Society*, 34 (2004), 91–110; Raphael Samuel, 'The discovery of Puritanism, 1820–1914: a preliminary survey', in Jane Garnett & Colin Matthew (eds), *Revival and religion since 1700* (London, 1993), pp 209–11. 18 J.S. Reid, *History of the Presbyterian Church in Ireland*, ed. W.D. Killen, 3 vols (2nd edn., Belfast, 1867), i, 410–12. 19 S.J. Connolly, *Religion and society in nineteenth century Ireland* (Dundalk, 1985). 20 For the Presbyterian understanding of these theological themes see, A.R. Holmes, 'Millennialism and the interpretation of prophecy in Ulster

scheme of choice for Presbyterians was postmillennialism, an optimistic creed that envisioned the ushering in of the millennium and the downfall of the papal Antichrist before the second coming of Christ at the end of time through temporal and spiritual progress in the form of revivals, missionary success, philanthropic work and scientific progress. Consequently, Presbyterians believed that popery and its offshoot Puseyism had to be challenged and overcome in order to bring about the millennial reign of Christ.

The influence of Puseyism was detected in the late 1830s, early 1840s during the controversy involving Presbyterians and Anglicans in Derry over the scriptural character of Presbyterianism, the church–state tensions in Scotland, and the questioning of the legality of marriages performed by Irish Presbyterian ministers. Those who advocated Presbyterianism in the Derry controversy through *Presbyterianism Defended* (1839) and *The Plea of Presbytery* (1841) had the best of the arguments in favour of the biblical basis of the organization and ritual of their church and, according to one denominational historian, demonstrated that they were no longer in awe of the established church and were ready and willing to engage in debate as equals.[21] *Presbyterianism Defended* was hailed by the periodical of the Reformed Presbyterians (also known as the Covenanters) as a timely repost to the Puseyite enemies of Presbyterianism.

> At a time when some dignitaries, and other ministers of the Church of England, are inflicting serious injury on the cause of our common Protestantism by their high pretensions, and by propounding Popish dogmas, we think the extensive circulation of such a work calculated to advance the cause of genuine Presbyterianism, which we hold to be of *Divine right and original*.[22]

The debate was also linked to the bicentenary of the so-called Second Reformation in Scotland and the example of the Covenanters.[23] The Second Reformation between 1638 and 1643 began with the signing of the National Covenant in 1638 and the meeting of the General Assembly in Glasgow later that year, which had been called by Charles I under pressure from Scottish Presbyterians. When he attempted to terminate its proceedings, the members of the Assembly continued to meet in defiance of his representatives and passed a series of acts abolishing episcopacy, rejecting the Articles of Perth and the *Book of Common Prayer*, and establishing the Presbyterian form of church government in Scotland. The Revd

Presbyterianism, 1790–1850', in Crawford Gribben & T.C.F. Stunt (eds), *Prisoners of hope? Aspects of evangelical millennialism in Scotland and Ireland, 1800–1880* (Carlisle, 2005), pp 150–76; 'The uses and interpretation of prophecy in Irish Presbyterianism, 1850–1930', in Crawford Gribben & A.R. Holmes (eds), *Protestant millennialism, evangelicalism, and Irish society, 1790–2005* (Basingstoke, 2006), pp 144–73. **21** Full details may be found in, Thomas Croskery & Thomas Witherow, *Life of the Rev. A. P. Goudy, D.D.* (Dublin, 1887), pp 71–87. **22** *Covenanter*, new ser., 6 (1839), 191. **23** *Presbyterianism defended, and the arguments of modern advocates of prelacy examined and refuted, in four discourses* (Glasgow, 1839), p. iv.

John Brown, minister of Aghadowey, travelled to Glasgow in 1838 to deliver a series
of sermons in support of the Home Mission of the Synod of Ulster and, in the
process, became caught up in the bicentenary commemoration. In the Hope Street
Gaelic church on 21 November 1838, Brown delivered a sermon in which he
defended the Covenanters from the criticisms levelled by Gilbert Burnett and Sir
Walter Scott. Brown emphasized the Scottish and Irish Presbyterian struggle for
freedom against prelacy, arbitrary government and oppression, and with ease
conflated the story of the Covenanters with that of the Glorious Revolution,

> and with sentiments of the highest respect for the memory of the great and
> good men, whose indomitable love of religion and freedom upheld them in
> uprearing the banner of the Covenant, until William III allured thereby to our
> shores, secured to us, we trust, permanently and forever, the right of worship-
> ping God according to our consciences, without molestation, without injury
> and without fear!

He ended his sermon with a call to Presbyterians in Scotland and Ireland to support
one another 'as in former times' so that 'amidst our contendings against error, and our
efforts to advance the truth, we shall remember each other before the throne of grace,
and remain united under the same banner, until all nations shall enjoy a lasting
jubilee, being subject to the Prince of Peace'.[24]

According to Brown's preface to the printed version of his sermon, the bicentenary of the Scottish Second Reformation had been commemorated with special
religious services in and around Derry.[25] The celebration of that anniversary may
have been confined to a specific area, but the entire denomination was involved in
the bicentenary commemoration of the formation by Scottish ministers of the first
presbytery in Ireland on 14 June 1842.[26] The commemoration involved public meetings and religious services during which appropriate speeches and sermons were
delivered. A number of common themes emerged from these, including the history
of the Presbyterian Church in Ireland since 1642, God's providential care and plan
for the church, the Bible-based constitution of Presbyterianism, Presbyterianism as
the friend of the people and advocate of liberty, and the world-wide aspect of the
denomination. Speeches also emphasized the reciprocal nature of the relationship
between the Scottish and Irish churches, calling on Irish Presbyterians to repay the
debt they owed to Scotland since 1642 by supporting Chalmers and the evangelical
party against the forces of Erastianism. Presbyterians in Ireland overwhelmingly
supported the Scottish evangelicals and immediately recognized the Free Church
'alone as the legitimate representative of those from whom the Presbyterian Church

24 John Brown, *1638; or, the Covenanters; a sermon preached in Hope-Street Gaelic Church,
Glasgow, on the 21st November, 1838* (Glasgow, 1839), pp 11, 24.   25 Ibid., p. 2; *Presbyterianism
defended*, p. iv.   26 For reports of the various meetings see, B[anner of] U[lster], 14 June 1842;
17 June 1842; 24 June 1842; *Londonderry Journal*, 14 June 1842.

in Ireland has always regarded it the noblest distinction to be descended' and only resumed links with the established Church of Scotland in 1885.[27] The shock of the Disruption of 1843, and the ongoing challenge to the legality of Presbyterian marriages in Ireland, led to the articulation of a distinctive Presbyterian political position which challenged both the continued ascendancy of the Church of Ireland in public appointments and state patronage and Henry Cooke's policy of Tory pan-Protestant unity.[28]

Another prominent theme of the bicentenary commemorations was the decisive role played by Presbyterianism in the prosperity of Ulster and its ability to have the same impact upon the rest of Ireland. The Presbyterian newspaper, the *Banner of Ulster*, pointed to the 'singular coincidence' between the progress of Presbyterianism and the progress of the population, agriculture and commerce of Ulster, especially the growth of Belfast.

> There is strong and unimpeachable evidence in these facts, that the easiest mode to improve any country is to improve its people; and that the surest method of making a people free, and keeping them free, is to implant amongst them a knowledge of the Gospel, and preserve it in its purity and truth.[29]

The Moderator of the General Assembly, John Edgar, believed that if his contemporaries planted Presbyterianism in the form upheld by their forefathers they could transform the Shannon, the Barrow, the Suir, or the Lee into the Lagan or the Bann.[30] Underlying this theme was the belief that Catholicism had retarded the economic, cultural and religious advance of Ireland. This was reflected in the final stanza of a poem by William McComb composed to celebrate the bicentenary and which referred to the killing of Protestants in Ulster by Catholics in 1641.

> Two hundred years ago, the hand of massacre was nigh;
> And far and wide o'er Erin's land was heard the midnight cry;
> Now Presbyterian Ulster rests, in happiness and peace,
> While crimes in distant provinces from year to year increase;
> O Lord! their bondage quickly turn, as streams in south that flow,
> For Popery is the same it was two hundred years ago.[31]

For Presbyterian evangelicals, the obvious response was to propagate biblical Christianity among the Catholics of Ireland. Consequently, Edgar was instrumental in forming the Bicentenary Fund which quickly amassed £14,000 to support itinerant preaching, the formation of schools, and the erection of meeting houses in the south of Ireland.[32]

---

27 *MGA*, I (1843), 220; VI (1885), 906–7.   **28** The best treatment of these themes currently available is R.F.G. Holmes, *Henry Cooke* (Belfast, 1981).   **29** *BU*, 10 June 1842.   **30** *BU*, 14 June 1842.   **31** *McComb's Presbyterian almanack and Christian remembrancer* (1843), p. 62. **32** W.D. Killen, *Memoir of John Edgar, D.D., LL.D.* (Belfast, 1867), pp 148–51. Also, W.D.

In 1860 Irish and Scottish Presbyterians joined to commemorate the tercentenary of the Scottish Reformation. Reflecting the concern of British Protestants more generally with the resurgence of political Catholicism, a four-day conference began in Edinburgh on 14 August with the express aim of protesting against the ecclesiastical despotism of Roman Catholicism.[33] A number of Irish Presbyterian ministers were involved in this conference, including Professor W. D. Killen of the Presbyterian College, Belfast (better known as Assembly's College), who delivered one of the main addresses, 'The hand of God in the Reformation'. Killen noted that 'the practical results of Popery and Protestantism have been proved by a comparative trial of three hundred years, and the finger of Providence now points to the countries of the Reformation as the lands of progress, prosperity, and freedom'.[34] Reflecting the views of Irish Presbyterians more generally, he also predicted that the electric telegraph, a direct outcome, he claimed, of the Protestant Reformation, would in due time transmit around the world the news that the papal antichrist, '"Babylon the Great, is fallen!"'[35] Similar themes were aired in a speech delivered by William Johnston of Ballykilbeg who dwelt upon 'the religio-political nature of Antichrist'.[36] Other papers by Irish Presbyterians reported on the progress of the 1859 revival, the benefits of open-air preaching, and the duty of Scottish Presbyterians to support the evangelization of Ireland.[37]

More generally, Presbyterians in England, Ireland, and Scotland agreed to set aside 20 December 1860 as a day of thanksgiving for the Reformation in Scotland, with the Irish General Assembly further recommending 'to the ministers of this Church on that day to call special attention to the aspects of the times in connexion with the movements of the Papacy'.[38] The religious services held throughout Presbyterian Ulster compared Protestant liberty with Catholic tyranny, and detailed the civil and religious benefits that resulted from the Reformation.[39] Some writers drew a clear connection between the Scottish Reformation and the Glorious Revolution. The Revd James Warwick of Joymount congregation in Carrickfergus, the scene of the meeting of the first presbytery and William III's arrival in Ireland, proclaimed,

> If a memorial be erected to Garibaldi on the spot where he first landed in Sicily to give freedom to that land, ought we not to commemorate in this town the Scottish Reformation, which brought us many blessings; and among others, the civil and religious liberty which William III established? What Presbyterian is ashamed, then, to speak of the Scottish Reformation, with which John Knox is identified? What lover of civil and religious liberty is afraid to speak of the Revolution of 1688, with which William is identified? If it had not been for the former, the latter would not have occurred, and

Killen (ed.), *Select works of John Edgar ,D.D. LL.D.* (Belfast, 1868), pp 447–58. **33** *Presbyterian almanack* (1861), pp 62–3. **34** J.A. Wylie (ed.), *Tercentenary of the Scottish Reformation, as commemorated at Edinburgh, August 1860* (Edinburgh, 1860), pp 140–7. **35** Ibid., p. 147. **36** Ibid., pp 282–3. **37** Ibid., pp 270–2, 272–3, 273, 274–6, 287–91. **38** *MGA*, ii (1860), 892; *Missionary Herald* (1860), 545–6. **39** *BU*, 22 Dec. 1860; 27 Dec. 1860.

William would never have sat on the Throne of these realms, as the Prelatists, to a large extent, and the Roman Catholics altogether, were satisfied with James; but the Presbyterians and Puritans supported and encouraged William, and Carrickfergus, in the person of its then Mayor, welcomed him to Ireland.[40]

For Presbyterians in Ireland, 1872 was a busy year for commemorations as it saw the tercentenary of the death of John Knox (20 November), the formation of the first English presbytery (10 November), the St Bartholomew's Day massacre (24 November), and the beginnings of the Dutch Revolt. A committee appointed by the General Assembly to co-ordinate the celebrations directed that on or about the anniversary of the death of Knox, public meetings were to be held in each presbytery to draw attention 'to the distinctive principles of Presbyterianism, to its witness for the truth of Christ, to the remarkable growth and progress of the Presbyterian Church, to its origin and place in Ireland, and to the Providence of God in its history'.[41] In addition, on Sunday, 24 November, ministers were to focus the minds of their congregations on 'those great doctrines of the Bible which were vindicated at the Scottish Reformation, and to which the Presbyterian Church bears a continuous testimony'. A circular was sent to every minister containing these plans and providing a brief overview of the life and teaching of Knox. It also outlined how the doctrines of Knox were brought to Ulster, the origin and development of Presbyterianism in Ireland, its role in forming the Presbyterian Church in America, their advocacy of religious freedom, and their stand against Rome. The Assembly was told in 1873 that there was good reason to believe 'their recommendations were generally adopted'.[42]

The main event of the 1872 commemorations was held in Rosemary Street meeting-house in Belfast where Thomas Witherow, professor of Church History at Magee College, Derry, from 1865 to 1890, delivered a lecture entitled, 'John Knox and His Times'. Witherow was too good a historian not to acknowledge that Knox had 'a certain flavour of intolerance' and too much of a royalist to accept Knox's condemnation of female monarchs when it was quite obvious to him and his audience that Victoria far-surpassed Mary, Queen of Scots, in moral character and true piety. Nevertheless, he thought that the spirit and teaching of Knox were needed to extend the experience of the Scottish Reformation to the whole of Ireland. 'The highest honour that we can pay to such a man is not to praise him and do nothing, but to follow his example so far as our circumstances permit of its being done.' Reflecting the concern of evangelical Protestants more generally at this time with the influence of Ritualism within Anglicanism, Witherow pointed out that 'the time can never come, when the religious principles of which Knox was the representative,

---

40 *BU*, 22 Dec. 1860.   **41** For these details see the information leaflet issued by the General Assembly, *Tercentenary of the death of John Knox* (Belfast, 1872), p. 1; *MGA*, iv (1872), 334–5.   **42** *MGA*, iv (1873), 523.

or the high moral qualities that distinguished him as a man, could be hurtful to society, or could be dispensed with without loss'.[43]

The same themes were rehearsed at the commemoration of the four-hundredth anniversary of the birth of John Knox in 1905. In cities and large towns across the province a 'considerable number' of public meetings were convened. On 21 May the generality of ministers brought details of the life and work of Knox before their congregations, especially his contributions to secular education, church government, civil and religious liberty, and to the maintenance of a pure gospel. It was clear to many that they needed a modern-day Knox to deal with the challenges of industrial and urban expansion and the implications of scientific theories about the origins of man and historical criticism of the text of Scripture. At the meeting in Randalstown, the 'impression was felt that in these days of tampering with revealed truth a second religious Reformer of a similarly honest and brave spirit with John Knox was emphatically required'.[44] The main celebration on 6 June took place in the new Assembly Buildings, located in Fisherwick Place, Belfast. Built in a Scottish Baronial style, this new building was the symbol of an assertive Presbyterianism, proud of its role in the development of one of the most prosperous cities in the British empire, and indicative of the attachment of Presbyterians to their Scottish roots. According to the commemorative brochure of a fund-raising event held in the building in November 1905,

> Belfast is an object lesson of the thrift, enterprise, and stubborn perseverance of the Scotch Presbyterian. In it and its phenomenal growth are represented in summary the characteristics of the Ulster Scot and the qualities which transformed a barren waste into a smiling and prosperous province.[45]

Addresses were delivered at the celebrations in June by William Watson, a Presbyterian minister in Birkenhead, and C.G. McCrie, grandson of the historian Thomas McCrie. The latter told his audience that they should honour Knox as he was the 'restorer of the Church's faith' and the 'fearless assertor of his country's free-doms' by beginning the struggle for civil and religious liberty that was continued through the Second Reformation and the Covenanters and secured by William III.[46] The General Assembly expressed the hope that the attention directed towards 'the life and work of the greatest of the Scottish Reformers may deepen and confirm the loyalty of all the members of our Church to the evangelical truths they lived and laboured to vindicate'.[47]

---

43 Thomas Witherow, *John Knox and his times: a lecture: delivered (by request of the Presbytery of Belfast) … November 20, 1872, on the tercentenary of the death of John Knox, in May Street church, Belfast* (Belfast, 1872), pp 15–16. **44** *Witness*, 26 May 1905. **45** *Grand United Church Extension bazaar, New Assembly Buildings, Fisherwick Place, Belfast, Wednesday, Thursday, Friday and Saturday, November 15th, 16th, 17th, and 18th, 1905* (Belfast, 1905), p. 7. **46** *Witness*, 9 June 1905. The same themes were rehearsed in a popular biography of Knox written by the Revd Andrew Gilchrist, minister of Holywood. *John Knox: his life and work* (Belfast, 1905). **47** *MGA*, x (1904), 1017–18.

Presbyterian interest in their Scottish origins was further demonstrated by the formation of the Presbyterian Historical Society of Ireland in 1907, which traced its origin back to 1877 and the interest expressed by American Presbyterians in their Ulster-Scots roots. According to one of its secretaries, J.W. Kernohan, the history of Presbyterianism in Ireland was 'a noble one' that played

> an important part in obtaining civil and religious liberty, and in working for the moral elevation of the people. By preserving its highest traditions, and setting out the worthy examples of the past, it gives an inspiration to the present generation to emulate and outdo their predecessors, and to work for the good of the Church and its people.[48]

In the midst of the third home rule crisis in 1913, the Historical Society organized the three-hundredth anniversary of the arrival from Scotland of Edward Brice as the first Presbyterian minister in Ireland. Following the general tendency of Presbyterians to conflate the histories of Ulster and of their own church, the official report of the Society pointed out that 1913 marked the tercentenary of both Brice's arrival and the formation of the Belfast Corporation. As the story of Presbyterianism was so closely linked with the tempestuous political history of the province and its economic prosperity, the denomination was 'as important, if not so powerful, as an Established Church'.[49] The writers of the report, Kernohan and his fellow secretary A.G. Crawford, also noted that while 1642 saw the introduction of an organized presbytery, it was 'thought proper' to mark Brice's arrival as it saw 'the beginnings of a form of worship that has had a profound influence on the character of a race which has played a large part in the Old and New Worlds, particularly as pioneers of civilisation, and as framers of constitutions. Had it not been for the Ulster Scot, his industry and energy, the Plantation of Ulster, it is agreed, would have been a failure.'[50] In a circular addressed to every minister within the church, the moderator for 1912, Henry Montgomery, directed a special sermon to be preached from every pulpit in May. He drew attention to the beneficial impact Presbyterian religion, despite its humble beginnings, had upon the country, the stand taken by Presbyterians 'for the great causes of the centuries, and at unspeakable cost has contended for civil and religious liberty'. With obvious application to the political turmoil of the time, Montgomery suggested that each minister preach on these themes,

> giving some account to the inspiring story of our forefathers who planted the Presbyterian Vine in this land, the story of their struggles and of their

---

48 J.W. Kernohan, *The Presbyterian Historical Society of Ireland: its story and aim* (Belfast, [1912]), p. 6.   **49** *Education in Ulster: narrative of early attempts towards the establishment of a Presbyterian university. Reports of the Presbyterian Historical Society of Ireland, 1912–1914* (Belfast, 1914), p. 5. A full report and details of the celebrations will be found on pages 5–7.
50 Ibid., p. 5.

unflinching fortitude and faith in dark and trying times, and of their ultimate success.[51]

The climax of the tercentenary commemorations was held in the Assembly Hall on 3 May. Addresses were delivered by Donald McMillan, who brought the sympathy of the Church of Scotland and promised as in times of trial in the past its full support against home rule, and by two Irish professors, James Heron and F. J. Paul. These were subsequently published and the volume quickly sold out.[52] In his paper entitled 'The Progress of Three Hundred Years', Heron reminded his brethren that behind them lay,

> a noble history, a history of incessant labour and poignant suffering and immense sacrifice for truth and righteousness, and to secure the blessings of civil and religious liberty, a history of which any community may well be proud and thankful, and which is well fitted to inspire, to uplift, and quicken
> ...

He asked those present to draw inspiration from the devoted Presbyterians of the past who cultivated their church and often watered it with their own blood. 'Let us be true to the heritage they have left us, and not surrender lightly what they have won for us at great cost.'[53] Kernohan, and others, drew out the clear implication of the story of Irish Presbyterianism and its Scottish origins for the immediate political context. 'With the shadow of Home Rule on the horizon, in which, with practised vision, they can detect the hand of Rome, it may be safely concluded that the spirit of their forefathers is not dead, nor have they forgotten it.' 'Well versed', he continued, 'in the history and meaning of ecclesiastical tyranny, they may be relied on to give a good account of themselves, while, at the same time, endeavouring to live on equal terms and in harmony with their countrymen of every denomination.'[54]

Presbyterians in Ireland in the nineteenth century had a distinct understanding of their Scottish origin and character that was recalled and refined in response to a variety of internal and external developments. These included the reformation of Presbyterian church life in the first decades of the century, the emergence of ritualism within Anglicanism, the re-organization of the Catholic church in Ireland, and the rise of Irish Catholic nationalism that culminated in the three home rule crises between 1885 and 1914. The Irish Presbyterian commemoration of their Scottish origin and character was an expression of a commitment to evangelical principles,

---

51 *Witness*, 25 Apr. 1913. **52** *Addresses on the occasion of the celebration of the tercentenary of Irish Presbyterianism: delivered in the Assembly Hall, Belfast, the third day of June, 1913* (Belfast, 1913). **53** Ibid., p. 20. **54** Ibid., p. 34. See also the editorials in *Witness*, 25 Apr. 1913; *Belfast News-Letter*, 4 May 1913; *Northern Whig*, 4 June 1913.

denominational self-confidence, and a provincial chauvinism held more widely by protestants in Ulster. It allowed them to define and articulate a narrative of religious and political freedom against the tyranny and ascendancy embodied within Roman Catholicism and, more problematically, Anglicanism. This ambiguity illustrates more generally their precarious, and often-misunderstood, place within Irish society, perched between Presbyterian Scotland, Protestant England, and Catholic Ireland. Presbyterians have always maintained that they are an all-island church (the official title of the denomination is the Presbyterian Church in Ireland) and ministers and communities north and south of the border established in 1920 have always asserted their Irish identity. Yet owing to their concentration in the province of Ulster, Presbyterians have a strong sense of provincial identity and tend to use interchange-ably 'Ulster' and 'Irish' depending on specific circumstances. An examination of the Irish Presbyterian commemoration of their Scottish past demonstrates this ambiguity and that their Ulster character, inextricably linked with their sense of Britishness, became more pronounced as the partition of the island became inevitable.

'The third character': the articulation of Scottish identities in two Irish writers

FRANK FERGUSON

This essay will examine the articulation of Scottish culture and literary identity in the works of two poets, Samuel Thomson (1766–1816) and William Hamilton Drummond (1778–1865). The legacy of Scottish culture and literature is prominent in the work of these individuals. They engage with Scotland on various literary, cultural and political planes. Their work can be viewed a series of declarations of unity with, and discussions of difference and otherness to Scotland, which symbolizes their personal and political commentaries as Irish patriots upon the constitutional Union of Great Britain and Ireland in the early 1800s. As such, their complex literary statements interrogate what has been perceived as an 'ideological community' between Scotland and Ireland, which comprised 'a common ground of ideas and assumptions, firmly anchored in religion, culture and politics'.[1] Both Thomson's and Drummond's works test the assumption that membership of a common community made them always desirous, or able to make positive statements about the Scottish elements of their identity. Furthermore, while both poets inhabited this 'ideological community' there were several other communities that they also moved within and aspired to colonize that informed their literary practice. Also, the impact of the Act of Union with Great Britain and Ireland of 1800/1 cannot be underestimated in the effect it had upon these writers. It was to them the 'rhetorical issue of Irish politics, the thing to be for or against, the simple reason for everything'.[2] However, the political and administrative *Union* was by no means the only matter of discussion in their work. These poets advanced alternative conceptualizations of union in cultural, religious, scientific and philosophical terms that complicate our understanding of north of Ireland Presbyterian reactions to the events of the 1790s and 1800s.[3] And, as such they offer an insight into the mentality of Presbyterian attitudes to union with and difference to Great Britain.

The impact of Scottish settlement in Ireland, which ranged from the state sponsored and private plantations of the seventeenth century to the countless familial and individual migrations of subsequent centuries, has had a profound effect on the political, religious and cultural landscapes of Ireland. This is particularly marked in the

---

1 Elaine McFarland, *Ireland and Scotland in the age of revolution* (Edinburgh, 1994), pp 1–3.
2 Roy Foster, *Modern Ireland, 1600–1972* (London, 1989), p. 290. 3 For a discussion of northern Presbyterian literature concerning the 1798 rebellion see Ian McBride, 'Memory and forgetting: Ulster Presbyterians and 1798', in Thomas Bartlett et al., *1798: a bicentenary perspective* (Dublin, 2003), pp 478–96.

literary record and has recently received renewed interest from scholars. Irish writers, from the north-east of Ireland, who were part of the Scottish diaspora, have sought to negotiate the mixture of Scottishness and Irishness that formed their unique cultural inheritance in numerous ways in their poetry and prose. In the nineteenth century this resulted in an eclectic and creative proliferation of texts that sought to articulate north-east Ulster's distinctive Hiberno-Caledonian identity, whereby writers simultaneously affirmed their pride in being Irish, with a similar desire to be seen as being Scottish as well. The coastal counties of Ulster, Donegal, Derry, Antrim and Down, which had the witnessed the greatest impact of Scottish settlement and culture in the previous two centuries, saw a further sea crossing in this period, that of literary genre and criticism, with poetry in particular proving a popular medium. Although these poets, in the main, viewed themselves as unreservedly Irish, they perceived themselves as sharing much in common with the communities of south-western lowland Scotland from which their families were often descended. This inheritance included Presbyterian belief and practice, an intellectual climate shaped by the Scottish enlightenment and propagated in Ireland by the many ministers, doctors and lawyers who had received their education in Scotland; and a multitude of familial, economic, cultural and personal connections that meshed communities on both sides of the North Channel together. However, despite all the many factors that complicated their national identity, their patriotic attachment to Ireland was evidenced profoundly and profusely throughout their poetry and it is this patriotic attachment that is of relevance to this essay. At the beginning of the nineteenth century their work provides a means to map the situation of northern Presbyterians in the aftermath of the failed United Irish rebellion and the union with Great Britain. This poetry contains many references to the concept of union. Their aspiration to reconfigure their role as Irish poets (with Scottish affinities) within a new political union with Great Britain and Ireland, can be read as an attempt to step beyond the bounds of national literature and into a form of transnational discourse. However, a reading of their work demonstrates that this was often a fraught and unsustainable ambition: one that required considerable encryption and which was contingent on a dedicated readership that was aware of subtle nuance and coded utterance. For some it was more prudent to return to the safer ground of conservative neo-classical epic, where matters of Ireland's literary culture, like its national destiny were placed into the control of the British crown and its representatives.

The essayist John Gamble remarked in the advertisement of his *Views of Society and Manners in the North of Ireland* (1819) that there was a third character type in the north of Ireland, that was neither Irish or Scottish, but a mixture of the two. This 'peculiar people' whose 'Irish vivacity' enlivened their 'Scottish gravity' and 'Irish generosity' ameliorated their 'Scotch frugality' Gamble attempted to make better known to the outside world.[4] The recourse to describing the blending of Irish and Scottish traits in

---

4 John Gamble, *Views of society and manners in the north of Ireland* (London, 1819), p. iv.

the north of Ireland in this period prefigures the racialist discourse of the latter part
of the nineteenth century during the home rule debates that sought to firmly disas-
sociate non-Gaelic, Scottish-descended planters in the north from nationalist Gaels
in the south. Prior to this the mixture of traits was generally viewed positively, with
the perceived weaknesses of one national stereotype being counterbalanced by the
strengths of the other. This is corroborated by Samuel Thomson's poem, first
published in 1799, 'To Captain M'Dougall, Castle Upton, with a copy of the Author's
Poems.'

> I love my native land, no doubt,
> Attach'd to her thro' thick and thin;
> Yet tho' I'm *Irish* all *without,*
> I'm every item *Scotch within.*[5]

    The biographies of Samuel Thomson and William Hamilton Drummond under-
score the proximity of Scotland and Ireland. They were descendants of Scottish
settlers. Both were of a similar age, Samuel Thomson was slightly older, being born
in 1766 while Drummond was born in 1778. They were both born in southern
districts of Co. Antrim, Thomson a few miles outside Belfast at Carngranny, between
the present day Mallusk and Templepatrick, and Drummond in the port of Larne.
They were both Presbyterian. Drummond, a Unitarian, was associated with the more
theologically radical Presbytery of Antrim, which was not subject to the
Calvinist/Trinitarian Westminster Confession of faith. Thomson was more orthodox
in his faith, and was accused of displaying strong Calvinistic tendencies by his friends
in his later years.[6] Journeys made to Scotland and experiences there were to play
pivotal roles in their lives. Drummond had studied for the ministry at Glasgow in the
1790s. Thomson had made a pilgrimage to see Robert Burns in 1794, one of the few
so-called 'weaver poets' of Ulster to have accomplished this feat. Scotland figures
prominently in the work of the poets as provider of literary and linguistic inspiration.
Much of Thomson's verse shares the linguistic and literary vernacular culture of
Lowland Scots tradition. Drummond's work, while not following this route, situates
itself within another arena of Scottish letters, the field of literary antiquarianism
popularized by James Macpherson and his controversial translations of the poetry of
Ossian.[7] Drummond, like several Irish poets writing after Macpherson's chauvinistic
attitude to Ireland's early poetry, stakes a claim for the Ossianic verse for Irish letters,
and as will be argued portrays Scotland and her heroes as aggressors and usurpers.
    Another common quality ascribed to these poets has been queries over the

5 Samuel Thomson, *Simple poems* (Belfast, 1806), p. 89.   6 The Co. Antrim poet James Orr
charged Thomson with this after reading his 1806 collection of poems; see John Gray &
Wesley McCann, *An uncommon bookman: essays in memory of J.R.R. Adams* (Belfast, 1994), pp
129–30.   7 See Fiona Stafford, *The sublime savage* (Edinburgh, 1988); Howard Gaskill, *Ossian
revisited* (Edinburgh, 1991); Clare O'Halloran, 'Irish re-creations of the Gaelic past: the
challenge of Macpherson's Ossian', *Past and Present*, 124 (1995), 69–95.

quality of their work. They have been accused of being derivative imitators of the models they aspired to emulate. Terence Brown in *Northern Voices* claimed that much of late-eighteenth-century Ulster writing was 'frozen in statuesque Augustan impotence'.[8] However, this essay would like to argue that these poets assumed and manipulated this tone and style for a number of strategic reasons. This was done to conceal their earlier radical pronouncements under the guise of being loyal subjects to the new constitutional arrangements. Their compliance to British form and genre stood as a declaration of their loyalty to crown and constitution. Their articulation of and fluency with English and Scottish poetic modes suggests to readers their similarity and equality to English and Scottish poets. But in their very statements of unity they betray anxieties about their contemporary situation, and despite their attempts to demonstrate their apparent consent to the concept of union, one is not entirely convinced.

There is one major contrast between Thomson and Drummond and that is their respective class positions. Drummond was of the 'middle sort': a university-educated Presbyterian minister and schoolmaster. Samuel Thomson was a poor hedge-school master from a labouring background, who was dependant upon subscriptions for the production of his poetry, although he sought in his later collections the protection of upper-class patrons. Both had sought in the 1790s to find a voice in the burgeoning cultural life of Belfast where for a time the rhetoric of civic virtue and the ideals of the American and French revolutions were espoused alongside declarations of the aims of the United Irishmen.[9] After the United Irish Rebellion was crushed in 1798 and a Union with Great Britain pushed through in 1800/1 Drummond and Thomson found it necessary to frame their opinions according to the new political climate; one in which optimism for a new regime in France had been replaced by the imperial tyranny of Napoleon and hopes for reform in Ireland had been vanquished under government reaction and sectarian warfare. Drummond had become a founder member of the Belfast Literary Society that aimed at:

> fostering the rising taste of their native province, and throwing additional light on a district that has of late attracted the curiosity of philosophers, and with respect to which, they enjoy so many local advantages ... to promote the improvement of their own vicinity, and disseminate a knowledge of their native country.[10]

It was agreed that the one thing that this association would not do was to discuss politics. In a sense these poets had much to conceal in the decade after the rebellion. They had shared enthusiasm for the United Irishman movement of the 1790s and

---

8 Terence Brown, *Northern voices: poets from Ulster* (Belfast, 1974), p. 16. **9** For a description of Belfast's commemoration of the French Revolution in the early 1790s see A.T.Q. Stewart, *A deeper silence: the hidden origins of the United Irishmen* (Belfast, 1993), pp 146–7. **10** *Select papers of the Belfast Literary Society* (Belfast, 1808), p. 1.

had both written poetry espousing radical sentiments. Thomson had contributed many poems to its newspaper, the *Northern Star*, and, as Liam McIllvanney has recently demonstrated, he had been among a group of poets who had taken Robert Burns to task for his apparent apostasy in the writing of his poem celebrating 'The Dumfries Volunteers'.[11] Drummond had been one of the Presbyterian ministers suspected of involvement with the United Irishmen. This appears to be due to his publishing two long poems through the *Northern Star* press, *Hibernia* and *The Man of Age* (1797). *The Man of Age* in particular displays many similarities to radical Jacobin-style epics of the period in its simple metrics and impassioned condemnation of the persecutions which 'round green Erin sweeps/ whilst justice slumbers and whilst vengeance sleeps'.[12] Such productions did not escape the attention of the authorities. In Belfast, after the battle of Antrim where a United Irish army was routed, a cavalry officer is said to have placed a pistol at Drummond's head and said, 'You young villain, it is you and the like of you, that have brought this upon us with your infernal poetry'.[13]

In the aftermath of the suppression of the Rebellion and the ratification of the Union between Great Britain and Ireland, Thompson's and Drummond's work became much less overtly radical in expression. And like many better-known Romantic poets such as William Wordsworth, Samuel Taylor Coleridge and Robert Southey, their later work drew charges of apostasy and quietism from contemporaries who maintained true to their youthful ideals. However, while their political opinions may have become more conservative in the 1800s their intimations of personal unions with their Scottish identity, or disinclination towards Scottish history and myth act as imaginative and figurative alternatives to the official Act of Union and stand as a means to recuperate personal and communal selfhood in the face of national trauma.

In his lifetime Samuel Thomson produced three volumes of poetry, and contributed numerous poems to the radical *Northern Star*, the paper of the United Irishmen, and to the liberal *Belfast Newsletter*. His first collection, published in 1793, *Poems on Different Subjects partly in the Scottish Dialect*, was dedicated to Burns and 'rustics of the present age'.[14] As its title suggests it contains many poems in the same vein as Burns' Kilmarnock edition. All of his collections of poems were funded by subscriptions by friends, family and local networks of support. There are prominent northern United Irishmen listed as subscribers and addressed in the poetry, such as Luke Mullan, a neighbour from Roughfort, Co. Antrim and fellow contributor to the *Northern Star*.

11 Liam MacIllvanney, *Burns the radical* (Phantassie, East Lothian, 2002), pp 235–9. 12 William Hamilton Drummond, *The man of age* (Belfast, 1797), p. 1. 13 Quoted in Ian McBride, *Scripture politics: Ulster Presbyterians and Irish radicalism in the late eighteenth century* (Oxford, 1998), p. 204. 14 Samuel Thomson, *Poems on different subjects partly in the Scottish dialect* (Belfast, 1793), p. iii.

Thomson's later collections, produced in 1799 and 1806, rely more heavily on gaining the patronage of local landowners and military personnel. The rebellious nature of his early poetry in the *Northern Star* becomes much less apparent in his work after the rebellion and he is determined to appear as a poet in retirement, a simple poet for the delight of country readers. His 1799 volume, *New Poems on a Variety of Different Subjects*, stems from a determination to write from:

> the rural cot, the humble habitation of the *man* of *labor*: where far apart from political clamor and city bustle, the vigorous sons of Simplicity count their days of innocence beneath the bowers of Content.

And he is quick to suggest that 'here no treason lurks'.[15] Despite these assurances his later poems contain covert statements concealed within his adaptation of vernacular and polite literary traditions to register dissent about the Union and failure of the United Irish enterprise.

One poem of Thomson's that does appear occasionally in Irish anthologies is his 'To a Hedgehog', although much of its philosophical thrust is disguised beneath its prosaic subject matter.[16] Written in the same Standard Habbie stanza form of Burns' 'To a Mouse', this is an Ulster-Scots vernacular poem very much in the same sentimental and philosophical tradition. Carol McGuirk has argued that such poems belong to the genre of Horatian satire, in which a poet observes a subject and closes with a maxim or philosophical statement.[17] Despite its appeal as a rather blunt weapon of country burlesque, this verse variety is a considerably sophisticated and subtle form when used by a skilful poet. It lends itself to ambiguity and satire, as it was employed as frequently for mock elegy and comic flytings as it was for serious elegy and contemplation. It was also a genre in which political statements could be made that would have been apparent to an audience knowledgeable about the poetry, but that would be less obvious to those unfamiliar with the nuances of the vernacular and oblivious to its various hidden meanings. The focus on rural subject matter allowed the poet to articulate the hardships of country life through what was assumed to be a sentimental animal poem.[18] There was also a broader national dimension to such poetry as well. Lowland Scots vernacular poetry had been used, at least from the times of Allan Ramsay in the aftermath of the 1707 Union with England, as a means to maintain cultural distinctiveness in Great Britain despite the disappearance of ones parliament.

In this poem the speaker becomes the elegist for the 'rougher subject' (line 1), the hedgehog.[19] This situates the poem very much within the Lowland Scots vernacular tradition in which everyday objects are used to make philosophical statements on life.

---

15 Samuel Thomson, *New poems on a variety of different subjects* (Belfast, 1799). **16** See for example John Montague's *Faber book of Irish verse* (London, 1975). **17** Carol McGuirk, *Robert Burns and the sentimental era* (Athens, GA, 1985), p. 223. **18** See Andrew Noble, *The Canongate Burns* (Edinburgh, 1990), pp 96–7. **19** See appendix for the complete poem.

The formal maxim of the poem attempts to join Irish and Scottish people together in their condemnation of superstitious thinking, 'witch-craft and omens' and other forms of 'hotch-potch muck' (line 10). On one level Thomson applies a rational, enlightened interpretation of a natural phenomenon to point out the failings of the supercilious in his community, and articulate his sympathetic attachment to nature. He also criticizes those who would contemplate the countryside as a place of pastoral idyll. His hedgehog becomes as symbol of the rural poverty suffered by Irish cotters, who like the hedgehog, must gather wind-fallen fruit and steal milk to survive the winter. In his discussion of the fiendish animal, literally a joke begotten by 'Belzie' the devil, there is an allusion to the hunted and demonized United Irish cause (line 4). They too 'dinna want for pikes' and they too fared badly against the figures of authority and law. With his desire for the animal to evade the sheepdog's wrath we see where Thomson's sympathies lie. The aptly chosen prefatory verse from William Broome's 'The Coquette' plays with reader's expectation for an early-eighteenth-century witty debate on sexual etiquette, only to be offered an elegy and demand to a 'hurchin', a hedgehog or an uncouth, unkempt person to remain safely at home, and a tantalizing thought is threaded through the poem, that the unguarded beauty that Thomson suggests, is like the United Irish cause one protected with pikes and the threat of violence.[20]

While Thomson was keen to shatter the readers' expectations of a pastoral idyll in his treatment of Irish nature, he was voluble in his praise of another motif in the pastoral canon, male friendship in a country setting. Indeed, Thomson's discussion of rural life becomes underscored with his fascination with the persona of the character Damon, his friend and confident, who figures in numerous poems in his 1799 collection, in 'Lyle's Hill, a Rhapsody', 'Crambo Cave', 'The Fairy Knows, or Damon's Birth Place', 'November' and 'Acrostic – To Damon'— 'Just such a bond of union, as of old,/ Saul's son and David did together hold'. Damon as a symbol of a shepherd swain was a commonplace in eighteenth-century poetry. And one that Thomson could have read in any number of literary miscellany, such as John Aikin's *Elegant Extracts*. It also appears in numerous poems by the Scottish poet, Robert Fergusson with whom Thomson would have been familiar. There is some confusion over who Damon may be and the actual nature of the relationship between the two.[21] The acrostic spells out John Williamson Junior in his second volume of poems, but in the 1793 volume Luke Mullan had been an earlier Damon, although the theme was not as developed as in 1799. The figure of Damon also had classical political overtones, as the classical story of Damon and Phintias or Pythias was one of a number of stories about friendship under tyranny, and as such can be read as an allegory of events for 1799.

20 William Broome, *Poems on several occasions* (London, 1739), p. 225.   21 Bridget Keegan, 'Romantic labouring-class pastoral as eco-queer camp', *Romanticism on the net* 36–37 (Nov. 2004–Feb. 2005), www.erudit.org/revue/ron/2004/v/n36-37/011134ar.html, accessed 1 June 2006.

As much as another means to make political statements, Damon, acts as a vehicle to promote Thomson's own poetic identity. Just as both Dorothy Wordsworth and Samuel Taylor Coleridge were employed by William Wordsworth as enablers of his vision of himself, Thomson appropriates Damon as his perfect audience. Damon is the friend, special companion and listener that provides him with the assurance that he is a poet. Their David and Jonathan relationship allows Thomson to articulate a complex and passionate assertion of brotherly love, and propose a system of perfect human coexistence at a time when alternative Utopian systems of Brotherhood had either been dismantled or outlawed in Ireland. One example of this is the 'Elegiac Lines Written on the Last Night of the Year 1798', where the figure of Damon, as shepherd singer is used to provide a commentary on the events of 1798:

> Fare well with all the scenes of guilt and woe,
> Thy every folly, and thy every crime!
> O! had Oblivion kept thee still below,
> Thou luckless period of revolving time!
>
> While we the insects of this fleeting day,
> For acts of treason stand indict'd there:
> Impatient Ruin howls to drag his prey,
> To the hopeless territories of Despair![22]

Thomson's transition from republican bard to poet in country retirement was hardly out of keeping with other poets of the time. However, his retreat did not signal capitulation or silence. In the later stages of his literary career his manipulation of Scots vernacular and British Augustan forms suggest a coded and covert language in his poetry that allows him to safely make pronouncements on the contemporary situation in Ireland.

William Hamilton Drummond's writing of an epic on the Giant's Causeway in Co. Antrim offers slightly different conclusions on the north of Ireland in the early nineteenth century and the place of Scotland and Scottish literary legacy within Irish cultural identity. Drummond's poem extols the Causeway as a grand site of the sublime and the picturesque. He becomes a literary-antiquarian cataloguer of the matter of the north of Ireland for scientific, literary and spiritual celebration, and most of all to praise the north as a site of the blessing of providence, improvement, industry and peace within the Union.[23] Unlike Thomson, Drummond was not

---

22 Thomson, *New poems on a variety of subjects*, p. 82. **23** For a comparison to Drummond's patron, Thomas Percy's antiquarianism See Nick Groom, *The making of Percy's Reliques* (Oxford, 1999). For a memoir of Drummond's life see John Scott Porter (ed.), *William Hamilton Drummond: posthumous sermons* (Dublin, 1867).

content to trace the local, the vernacular and the communal. His vision was for the epic and for a poem that would redefine the north of Ireland and hopefully rehabilitate his public character in the process.

After his unhappy encounter with authority, Drummond's revolutionary ardour understandably cooled somewhat. He continued to write from his base at Belfast and gained prominence in literary circles there as teacher, minister and poet. He gained patronage from Thomas Percy, Anglican bishop of Dromore, famous for his *Reliques of Ancient English Poetry*, who helped him gain contacts with the remnants of Johnson's Club in London and with the Scottish publisher Robert Anderson who likened his patriotic epic on *Trafalgar* (1806) and its description of death of Nelson to Pope and Erasmus Darwin.[24]

The Giant's Causeway is a poem about union and unities, a compendium of scientific exposition, travel-guide, mythic romance, and homily that acts as a declaration of the peaceful and patriotic intentions of Ireland towards to world. *The Giant's Causeway*, as its preface announces, is described as the great artefact of Ireland:

> The coast of Antrim has long been a subject of laudable curiosity, as it furnishes a fine field for geological enquiry, and presents a grand and novel spectacle to the eye of taste, in the wild sublimity of its promontories, the fantastic winding of its bays, and the romantic variety of its cliffs and rocks ...[25]

It is the place where the Irish muse can fully be reactivated, in Nature, and where the traveller, painter and poet, can discover 'Dalriada's wild romantic shore' with the awe inspiring grandeur that only Ireland is said to possess exists:

> Swift torrents foaming down the mountain side,
> Rocks that in clouds grotesque their summits hide,
> Gigantic pyramids, embattled steeps,
> Bastions and temples nodding o'er the deeps,
> Aerial bridges o'er vast fissures thrown,
> Triumphal arches, gods of living stone,
> Æolian antres, thunder-rifted spires,
> And all the wonders of volcanic fires,
> Here broken, shattered, in confusion dread,
> Towers, bridges, arches, gods and temples spread:
> Stupendous wrecks, where awful wildness reigns!
> While all th' ideal forms which fancy feigns
> Sweep the dun rack, and to the poet's eyes,
> In many a strange embodied shape arise.[26]

24 See Robert Anderson to Thomas Percy [13 July 1806], in John Nichols (ed.), *Nichols illustrations*, vii (London, 1831), pp 164–5. 25 William Hamilton Drummond, *The Giant's Causeway: a poem* (Belfast, 1811), p. v. 26 Ibid., p. 1.

Ultimately the causeway is the 'Great fane of God! where nature sits enshrined', a site for Christian redemption and edification after one is led through a picturesque itinerary of myth, science and topographical description. If Scotland is a place full of linguistic, literary and physical connections with Thomson, with Drummond it is a place of threat, danger and marauding armies where Irish heroes are provoked into battle. Drummond continues the long Irish Scottish antiquarian spat of the eighteenth century initiated by James Macpherson, and employs Ossianic precedents to give a mythic reason for the construction of the Causeway.

> From Albin oft, when darkness veiled the pole,
> Swift o'er the surge the tartaned plunderers stole,
> And Erin's vales with purple torrents ran,
> Beneath the claymores of the murd'rous clan;
> Till Cumhal's son, to Dalriada's coast,
> Led the tall squadrons of his Finnian host,
> Where his bold thought the wondrous plan designed,
> The proud conception of a giant mind,
> To bridge the ocean for the march of war,
> And wheel round Albin's shores his conquering car.[27]

Drummond diminishes the recent failed revolution with this confection, substituting myth for history, and replacing north Antrim with a romantic land of the Celtic Golden age, in which artist warrior gods labour to fashion a road across the sea to lay siege to Scottish insurgents. This in itself is an intriguing construction of national identity that places Drummond's own Scottish forebears as alien, other and dangerous, there is no Scottish on the inside, Irish on the outside dichotomy with him.

A fascinating piece of antiquarian legerdemain in the poem that appears to have been overlooked by critics is Drummond's use of Gothic heroes in the causeway.

> Rise mighty Odin, rise in power divine,
> And sink to Hela's gulf our foes and thine,
> These sons of Frost, whom mad ambition goads
> To brave thy power, and scale thy blest abodes."
> Throned on dark clouds, dread Odin heard from far,[28]

Odin and the sons of frost, from Scandinavian mythology, are invoked by the Scots to save them from the onslaught of the Irish. As convoluted as this might appear, there are a number of reasons why Drummond would take this course of action. On a personal level, it can be seen as a cynical ploy to ingratiate himself with Thomas Percy, who had edited Henri Mallet's *Introduction to the History of Denmark* in 1770.[29]

27 Ibid.,pp 9–10. **28** Ibid.,p. 14. **29** Thomas Percy (ed.), *Northern antiquities or a description*

There are also more fundamental reasons why Drummond might choose to invoke the Goths in this poem. Percy had been the first English editor to suggest that Celts and Goths were of two distinct races, and to suggest a cultural superiority of Goths over Celts in his antiquarian editing projects. It is the Goths, the prototypical English who rescue the warring Celtic heroes in Drummond's epic, certainly an ultra loyalist interpretation of events in Ireland in the 1798. To compound this, the Gothic solution to the epic battle is enchantment and magic, that petrifies the heroes, and leaves them, to invert Brown's words, frozen in Augustan potence.

> But by enchanted spells unnerv'd they stood,
> Fixed to the beach, till horror chilled their blood,
> And total change pervading nerve and bone,
> Hard grew their limbs, and all were turned to stone.
> Now oft their shadowy spectres, flitting light,
> Croud to their favourite mole at noon of night,
> In fancy's eye, the curious toil pursue,
> And all the tasks that pleased in life renew.
> One, huge of stature, dark beneath the gloom,
> Grasps in his brawny hand the mimic loom;
> One rides the lion rock; in cadence low,
> One bids the organ's beauteous structure blow;
> While far aloof on yon lone column's height,
> Their Lord and Hero glories in the sight.[30]

It is this battle and its resolution that, pre-eminent in the first book of the poem, arguably more important than the scientific and travel itinerary that follows later that propels Drummond's paean to 'fair Improvement, on the wheels of Time,/Rejoicing, moves o'er Dalriada's clime' where Belfast, not Edinburgh, is honoured as the 'Athens of the land'.[31]

Drummond's propensity to shift his national and cultural allegiances illuminates the difficulty in defining the variable 'third character' of northern Irish Presbyterian poets. Texts such as *The Giant's Causeway* testify that this character was a complex phenomenon, which could not be as easily articulated as John Gamble's sketchbook would assure us. Furthermore, the 'Scottishness' of Drummond and Thomson cannot be understood as simple acts of imitating Scottish poets, but an extended cultural dialogue with and negotiation of Scottish influences that developed through the vicissitudes of personal, social and political change as well as a heightened awareness of the dictates of literary fashion and marketplace. In Samuel Thomson's and William

of the manners, customs, religions and laws of the ancient Danes (London, 1770).
30 *The Giant's Causeway*, p. 16.   **31** Ibid., p. 30.

Hamilton Drummond's poetry Scottishness and Scottish cultural artefacts were invoked, plundered, cannibalized, celebrated and appropriated to suit the needs of the individual poets. While Thomson and Drummond both existed within a shared ideological community of Scottish and Irish Presbyterianism, they perceived themselves as Irish patriots, shaped by the political, theological and cultural concerns of their own nation, province and locale. Scotland provided a major component of their literary language: but it was often subsumed within their grander aspirations to write as Irishmen who could also call upon alternative tropes, genres, writers and schools of classical, Augustan, other British and Irish verse in their search to articulate their poetical animus.

In this regard Thomson's and Drummond's writing after the 1798 rebellion corresponds to literary approaches adopted by Romantic period poets elsewhere in Britain and Ireland. Their invocation of the cults of simplicity, picturesque retreat and the national epic mirror those implemented by other poets of the early nineteenth century and provide them with a safe platform for the continuation of their work in post-revolutionary settings. Thomson's Scotland becomes a land of sensibility that he feels a compromised attachment to, whereas Drummond views it as a potentially dangerous mythic location that requires intervention by proto-Britons to protect him. The debating of their 'third character' in their work as much as it reads like an uncontroversial exploration of personal interiority and almost jocular exposition of national identity is in reality a coded reaction to the concept of unity within the United Kingdom. Indeed, their desire to examine the less contentious relationships between Ireland and Scotland is a grand enabling metaphor that permits Thomson and Drummond respectively to criticize or praise the Union of Great Britain and Ireland.

APPENDIX

To a Hedge-Hog.

'Unguarded beauty is disgrace.'
BROOME.

WHILE youthful poets, thro' the grove,
Chaunt fast their canny lays o' love,
And a' their skill exert to move
            The darling object;
I chuse, as ye may shortly prove,
            A rougher subject.

What sairs to bother us in sonnet,
'Bout chin an' cheek, an' brow an' bonnet?
Just chirlin like a widow'd linnet,
            Thro' bushes lurchin;

Love's stangs are ill to thole, I own it,
              But to my hurchin.

Thou grimest far o' gruesome tykes,
Grubbing thy food by thorny dykes,
Gudefaith *thou* dinna want for *pikes*,
              Baith sharp an' rauckle; [loose or ramshackle]
Thou looks (L—d save's) array'd in spikes,
              A creepin heckle!

Some say thou'rt sib kin to the sow, [blood kin]
But sibber to the deil, I trow;
An' what thy use can be, there's few
              That can explain;
But naithing, as the learn'd allow,
              Was made in vain.

Sure Nick begat thee, at the first,
On some auld *whin* or thorn accurst;
An' some horn-finger'd harpie nurst
              The ugly hurchin;
Then Belzie, laughin, like to burst,
              First ca'd thee *Hurchin!*
                          [unkempt/uncouth person]

Fok tell how thou, sae far frae daft,
Whar wind fa'n fruit lie scatter'd saft,
Will row thysel', wi' cunning craft,
              An' bear awa
Upon thy back, what sairs thee aft
              A day or twa.

But whether this account be true,
Is mair than I will here avow;
If that thou stribs the outler cow, [squeezes the last drop
    of milk, wintering out]
              As some assert,
A pretty milkmaid, I allow,
              Forsooth thou art.

I've heard the supercilious say,
To meet thee on our morning way,
Portends some dire misluck that day—
              Some black mischance.
Sic fools, howe'er, are far astray
              Frae common sense.

Right monie a hurchin I hae seen,
At early morn, and eke at e'en,
Baith setting off, an' whan I've been
                    Returning hame;
But Fate, indifferent, I ween,
                Was much the same.

How lang will mortals nonsense blether,
And sauls to superstition tether!
For witch-craft, omens, altogether,
                    Are damn'd hotch-potch mock,
That now obtain sma credit ether
                Frae us or Scotch fok.

Now creep awa the way ye came,
And tend your squeakin pups at hame;
Gin Colley should o'erhear the same,
                    It might be fatal,
For you, wi' a' the pikes ye claim,
                Wi' him to battle.

From Scotland's storied land: William McComb and Scots-Irish Presbyterian identity

PATRICK MAUME

The Belfast schoolteacher turned bookseller William McComb (1793–1873) was regarded as 'the laureate of Presbyterianism'.[1] Through such publications as *McComb's Presbyterian Almanac* (1840–89) he sought to disseminate to an Ulster Presbyterian audience a sense that they were part of a worldwide Evangelical culture at its purest in the tradition deriving from the Scottish Reformation and destined to find definitive expression in a world dominated by an united Presbyterian Church.

This paper, based on a survey of the *Almanac* and on McComb's 1864 *Poetical Works*, is mainly focused on McComb's later career, when he and Henry Cooke diverged in terms of politics – though not religion. It examines his literary models, his verses on the links between Scottish and Irish Presbyterianism, and how the writings of the early-eighteenth-century Presbyterian millennialist Robert Fleming contributed to McComb's move from expecting imminent apocalypse in the 1840s to a vision of universal Presbyterian triumph in the mid-Victorian era.

McComb was born in Coleraine in 1793, the son of a draper. While serving his apprenticeship in Belfast he joined a friend in founding a Sunday school in Smithfield to counteract an establishment described as having been founded to disseminate the doctrines of Thomas Paine. (The United Irish activist James Hope was then living in Brown Square, a nearby weaving district at the top of the Shankill.)[2] McComb received the assistance of the predominantly Anglican Sunday School Society for Ireland and soon thereafter abandoned drapery for school-

1 Robert Jeffrey, *The Indian mission of the Irish Presbyterian church* (London, 1890), p. 63. 2 Cathal O'Byrne, *As I roved out* (Belfast, 1946), pp 79–82. 3 Irene Whelan, *The Bible war in Ireland: the 'second reformation' and the polarization of Protestant-Catholic relations, 1800–1840* (Dublin, 2005) p.109. My belief that McComb is the anonymous Belfast correspondent whose letter is reproduced by Whelan from William Urwick, *Biographical sketches of the late James Digges La Touche, Esquire* (Dublin, 1868) is based on the similarity between the writer's account of his activities and that in McComb's 1873 *Belfast Newsletter* obituary. For the Anglican La Touche's willingness to co-operate with Nonconformists to further the Evangelical cause, see Whelan, *Bible war in Ireland*, p. 62; for his friendship with McComb see Norman Vance, *Irish literature: a social history* (London, 1990), p. 141.

teaching.[3] Thus began a lifelong career of charitable work and evangelical activity which brought him into touch with such figures as Henry Cooke and the earl of Roden, and into conflict with Catholic ecclesiastical authorities. (In 1822–4 the parish priest of Belfast, William Crolly, ordered Catholic children withdrawn from McComb's school in Brown Square on the grounds that the school authorities were trying to convert them to Protestantism.)[4] In 1828 he became a bookseller, publishing the pro-Cooke journal, *the Orthodox Presbyterian* (1829–40), and many other religious titles; the Belfast Linenhall Library has over 120 titles (a few non-religious) published by him, and by 1859 McComb had printed 50,000 copies of Sidney Hamilton Rowan's school edition of *The Assembly's Shorter Catechism*.[5] In 1841 he compiled *The Repealer Repulsed*, a satirical account of Daniel O'Connell's January 1841 visit to Belfast and evasion of Cooke's challenge to debate civil and religious liberty.[6]

McComb had begun writing verse by 1815 when he celebrated the battle of Waterloo ('Waterloo – Wellington – Erin go bragh').[7] His first collection, in 1817, was dominated by a long poem mourning the dead harper Denis O'Neill. This incorporates an antiquarian account of Irish minstrelsy beginning with Noah's flood, garnished with antiquarian footnotes,[8] and including a lament over the battle of Clontarf (though discreetly omitting the Norman Invasion as it skips from 1014 to the Belfast Harp Festival of 1792). In Augustan couplets, McComb hails O'Neill as an Ossianic figure:

> Seek ye the bard's empassion'd fire,
> As erst he swept the trembling wire?
> Enshrined with Ossian's hallowed throng,
> There see the hoary son of song!
> Enwrapt in CAROLAN's embrace,
> O'NEILL, the last of minstrel race,
> Encircled with a druid band,
> Receives the crown from ULLIN's hand:

---

4 Ambrose Macaulay, *William Crolly, archbishop of Armagh 1835–49* (Dublin, 1994), pp 22–8. 5 John A. McIvor, *Popular education in the Irish Presbyterian church* (Dublin, 1969), p. 93. 6 The 2003 UCD Press reprint of *The repealer repulsed* (ed. Patrick Maume) provides a brief outline of McComb's career (pp vii–xi). Andrew Holmes notes that the F.J. Biggar catalogue in Belfast Central Library and a copy of *The repealer repulsed* in Assembly's College name the journalist and tenant-right activist James McKnight (1801–76), then editor of the *Belfast Newsletter* as a contributor if not the principal compiler. An assessment of this claim, and of the relations between the two men, must await further research on McKnight, but it should be noted that McComb's name is on the (otherwise anonymous) text as publisher, that much of the text consists of Cooke's reported speeches and McComb was Cooke's semi-official publisher, and that the pamphlet's use of parody and mock-heroic resembles McComb's 'Grey Seer' columns in the *Presbyterian Almanac*. 7 Reprinted in William McComb, *Poetical works* (London/Edinburgh/Belfast, 1864), pp 166–7. Hereafter cited as *PW*. 8 *PW*, pp 23–30

> Lives there a bard, that would not die
> To join the sainted revelry![9]

As this suggests, the Ossianic bard – simultaneously Scottish and Irish – was to be one of the models for McComb's self-presentation, though often with a certain self-deflation. (The poem closes with a Moore-style apology for daring to handle 'Ultonia's harp').[10] McComb's attraction to the Ossianic figure derives from a variety of sources, including literary fashion, contact with O'Neill (who taught classes for the Belfast Harp Society in 1808–13; a footnote mentions that McComb heard O'Neill 'play the beautiful air of Kitty Tyrrell'),[11] and – oddly for such a pronounced Evangelical – a hint that druidic 'natural religion' might have been more pleasing to God, as well as more Irish, than Catholicism. (McComb even quotes and apparently endorses John Toland's insinuation that the replacement of druids by monks at Derry was a change for the worse).[12] The poem's celebration of Brian Boru also allows McComb to assert his Irish patriotism without denying his Unionism.[13] This balance sometimes wavered; in the 1866 *Presbyterian Almanac*, when denouncing Fenianism, McComb contrasts the rule of Victoria with that of Brian, who never enjoyed a newspaper, slated house, glass window, or cup of tea.[14]

McComb's literary models were Scott and Campbell at their most declamatory,[15] the English Nonconformist Isaac Watts[16] (whose simple quatrains underlie McComb's most effective pieces – such as his verses on the 1798 heroine Betsy Gray, intended by McComb as an exercise in pathos rather than politics though his audience may not all have seen it in that light),[17] the hymn-writer James Montgomery (1771–1854),[18] perhaps Cowper (in simpler pieces such as McComb's humorous tribute to his cat Lily)[19] and Thomas Moore. He had some contact with the Burns family – his *Poetic Works* contain 'Burns' Seal, on receiving from his Granddaughter an Impression of the Poet's Seal',[20] and 'To Robert Burns Esq., Eldest Son of the Poet, on the occasion of his Visit to Belfast, Sept. 4, 1844'.[21]

However, there is very little Burnsian influence on McComb's verse; he almost never uses dialect (except for satiric effect in a few ephemeral contexts such as *The Repealer Repulsed*, part of whose attraction is that McComb speaks with greater vigour from behind a satirical mask than in his official publications). His Burns is the sentimental moralist beloved of the late-Victorian and early-twentieth-century Burns Society respectabilities whose outraged response to Catherine Carswell's

9 *PW*, pp 8–9. 10 *PW*, p. 22; McComb echoes Moore's 'Dear Harp of my country' (1815). 11 *PW*, p. 7n. 12 *PW*, p. 28. 13 *PW*, pp 17–20. 14 P[resbyterian] A[lmanac], (1866), 1. 15 'Campbell and Kosciusko', *PW*, pp 294–5. 16 For Watts and his extensive influence see Donald Davie, *A gathered church: the literature of the English dissenting interest, 1700–1930* (Oxford, 1978) 17 'Bessie Grey', *PW*, pp 357–8; *PA* (1860), 78–9. Compare 'Edmund and Ella', *PW*, pp 157–64, as an exercise in pathos. 18 'To James Montgomery, Esq., on his Visiting Belfast in 1842', *PW*, pp 202–3. 19 'Lily', *PA* (1857), 86; *PW*, pp 342–3; see also 'The Carpet', *PW*, pp 256–8 for an explicit invocation of Cowper as model. 20 'Burns' Seal', *PW*, pp 242–4. 21 'To Robert Burns, Esq.', *PW*, pp 290–2.

Burns biography is criticized by Edwin Muir;[22] like them McComb emphasized the poet's sentimental moralism while treating Burns' daemonic side as a personal failing quite separate from his poetic inspiration, playing it down to such an extent that it is virtually though not formally denied.[23]

McComb's *Presbyterian Almanac* first appeared in its mature form in 1841 (there had been a smaller precursor in 1840). Its cover was Presbyterian blue, and bore a portrait of John Knox. It was a self-consciously respectable and religious rival to such precursors as *Old Moore*, combining useful information and agricultural advice culled from other publications with news of Presbyterian activities worldwide and commentary on current events. Each edition was prefaced by a standard verse with adaptations commenting on the previous year's events. (Early editions also had a verse beneath each year in the calendar, commenting on anniversaries or on a series of linked themes.) The 1844 edition summarizes its contents as follows (year-specific items in plain type, recurring elements in italics):

> I give in likeness true this year,
> The father of our Zion dear – [Rev. James Elder of Finvoy]
> A patriarch whose hoary head
> Now slumbers with the ransomed dead.
> A faithful history I render
> Of Derry Walls and 'No Surrender'.
> I name each precious stone and gem
> That garnish New Jerusalem;
> And *tell of years of olden date,*
> *Of men who braved the martyr's fate,*
> *Of fields where first our sires did plant*
> *The banner of the Covenant.*
> *Each Minister is noted down,*
> *His congregation and post town,*
> *That he who runs may read and see*
> *The list of our Assembly.*
> *Its Foreign, Home and Jewish Mission*
> *I give with accurate precision*
> I hail the Church of Scotland – Free,
> Her dawn of Christian Liberty!
> Opposed to Puseyite succession,
> I trace the sires of our Confession, –
> The followers of Him, whose name,
> From Judah, not from Levi, came.
> *Of Churches then my pen narrates,*
> *Moravian – Wesleyan – Welsh – the States,*

22 Edwin Muir, *A Scottish journey* (London, 1935).   **23** 'Burns' Seal', *PW*, pp 242–4.

> *Knox, Calvin, Melville, Blair and others,*
> *I rank as Presbyterian brothers.*
> *I tell of Sun, and Moon, and Tides,*
> *Eclipses, Fairs, Post-Office guides;*
> *The penny-Postage and the Mails,*
> The Queen and the young Prince of Wales;
> *With skill Municipal declare*
> *The Council, Aldermen, and Mayor.*
> *Enigma, clear – obscure – sublime,*
> *For Bards to solve in flowing rhyme;*
> *And many strange and wondrous cracks,*
> *Not found in other Almanacks.*[24]

The opening years of the *Presbyterian Almanac* were overshadowed by the patronage dispute in the Church of Scotland, as Evangelicals led by Thomas Chalmers sought to secure that ministers should be elected by the congregation rather than nominated by a patron. Although Peel's Conservatives used figures like Cooke and Chalmers in rebuilding their party during the 1830s, they were unwilling to give the church so much power over its own affairs:[25] McComb lamented that they were 'opposed and persecuted by those very politicians under whose banners they had ranged themselves'.[26] The Evangelical view of the dispute was backed up in the *Almanac* between 1841 and 1850 in a serialized history of the Church of Scotland summarized from a work by the evangelical Revd A.M. Hetherington of Torphichen.[27] In the first Almanac McComb rallied his readers with an article on the 'Present Position of the Church of Scotland'; McComb clearly expected that some readers would not know of the dispute, or even of the existence of the patronage system in Scotland. He denounced the 'Moderate' supporters of patronage as crypto-episcopalians, descendants of those who crept into the Church of Scotland after 1688 through 'the too great liberality of Presbyterians', which McComb also blamed for the paucity of Presbyterian MPs:

> Whilst the emissaries of infidelity and debauchery [Owenites – *McComb's footnote*] and Popery may roam at large over the whole of broad Scotland, her Presbyterian ministers, because of their fidelity to Christ the King, and faithfulness of his people, are threatened, prosecuted, and prohibited, on pain of incarceration, from preaching even in the open air …

24 *PA* (1844), 1. 'Puseyite succession' refers to the Catholic, Orthodox and High Anglican view that ministerial/priestly orders are conferred through ordination by a bishop in succession from the apostles, upheld by followers of the Anglo-Catholic leader of the remnant Oxford Movement, E.B. Pusey. When the ex-Presbyterian Archibald Tait became archbishop of Canterbury, McComb mockingly enquired whether Puseyites believed his Presbyterian baptism invalidated his orders (*PA* (1869), 63). 25 Stewart J. Brown, *Thomas Chalmers and the godly commonwealth* (Oxford, 1982). 26 'Present position of the Church of Scotland', *PA* (1841), 59–62. 27 E.g. *PA* (1850), 62–4.

Now we ask the Presbyterians of Ulster, and of Ireland generally, will they sit coolly still while such things are doing? Will they suffer their brethren in Scotland, to be deprived of their liberties, have their ministers imprisoned, and their families reduced to beggary before their very eyes? ... if the Patronage triumphs there, it may soon be riveted upon us here ... Prove by your exertions for the Church of Scotland, that the cause of the martyrs is still dear to you, and that the blood of the Covenant still flows within your veins. Tell the British Parliament ... that your Presbyterianism is dearer to you than your life ... Tell those Members of Parliament who should represent you.. that they should advocate your cause and that of Scotland before the British Senate, or else, you will look out for those who will. Tell your landlords that conscience requires you, henceforth, to act independently as freeholders, and that you will support no candidate who will not support your principles and struggle for the Church of your forefathers.[28]

This call on Presbyterian tenants to defy their landlords is noteworthy from a supporter of Cooke, whose calls for a pan-Protestant alliance involved suspicion of tenant-right agitators and considerable laudation (sometimes echoed by McComb) for Church of Ireland Tory aristocrats.[29] McComb's most celebrated verses (whose opening, metre and language he redeployed in verses celebrating the tercentenaries of the Church of Scotland and the death of John Knox) were written after the 10 June 1842 bicentenary commemorations of the first Ulster Presbytery in Carrickfergus (modelled on the 1838 bicentenary celebrations of the Presbytery of Glasgow):[30] .

Two hundred years ago, there came from Scotland's storied land,
To Carrick's old and fortress town a Presbyterian band;
They planted on the Castle wall the Banner of the Blue,
And worshipped God in simple form, as Presbyterians do.
Oh, hallowed be their memory who in our land did sow
The goodly seed of Gospel Truth, two hundred years ago!

After contrasting the tiny founding presbytery with the expanding church of his own day, recalling the Sixmilewater revival and celebrating the newly-begun missionary activities of Irish Presbyterianism, McComb equated the looming patronage issue with the persecution of Covenanters under the later Stuarts:

Two hundred years ago was seen the proud and mitred brow
Frowning on Scotland's envied kirk, as it is frowning now;

---

28 'Present position of the Church of Scotland', *PA* (1841), 59–62. **29** *Repealer repulsed*, pp ix–x, 193–4; 'The funeral of the late marquis of Downshire at Hillsborough, April 24, 1845', *PW*, pp 276–9; 'Lines on the laying of the foundation stone of the testimonial to the late marquis of Downshire, October 23, 1848', ibid., pp 280–1. **30** *PA* (1843), 60–1.

But enemies in church and state may threaten stern decree;
Her Ministers are men of prayer – her people still are free:
Nor threat, nor interdict, nor wile of Legislative show
Shall change the men whose fathers bled, two hundred years ago.

Two hundred years ago, o'er graves the bluebell drooped its head,
The purple heather sadly waved above the honoured dead;
The mist lay heavy on the hill – the lav'rock ceased to soar,
And Scotland mourned her martyr'd sons on mountain and on moor;
And still hers is a mourning Church; but He who made her so
Is nigh to aid her as he was two hundred years ago.

McComb finally contrasts peaceful Presbyterian Ulster with the rest of Ireland, where 'Popery is the same it was two hundred years ago'.[31] When the 'Disruption' took place in 1843 – with the secession of Chalmers and his followers, comprising almost half the ministers and more than half the laity, to form the Free Church of Scotland – McComb hailed Scotland's third reformation,[32] and wrote impassioned verses comparing it to the exodus of the Israelites from Egypt.[33] The Irish Presbyterian church entered communion with the Free Church, breaking with the remnant established Church of Scotland. For some years McComb publicized cases where Free Church congregations worshipped in the open air, like seventeenth-century Covenanters, because Highland landlords refused to allow them to build a church.[34] The principal aristocratic supporter of the Free Church was John Campbell, second marquis of Breadalbane; McComb regaled readers of the *Presbyterian Almanac* with a description of his mansion, Taymouth Castle.[35] A large and elaborate Berlin wool carpet woven by Belfast Presbyterian women was presented to Breadalbane on 23 October 1843, accompanied by a speech from Chalmers and some verses by McComb:

Look on the splendid centre-group, and see
The harp of Erin's ancient minstrelsy-
Hibernia sits, as if enthroned in song,
Sweeping, with rapid hand, the chords along.
'Midst wreath of Scottish thistle, lo! I see
Breadalbane's arms in blazoned heraldry –
Breadalbane's honour'd name, his country's boast,
To Scotland's free-born Church a mighty host ...

McComb visualized Breadalbane explaining the significance of the carpet to Queen Victoria on her next visit to Taymouth (clumsily putting exuberant praise of the Marquis into that worthy's own mouth):

31 *PA* (1843), 61–2; 'Two hundred years ago', *PW*, pp 210–12.   32 *PA* (1844), 32. The first Reformation was led by John Knox; the second by the seventeenth-century Covenanters. 33 *PA* (1844); 'The Free Church of Scotland – the disruption', *PW*, pp 212–14.   34 *PA* (1848), (Duthil), 122; (1849), (Wanlockhead), 120.   35 *PA* (1844), 71–2.

This Carpet, wrought in curious needle art,
Is the free offering of the Irish heart:
Erin's fair daughters, who the needle plied,
To Scotland's church by sacred ties allied,
Felt deeply for her wrongs, and mourned to see
The hand that helped the slave assault the free.
They heard how great Breadalbane, wise and good,
Before the Senate and his country stood ...
When high-born nobles from the combat fled,
With dauntless step he to the rescue sped ...
And in this splendid trophy here you see
How Erin's daughters love the brave and free.[36]

In the 1840s McComb saw Ulster Presbyterians engaged in a worldwide struggle between Catholicism and Protestantism prefiguring the final apocalypse. The Oxford Movement, with its revival of Catholic-related sacramentalism within the Church of England, appeared a sinister portent; when noting the anniversary of the death of the American Presbyterian Andrew McLeod, McComb declared: 'M'LEOD, some thirty years ago, Foretold of Britain's night of woe; Of Puseyism's crafty reign, When the two witnesses are slain.' [37] (The two witnesses are Enoch and Elijah, expected to return to preach against Antichrist; their death at his hands opens the final tribulation.) McComb presents the Disruption of the Church of Scotland in the same terms:

> The Free Church has already presented a new centre of attraction to other churches, and it may, we think, be confidently expected, that through her instrumentality the true churches of the Reformation will be united more and more. The aspect of the times would seem to warrant the expectation, that a great struggle is approaching in which the Presbyterian Church will bear a distinguished part. The state of the Church of England now overrun with deadly and anti-Protestant error, fatally insensible to danger, together with the growing confidence and high-rated anticipations of the man of sin [i.e. the Pope] give warning of coming judgment; and who can tell, but that by the whole train of circumstances which has led the Free Church to her present elevated position, the Lord may have been preparing the way for a combined effort of his people against the common foe ...[38]

This is a neglected element in the alliance of evangelical Anglicans and Presbyterians, often seen simply as manipulation of the Presbyterians by Church of Ireland aristocrats; the blurring of denominational boundaries caused by shared evangelical

---

36 *PA* (1844), 70; 'The Carpet', *PW*, pp 256–8. **37** *PA* (1844), 16 ('Rev. Alexander McLeod died at New York 1833 aet. 59'.) **38** *PA* (1844), 62–4.

commitment and the periodic defection of individual evangelical Anglicans to Nonconformist denominations led some Presbyterians to expect the eventual conversion of their allies to Presbyterianism;[39] we shall see how in later years McComb predicted eventual Presbyterian world dominance. The obituary for Chalmers in the 1848 *Almanac* laments that like Moses God called him away when the battle looms, and urges new Joshuas to fight against Antichrist.[40]

McComb's narrative poem, *1848: The Story of a Year*, argues that the revolutions of 1848 vindicate the interpretation of the apocalypse put forward in *Apocalyptical Key: An Extraordinary Discourse on the Rise and Fall of Papacy* (1701) by the early-eighteenth-century Scotch Presbyterian commentator Robert Fleming (c.1660–1716), who attracted renewed attention after the French revolution was seen as fulfilling his prediction that a great chastisement of the papacy would begin with the downfall of the French monarchy in 1794, culminating with another great blow in 1848. Fleming did not expect this to bring the complete destruction of the papacy, but predicted another great chastisement in 1866. The downfall of the papacy would be followed by an outpouring of the Holy Spirit gathering of the nations to the Gospel light.[41]

In the 1850s and 1860s McComb moved away from his earlier quasi-premillennialist view (premillennialists interpret the Book of the Apocalypse as foretelling general apostasy culminating in the appearance of Antichrist, after which Jesus will return) to a more optimistic postmillennialist view based on Fleming's prediction of the Parousia. (Postmillennialists interpret the Apocalypse's reference to a thousand-year reign of Christ as meaning the diffusion of the Church throughout the world will produce a thousand-year period of peace, piety, and prosperity before the appearance of Antichrist and the Final Judgment.)[42] This shift from pessimism to optimism derived from several sources. There had been widespread expectation of

39 Grayson Carter, *Anglican Evangelicals: Protestant secessions from the Via Media 1800–1850* (Oxford, 2001) discusses this phenomenon. Note also McComb's view of the Lutheran Church of Sweden as illustrating the evils of Protestant Episcopalianism and his hopes for its conversion to Presbyterianism (*PA* (1855), 59). 40 *PA* (1848), 63; 'Tribute to the memory of the Rev. Dr. Chalmers', *PW*, pp 281–5. 41 *Oxford DNB* article 'Robert Fleming' by M.J. Mercer; http://www.ao.net/~fmoeller/fleming.htm (accessed 21 June 2006) by a present-day exponent of Fleming's system. 42 For a discussion of premillennialism, including the relevant biblical texts, see Paul Boyer, *When time shall be no more: prophecy belief in modern American culture* (Cambridge, MA, 1992). In the discussion following the original presentation of this paper in Derry in 2006, Andrew Holmes criticized the description of McComb as premillennialist in the pre-Famine period, stating that postmillennialism was overwhelmingly dominant among nineteenth-century Ulster Presbyterians; however, the identification of Puseyism with Antichrist is clearly premillennialist, though the suggestion that the Free Church of Scotland will defeat the forces of darkness and usher in a golden age suggests postmillenniallism. McComb may have been influenced by his contacts with Anglican Evangelicals (such as Charlotte Elizabeth Tonna – see her *Irish recollections* (Dublin, 2004 with preface by Patrick Maume) among whom premillennialism was extremely widespread, without definitively embracing it himself. Cf., tribute to Tonna, *PA* (1866), 100–1.

conflict between the France of Louis Philippe and Britain; although the role of perceived Catholic-continental threat was taken over to some extent by Napoleon III, the fact that Britain, almost uniquely, did not experience a major revolt in 1848 is presented in *The Story of a Year* as a sign of divine blessing (with Ulster's loyalty and supposed tranquillity attributed to Bible teaching – 'Heaven's bow of Gospel light effulgent shone, Stretching from Ulster's vales to loved VICTORIA's throne').[43] These fears were further dispelled by the alliance of France and Britain against Russia in the Crimea,[44] and the subsequent clash between France and the other major Catholic power, Austria, in northern Italy in 1859.[45] McComb noted that both powers seemed to regard the pope as 'a species of political nuisance'; he remarked in 1863 that Napoleon III and Victor Emmanuel would be greatly relieved if the pope emigrated to California or went to Ballinasloe to assist 'his faithful helper, [Archbishop] John [MacHale] of Tuam, to curse and to bluster'.[46]

The Oxford Movement within the Church of England abated after the secession of Newman to Rome (though the remnant centred around Pusey continued to arouse evangelical suspicion they never held the same strength and prestige),[47] and the flow of converts to Catholicism tailed off in the 1850s.[48] McComb welcomed the Ecclesiastical Titles Act (forbidding Catholic bishops to bear United Kingdom territorial titles, formally enacted July 1851) as a blow against Roman aggression and a sign that Whig appeasement of Catholicism was being abandoned.[49] Meanwhile, Lord Palmerston's ecclesiastical policy favoured the evangelical wing of the Church of England, promoting what McComb called 'excellent Calvinist bishops'.[50] (In the 1850s and 1860s McComb appears to have been a Palmerstonian Whig rather than a Derbyite Conservative like Cooke, although McComb is not known to have criticized Cooke and continued to praise him as a second John Knox; McComb even supported Disestablishment – which Cooke opposed to the last – as preferable to the alternative policy of concurrently endowing Romanism,[51] predicting that a disestablished Church of Ireland – a title which he disliked – would become Presbyterian in all but name.)[52] Palmerston could also be seen as a Protestant champion through his support for the Italian nationalist movement.[53] The *Presbyterian Almanac* in the late

43 *PW*, pp 142–4. **44** *PA* (1855), 3; (1856), 3–4. **45** *PA* (1860), 3–4, 61, 64. **46** *PA* (1863), 1. **47** Owen Chadwick, *The Victorian church part one: 1829–1859* (1970, London, 1987), pp 195–212. **48** Owen Chadwick, *The Victorian church part two: 1860–1901* (1970, London, 1987), p. 401. 'The Roman Catholics never regained the extraordinary sense of confidence and hope which the years, and the statistics, of 1844–54 bred in them'; see also pp 409–10. McComb notes the decline in *PA* (1866), 'Report on Popery', 59. **49** *PA* (1852), 4. **50** *PA* (1858), 62. **51** *PA* (1868), 2–3. Cf. also his 1869 profile of the leading Ulster Presbyterian Liberal MP Sir Thomas McClure (72) which devotes more space to Presbyterian ministers among McClure's ancestors than to McClure himself. McComb's comments on the damaging effect of Erastianism on the Prussian Church (e.g. *PA* (1854), 60–1; (1870), 70–1) can be seen as pointing in the same direction, though they are not necessarily incompatible with belief in the principle of establishment (McComb hoped the Prussian Church might yet become Presbyterianism – *PA* (1866), 67). **52** *PA* (1867), 75–6, (1869), 3; (1870), 1; (1871), 6. **53** For a hostile Irish Derbyite view of Palmerston's image

1850s and 1860s exalted over the crumbling power of Pius IX;[54] Garibaldi was eulo-
gized and Irish volunteers for the Papal Brigade mocked as chiefly effective in
fighting each other,[55] and learning from experience how much better off they were
under Queen Victoria than as temporal subjects of the pope.[56] Fleming's prophecy
of papal setbacks in 1866 was presented as foretelling the defeat of Catholic Austria
by Protestant Prussia,[57] and a prophecy that the First Vatican Council would be
engulfed by an earthquake was retrospectively seen as fulfilled by the Italian occupation of Rome.[58] Although McComb calculated the papacy would not finally
disappear until 2015,[59] he anticipated massive conversions to Protestantism on the
continent, and a general move by continental Protestant churches towards orthodox
Calvinism and Presbyterian church government.[60]

Reporting the 1860 tricentenary of the Scottish Reformation, McComb
announced:

> Whilst time is proving that other systems are behind the age, and becoming
> unfit for effective exertion, Presbyterianism has yet scarcely reached manhood,
> and is evidently girding herself for something greater than she has ever yet
> attempted. The days of ecclesiastical despotism are numbered, but
> Presbyterianism, which secures liberty without licentiousness, and unity
> without sameness, is the system which must eventually prevail all over
> Christendom. Steam has done much to prepare the way for its general estab-
> lishment.[61]

The belief in Victorian technological developments as both fruits of the Reformation
and divinely-ordained means for the expansion of Presbyterianism is characteristic of
McComb, as is his cannibalization of his 1842 'Carrickfergus Bicentenary Ode for
Reformation Tercentenary' verses emphasizing Presbyterian Ulster's debt to Knox
and the Scots Covenanters, implicitly equated with Old Testament Israel as a chosen
people:

> Three hundred years ago there dwelt, on mountain and in glen,
> In Scotland's chosen land a race of brave and stalwart men:
> From sire to son they handed down a heritage and name,
> Unsullied as Ben Lomond's snow, and spotless as the same.
> Oh, for the muse of Israel's bard! – oh, for a harp of gold!

as a Protestant champion see Alexander Charles Ewald, *The life of Sir Joseph Napier, Bart., ex-
lord chancellor of Ireland, from his private correspondence* (London, 1887).   **54** *PA* (1861), 4 (hopes
the pope will use the leisure attained by shrinkage of his dominions to study the New
Testament and the Westminster Assembly's Shorter Catechism to learn about 'the
Presbyterians, before whom he is doomed to fall').   **55** *PA* (1861), 93.   **56** *PA* (1861), 4;
(1862), 63.   **57** *PA* (1867), 97–8.   **58** *PA* (1870), 1–2; (1871), 71–2.   **59** *PA* (1856), 61 – i.e.
1260 years after the creation of the Papal States in 755.   **60** *PA* (1852), 63–4; (1859), 68.
61 *PA* (1861), 62–3.

To sing of all our fathers did in glorious times of old:
Their witness-bearing for the truth – their bold front to the foe –
Their faith, and hope, and holy love, THREE HUNDRED YEARS AGO ...

Three hundred years ago was owned, the standard of our faith
By Scottish Parliament, and freed from Antichristian scaith;
And Presbyterian worship hailed with national array,
Establishing its simple forms from thenceforth and for aye:
No other Church, of any land, in Reformation days,
Did e'er on Freedom's pedestal such high memorial raise:
In all its long contendings – in weal-time and in woe –
It nailed its banner to the Cross, THREE HUNDRED YEARS AGO ...

TWO HUNDRED YEARS AGO, there came to Ulster's fertile shore
A goodly race of faithful men, our birthright to restore;
We hailed them from the fatherland of mountain and of flood–
The sons of sires who fought the fight, resisting unto blood.
Hence Ireland's Presbyterian Church sends greeting on the day
When Scotland's Presbyterian Church holds Tri-Centenary.
The bulwark of our liberty to Scotland's sons we owe,
And to our martyred ancestors, THREE HUNDRED YEARS AGO.[62]

McComb had always been interested in technological progress:[63] now he declared it divinely ordained to spread Presbyterianism:

During the past year, the electric telegraph has been extending its influence. In a short time we expect to be able to convey messages in a few minutes to the United States. As a matter of convenience, all the Supreme Courts of the Presbyterian Church throughout the world may soon find it expedient to meet simultaneously. Then our Assembly, met in Belfast, Dublin, or Galway, may be receiving telegraphic messages from other Assemblies sitting in Edinburgh, London, New York, Paris, La Tour, Jerusalem, and Melbourne. All the Presbyterian Churches may thus be enabled to agree upon the same line of action, and may exhibit a specimen of ecclesiastical unity which will astonish the Romanists ...[64]

62 *PA* (1861), 9; 'Tri-centenary of the Reformation in Scotland', in *PW*, 353–5. 63 Cf. the calendar verses in *PA* (1847) which describe the wonders of the nineteenth century – railways, the electric telegraph, daguerreotype portraits, balloons, steam, penny postage, the atmospheric railway, the diving bell, Lord Rosse's telescope, the steam press and the Thames Tunnel – ending grimly with potato blight (p. 36). 64 *PA* (1857), 4. Cf. also 'The Atlantic telegraph cable' in *PW*, pp 337–8 and the Grey Seer's Ossianic raptures on the same subject in *PA* (1867), 97.

The *Presbyterian Almanac's* reports on developments in the reformed Churches of the globe encouraged readers to see themselves as part of a worldwide movement. McComb was always eager for signs that the Presbyterians of the British Dominions – or even the whole world – might coalesce into one body,[65] and hailed the resurgence of orthodox High Calvinism against 'neology' (that is, theological Modernism) in continental Protestant churches.[66] Moral progress was also embodied in the destruction of American slavery by 'President Lincoln, a good old Presbyterian, a patron of Sabbath-schools, and a lover of liberty',[67] for whom McComb penned an impassioned elegy ('Sound the loud trumpet! O'er land and o'er sea Jehovah hath triumphed – the Negro is free').[68] McComb liked to quote Jonathan Edwards' prediction that the final gospel revival would spread westwards from America,[69] and when gloating over the discomfiture of Irish Catholic nationalists who hoped the seizure of Confederate envoys from the British ship *Trent* would lead to war, remarked that as the two greatest Protestant powers Britain and America should never quarrel.[70] 'Presbyterians stand at the head of all American denominations in intellectual culture.' [71]

The election of Presbyterian presidents in the United States, like the activities of Presbyterian imperial heroes such as the missionary David Livingstone and Sir Colin Campbell, reliever of Lucknow in the 'Indian Mutiny', were cited as disproving 'the threadbare calumny that Presbyterianism is not a religion for a gentleman',[72] and supporting calls for Irish Presbyterians 'one-half of churchgoing Irish protestants' to receive their fair share of government posts and social recognition.[73] McComb highlighted the performance of Presbyterians as magistrates and civic officers and official recognition or favour shown to Presbyterians by the queen or the lord lieutenant.[74] The *Almanac* regularly covered the erection of new Presbyterian churches and institutions such as Magee College.[75]

McComb's optimism was encouraged by developments in Catholic and Nationalist Ireland. In the 1830s and 1840s O'Connell seemed an ever-present menace; *The Repealer Repulsed* links his Belfast visit to a papally-directed conspiracy against Protestant Ulster and equates his influence over the Whig governments of the

65 *PA* (1864), 1–2. **66** E.g. - Holland: *PA* (1853), 62; (1855), 59; (1867), 67; (1869), 67; (1870), 70–1; Geneva (where McComb emphasized the Reformation historian Merle D'Aubigne as champion of orthodoxy), (1851), 64; (1853), 64; (1854), 58–9; (1869), 68; Prussia: (1855), 59–60; France (1850), 66–8; (1851), 64; (1854), 60. **67** *PA* (1861), 4. Lincoln had Calvinistic Baptist parents and sometimes attended Presbyterian services but was never a formal member of any church. **68** *PA* (1861), 11. McComb's abolitionism is expressed in *PA* (1862), 1; (1865), 1 and in 'To Mrs. Harriet Beecher Stowe – On Her Arrival in Britain', *PW*, pp 319–20. **69** *PA* (1853), 64–65. **70** *PA* (1862), 1. **71** *PA* (1870), 2. **72** *PA* (1858), 3–4. McComb notes the Presbyterianism of American President Buchanan (cf. also *PA* (1859), 57) and takes credit for General Havelock, another leading figure in the Indian repression of 1857, as 'a Calvinistic Baptist, nourished by the milk of Presbyterian preaching'. He noted the 'fiendish joy' of some Irish Catholic papers (probably A.M. Sullivan's *Nation*) at the prospect that the Sepoys might prevail, *PA* (1858), 4. **73** *PA* (1866), 71. **74** See *PA* (1851), 4; (1864), 2. **75** *PA* (1866), 1.

1830s with persecution of Protestants in the 1640s, under James II and in the 1798 Rebellion.[76] With O'Connell's death and the collapse of the Repeal movement, the enemy seemed deprived of coherent leadership; no threat of equal stature appeared in McComb's lifetime. Although the *Presbyterian Almanac* noted the growing Romanization of the Catholic Church in Ireland under Cardinal Cullen, and the Fenian movement,[77] both are ridiculed as effective only in proving 'papist' malevolence;[78] the nascent home rule movement is dismissed as the work of windbags who do not realize that without the Union Ireland would be torn apart by factions.[79]

McComb lauded the Revd John Edgar's policy of Irish-language evangelization in Connacht and Munster. He argued that Scottish Highlanders and Gaelic Irish were the same people, pointing out that the seventeenth-century Scottish General Assembly referred to Scots Gaelic as 'Irish' and even to Gaelic-speaking areas as 'Irish parishes'; the current religious difference between the two he attributed to Irish Episcopalian negligence:

> The Scottish Highlanders are now a race as civilised and moral as any in Europe, and why? The "Ard-Eaglais na h-Alba"... treated them as rational beings, afforded them religious instruction in its own language, and ... the Highlanders are, for the most part, devoted Protestants.[80]

He saw the Famine as a heaven-sent opportunity for evangelization; the peasantry would see that where priests were powerless to help them the generosity of Ulster and Scotland would bring relief.[81] (McComb's support for voluntary relief efforts – he wrote poems proclaiming 'Come to the Rescue' and supporting a 'Bazaar for the Famishing Poor in Connaught'[82] – was accompanied by complaints that the rate-in-aid subsidized thriftless papist Connaught at the expense of hardworking Presbyterian Ulster.)[83]

Although McComb published technical advice on potato blight (suggesting it might be overcome by planting potatoes in winter instead of spring,[84] or advocating dry ashes as manure and docks as pig-feed),[85] he emphasized that it was the will of God, to be met with submission and prayer.[86] After prematurely hailing the 1847 harvest as divine interposition to save the people,[87] he decided the blight would last

---

76 *Repealer repulsed*, pp 168–85. **77** *PA* (1867), 68; *PA* (1866) 3; (1867), 3. **78** *PA* (1868), 2–3; (1870), 2. When Cardinal Wiseman toured Ireland McComb commented that a Cardinal in full canonicals helped one to visualize the Scarlet Beast of the Apocalypse (*PA* (1859), 3–4). **79** *PA* (1873), 6. **80** *PA* (1841), 75. **81** *PA* (1848), 56. **82** *Collected poems*, pp 194–6; 'Call to prayer', pp 196–7 endorses the general Fast Day of 24 March 1847, while 'Harvest hymn', pp 197–8 prematurely proclaimed that the harvest of 1847 showed God's wrath had been turned away. **83** *PA* (1850), 4. **84** *PA* (1847), 10–11. **85** *PA* (1849), 79–80. **86** *PA* (1846), 28; see also 'Come to the rescue', *PW*, pp 194–5; 'Bazaar – for the famishing poor in Connaught', *PW*, pp 195–6; 'Call to prayer – suggested by a proclamation from the queen for a general fast, on the 24th March, 1847', *PW*, pp 196–7. **87** *PA* (1848), 8–11; see also 'Harvest hymn – call to praise and prayer', *PW*, pp 197–8

a Biblical seven years;[88] looking back at the end of that period, McComb declared it
had wrought as great a change as if the pope turned 'Mahommedan' or the Council
of the Tenant League were elected to parliament.[89] He offered a harshly punitive
explanation (though it should be borne in mind that supporters of the view that the
Famine represented divine punishment did not necessarily believe it wrong to relieve
the starving):

> Our opinion is that if Sabbath breaking and Romanism were banished out of
> the land, there would be nothing to prevent the growth of our favourite
> vegetable. When we see it announced in the newspapers that five hundred
> priests in Connaught and Munster have renounced their errors, and applied
> for admission into the General Assembly, we shall have as fine crops of
> seedlings and flat reds as ever gladdened the heart of an Irish farmer.[90]

In the subsequent decade McComb saw the Famine as preparing Ireland's economic
regeneration. He hailed William Dargan's 1853 Dublin International Exhibition as a
daystar of hope,[91] and excerpted newspaper comments about growing prosperity and
rising wages.[92] In 1861 McComb reprinted an article by Edgar pointing to the
purchase of Irish land by Scots farmers and landlords under the Encumbered Estates
Act and the activities of Presbyterian missionaries in the three southern provinces as
proof that 'Ireland owes Presbyterians much in her soil and her people. In both they
are making her as the garden of the Lord'.[93] Converts from Catholicism during the
1859 Ulster Revival (which McComb noted coincided with the Scottish
Reformation tercentenary),[94] were hailed as 'first fruits of a glorious harvest all over
St Patrick's land ... What Presbyterians make Ulster, they will make Munster and
Connaught; revived Ulster will break forth on the right hand and on the left, and all
Erin shall yet see the salvation of God.'[95]

McComb's writings were not all so sombre. A popular feature of the *Almanac* was
'The Old Grey Seer of the Bracken Tower'.[96] This persona was based on the
legendary seventeenth- (or sixteenth-) century Highland prophet Coinneach Adhair,
the 'Brahan Seer'[97] (from Brahan in Wester Ross; McComb's version is first called
'brechan', which he takes as meaning 'bracken', before changing it to the standard
English word).[98] The Seer commented in pseudo-Ossianic style on his age and

(written Cultra, 23 Aug. 1847). **88** *PA* (1850), 3. **89** *PA* (1851), 4. **90** *PA* (1849), 6.
91 *PA* (1854), 3. **92** *PA* (1857), 86–7. **93** McComb gives particular praise to Allan
Pollock, whose 1854–7 attempts to clear his newly-purchased Connemara estate provoked
vigorous and successful resistance by his tenants: see Paul Bew, *Ireland: the politics of enmity
1789–2006* (Oxford, 2007), p. 242. **94** *PA* (1860), 4, 69–71. **95** *PA* (1861), 70–3; see also
1853. **96** McComb attempted to discontinue this feature in 1860 but it was brought back
by popular demand. **97** Alexander Mackenzie, *The prophecies of the Brahan Seer* (1877)
available online at http://www.geocities.com/Athens/Forum/8287/brahan.html (accessed
21 June 2005); see also the BBC profile at http://www.bbc.co.uk/legacies/myths_legends/
scotland/western/index.shtml (accessed 21 June 2005). **98** *PA* (1846), 90–1; the change to

waning vitality, described annual Hallowe'en visits to his tower and its bracken-filled surroundings, whose inutility fitly represented the realms of fantasy, communed with the 'spirits' of his correspondents, and reviewed the previous year in pseudo-bardic style (with occasional prophecies of such auspicious events as the reconquest of Rome)[99] before unveiling the annual 'Enigma' (a verse riddle, to be answered in a verse composition on the same theme). Some early columns present the Seer as a mildly Faustian figure like Michael Scott, whose enigmas are presented as challenges by malign spirits who will destroy him unless readers solve the mystery.[1] In later Almanacks he becomes the vehicle for McComb's musings on death, faith and revisiting his native Causeway Coast.[2]

McComb sold his business in 1864 when he published his *Poetical Works*, though he continued writing for the *Presbyterian Almanac* (now published by James Cleeland of Arthur Street). He lived to welcome the prospect of the 1870 Land Act,[3] compose an elegy for Cooke (compared to David as a shepherd boy raised to kingship)[4] and call for the 1872 tercentenary of John Knox's death to be celebrated with a Belfast memorial column (presumably modelled on that in the Glasgow Necropolis):

> Three hundred years ago! 'tis true three cycles thus have run;
> And sure 'tis well in thought to dwell on what the Lord has done
> In freeing conscience from the grasp of bigotry and wrong;
> And making by the Word of God the feeble flock grow strong.
>   And shall this anniversary unnoted pass away?
> No, sons of true men let us all commemorate the day;
> And let us raise a column fair in future times to show
> Honour to Knox and his compeers three hundred years ago.[5]

In his last appearance as the Grey Seer (1872) McComb invoked Ossian to celebrate the meeting of Stanley and Livingstone.[6] His last known verses 'On the Death of Rev. James Morgan, my dear Pastor' were written on 8 August 1873,[7] just over a month before McComb's own death on 13 September.

McComb saw himself as living at the beginning of a Presbyterian golden age, but he embodied many of the trends which, as David Miller shows, transformed Ulster Presbyterianism from a cross-class community religion to one dominated by a cerebral and decorous middle-class piety, while the lower classes became unchurched or turned to revivalism.[8] He saw himself as the heir of Ossian, celebrating a divinely-driven epic of Presbyterian revival and evangelization, when in fact the self-deflating irony which accompanies the proclamations of the Old Seer prefigured the self-

---

'bracken' comes in (1851), 80. The 'lone tower' first features in *PA*, (1844), 98–9.   **99** *PA* (1862), 91–2.   **1** *PA* (1847), 83–4; (1848), 82–4.   **2** *PA* (1867), 97–9, (1870), 95–9.   **3** *PA* (1870), 2.   **4** *PA* (1869), 1–4; on p. 3 Cooke is called the most distinguished minister ever produced by the Presbytery of Ulster.   **5** *PA* (1873), 6.   **6** *PA* (1873), 7.   **7** *PA* (1873), 10. **8** David W. Miller, 'Did Ulster Presbyterians have a devotional revolution?', in James H. Murphy (ed.), *Evangelicals and Catholics in nineteenth-century Ireland* (Dublin, 2005), pp 38–54.

conscious provincialism of later Ulster kailyard writers. For later Presbyterian church-affiliated literati as late as the mid-twentieth century McComb remained an honoured name even though his works were increasingly neglected (in his work on the rhyming weavers John Hewitt still thought it necessary to make a brief and dismissive reference to 'that sanctimonious bookseller'),[9] but his social, political and religious hopes of a converted Ireland and a worldwide Presbyterian modernity, increasingly far-fetched by the time of his death, were driven from public memory with the collapse of the mid-Victorian order. The sardonic Belfast journalist Frankfort Moore escaped from an evangelical (Brethren) upbringing into polished agnostic derision and a cult of the eighteenth century; looking for an emblem of the provincial pretentiousness of mid-Victorian Belfast, he seized on

> Mr M'Comb's highly-decorated volume of poems – an ornament to the parlour centre table of the period, harmonising with the Berlin wool mats [Breadalbane's carpet!] and in no way clashing with the vivid green of the red curtains or the horsehair upholstery of the parlour ... the verse of a thoughtful, pious and educated man – a man of many sympathies and much good sense.[10]

9 John Hewitt, *Rhyming weavers* (Belfast, reprinted 2004) p. 103.   10 *Belfast Telegraph*, 27 Mar. 1924, 5; see also Patrick Maume (ed.), Frank Frankfort Moore, *In Belfast by the sea* (Dublin, 2007), pp 93-4 & n. 76, p. 93.

Thomas Chalmers and Irish poverty

PETER GRAY

In the wake of the implementation of the 1800 Act of Union many British (and some Irish) commentators continued to attribute the manifest problems of Irish governance and Irish socio-economic conditions to the 'incompleteness' of the Union itself. This developing awareness that legislative union alone could not address the underlying issues problematizing British-Irish relationships did not (in general) lead to any questioning of the logic of the constitutional tie, but often led to a demand for further integration – of institutions (including the executive and financial departments of the state), of the currencies and tariff barriers, and, rather more speculatively, of the moral and social condition of the Irish people with that of the population of Great Britain. This integrationist solution to the 'Irish difficulty' had particular appeal to Scots such as Joseph Hume, who regarded their own country's union with England in 1707 as source of its rapid social development, and hence the optimal model for Irish 'improvement'.[1]

The fear that Irish difference posed a disruptive danger to the British body politic increased in the wake of 1815 with the challenges raised by the mass Catholic and Repeal campaigns led by Daniel O'Connell, and the economic crises most overtly demonstrated in the 1817 and 1822 famines and the outbreaks of agrarian violence that attracted outbursts of despairing sympathy and outraged horror respectively in the British reading public. All of these 'backward' Irish characteristics stoked growing alarm in the context of the growth of Irish labour migration (both seasonal and permanent) facilitated by the introduction of cheap steamship transit across the Irish Sea in the 1820s, and fuelled by Irish rural distress and the lure of industrial employment in Great Britain (and, some xenophobic commentators claimed, by the more favourable welfare provision available there).[2]

Thus in the decades between the Union and the Great Famine the phenomenon of Irish poverty – and indeed the perception of poverty as a defining characteristic of Irish society – acquired ever growing attention in Britain. This stimulated a plethora of developmental theories and a rather smaller number of policy initiatives, none of which (at least before the introduction of the Board of Works and the National Education Board in 1831) appeared to make much difference to the dete-

---

1 For Hume, see Peter Gray, "'Ireland's last fetter struck off": the lord lieutenant debate 1800–67', in Terrence McDonough (ed.), *Was Ireland a colony? Economics, politics and culture in nineteenth-century Ireland* (Dublin, 2005), pp 87–101. 2 See, for example, John Ede, *Reflections on the employment, wages, and condition of the poor, showing the fallacy and injustice of recommending emigration as a remedy for the lamentable state of the English labourer, and tracing the evils of insufficient wages and ruinous poor's rates to their natural causes* (London, 1829).

riorating conditions of the Irish countryside. This preoccupation with poverty also, perhaps inevitably, focused attention on the question of institutional structures of poor relief and their applicability to Ireland, a country with no national poor law and only an unco-ordinated and underfunded network of public institutions for the alleviation of poverty, mostly in the form of medical charities.[3]

One dilemma confronting those considering the integration of Ireland into a 'British' welfare regime as a means of addressing the endemic and overflowing 'problem of poverty' was the absence of any single 'British' poor law. England and Wales, on one hand, and Scotland on the other, had separate national poor laws from the late sixteenth or early seventeenth centuries, but these had never been identical and had diverged further in both law and practice in the ensuing centuries. To complicate things further, by the early nineteenth century there were marked regional distinctions in relief practice within each of the two countries, and intense internal debates disputing both the nature and necessity of reform of their respective institutions. Campaigns for reform would lead to fundamental amendments of the 'old' English law in 1834 and of the 'old' Scottish law in 1845, but while there was some convergence, uniformity in welfare provision remained (and indeed remains) elusive.[4]

In retrospect it might appear inevitable that Ireland should have been granted a pared-down version of the workhouse-based new English poor law in 1838, but as late as 1836 this was far from clear. In the eyes of many theorists of union, Ireland's situation (and socio-economic backwardness) was cognate with that of Scotland in the aftermath of the 1707 Anglo-Scottish Union. This positive vision (surprisingly widespread both before and after the Famine) forecast a dynamic future for Ireland under the aegis of the Union, so long as backward-looking nationalists and agrarian secret societies were defeated (as the Scottish Jacobites had been in 1746), and obstacles impeding the dynamic potential of Irish economic growth (including overpopulation, endemic poverty and low expectations) were overcome. For many early nineteenth-century observers, the (largely voluntaristic) social institutions which had evolved in the poorer environment of Scotland, and apparently facilitated that country's remarkable economic growth since the mid-eighteenth century within the Union context, might be more easily transferable to Ireland than those of England, and assist in the necessary 'modernization' of the western island.[5] This preference was shared by some commentators in Ulster, where some Scottish-style parochial bodies (albeit generally underfunded) were already in existence.[6]

This 'Caledonianization' strategy appealed to a number of English and Irish

---

3 The best introduction to the history of poor law and its predecessors is Virginia Crossman, *The poor law in Ireland 1838–1948* (Dublin, 2006). **4** For regional variation within England, see Steven A. King, *Poverty and welfare in England 1700–1850: a regional perspective* (Manchester, 2000); for Scotland, see Rosalind Mitchison, *The old poor law in Scotland: the experience of poverty, 1574–1845* (Edinburgh, 2000). **5** *The Scotsman*, 17 Mar. 1830. **6** See for example, [John Macausland], *A letter to the right hon. Lord Goderich, on the deplorable condition of the helpless poor in Ireland, with a plan of relief, as at present partly in operation in several districts of the province of Ulster. By a member of a parochial poor relief committee* (Dublin, 1827).

Unionist commentators, but not surprisingly its principal advocates were Scots. Chief among these was Thomas Chalmers. The son of a merchant family in small-town Fife, Chalmers emerged, after his 'conversion' of 1808, as the leading Presbyterian evangelical clergyman of his generation. Always confrontational and controversial, Chalmers had taken a strong line in 1827–9 in favour of Catholic emancipation (believing the abandonment of penal exclusion would actually strengthen both the Union and the Irish Church establishment by undercutting Catholic grievances). By 1830 he was also anxious to extend the 'purifying' experiment in poor relief he had pioneered in the Glasgow parish of St John's in 1819–23 to Ireland (as well as to the rest of Scotland and, gradually, also to England).[7]

Chalmers received an opportunity to promote his Scottish programme for Irish amelioration before the Spring Rice committee of inquiry into the state of the Irish poor in 1830. The growing volume of demands for an Irish poor law from both countries (from Irish liberal Catholics such as Bishop James Doyle as well as British labour-protectionists and radical philanthropists such as Thomas Sadler and George Poulett Scrope) had put pressure on both the administration and parliamentary opponents of such a measure to offer some concrete response. There is little evidence to suggest that the ministers in 1828–30 had any sympathy for such an initiative, and certainly Wellington as prime minister made his opposition explicit in the Lords in 1828 and again in 1830.[8] Nevertheless, the most committed, and increasingly anxious, Irish opponents of any poor laws were becoming rattled. The liberal landowner and Co. Limerick MP Thomas Spring Rice had warned parliament in 1829 that even the public discussion of the matter was dangerous as it would raise unrealizable expectations in Ireland.[9]

There were precedents for such a manoeuvre. The select committees of 1804, 1822 and 1825, dominated by Irish landowners and 'experts' both on political economy and Irish conditions, had strongly recommended against any extension of poor laws to Ireland, and suggested alternative measures of improvement. Spring Rice, having been assured that the government would have no objection, moved in March 1830 that a new select committee of inquiry be formed to consider the state of the labouring poor in Ireland. Well aware that some might be sceptical as to the real purposes behind such a manoeuvre, he assured the house of his sincerity in seeking to elucidate and adjudicate between all opinions. At the same time, he took the opportunity to set out his own views: the distress of the poor in Ireland had been grossly exaggerated; they were, in fact, in a better position than the pauperized labourers of the south of England, and likely to advance further as Irish agriculture continued in its improving trajectory. Moreover, Ireland already had a magnificent

---

7 For Chalmers' life and ideas, see Stewart J. Brown, *Thomas Chalmers and the godly commonwealth in Scotland* (Oxford, 1982). 8 *Hansard's Parliamentary Debates,* 2nd ser., xix, cols 257–9 [1 May 1828]; xxiii, cols 367–8 [16 Mar. 1830]. 9 Ibid., xxi, cols 1142–3 [7 May 1829]. Spring Rice's case against poor laws in both countries was rigidly Malthusian, although he made the case for assistance to the country through emigration and public works.

system of asylums and hospitals for the sick, destitute and insane, which were a tribute to the charitable character of the Irish gentry.[10] For Spring Rice (also the leading parliamentary rebutter of O'Connell's repeal motion in 1834), the political assimilation of the two countries was imperative, but Ireland's backwardness rendered unacceptable any imitation of England's 'social constitution' manifest in its poor law.

Spring Rice sought to neutralize the demand for an Irish poor law based on the 'old' English model by ensuring his committee had a majority of rejectionists, and by giving a hearing to leading advocates of such a measure, including Bishop Doyle and the political economist J.R. McCulloch, while countering them with witnesses he was confident would effectively undermine them. One was the English moralist and poor law abolitionist J.E. Bicheno (who had recently completed a tour of Ireland and written up his observations as a popular book),[11] but the 'star' witness – then approaching the peak of his public influence in England as well as Ireland – was Thomas Chalmers. What Bicheno and Chalmers had in common was an evangelical Christian political economy that was grounded in Robert Malthus' pessimistic concern about lower-class immorality and fecundity, and scepticism about secular progress and human perfectibility.[12] Both located the fundamental cause of poverty and misery in the moral failings of the poor – their lack of foresight, self-help and sexual restraint – and in the indifference of the upper classes and the tendency of ill-designed institutions to encourage such attitudes (in England the poor law; in Ireland absenteeism and non-paternalist landlordism). Chalmers, moreover, had the additional authority garnered from having pioneered an experiment in voluntary poor relief, aimed at 'purifying' the traditional Scottish relief system from its subsequent accretions, in the Glasgow parish of St John's in 1819–23. Stewart Brown describes this as a determined attempt to recreate an ideal 'Godly Commonwealth' amid the social dislocation consequent on the rapid and unsettling industrialization and urbanization of the Scottish lowlands. It is clear, however, that Chalmers believed his Glaswegian model readily exportable to both Ireland and England.[13]

Chalmers' objectives in giving evidence to the committee were to justify the superiority of the traditional Scottish system of poor relief over its English rival (and to challenge the inroads the latter was starting to make in the practice of poor relief in the Scottish borders and cities), and to advocate his own perfection of the Scottish voluntarist approach in the St John's experiment. For Chalmers, the chief merit of the traditional Scottish system lay in its minimalism: 'the excellence of our system', he opined,

> when compared with that of England, is altogether of a negative kind. Our parochial charity, from the extreme moderation of its allowances, does not

---

10 *Hansard*, 2nd ser., xxiii, cols 183–202 [11 Mar. 1830].   11 J.E. Bicheno, *Ireland and its economy; being the result of observations made in a tour through the country in the autumn of 1829* (London, 1830).   12 For Chalmers and Christian political economy, see Boyd Hilton, *The age of atonement: the influence of evangelicalism on social and economic thought 1785–1865* (Oxford, 1988), pp 39–40, 55–70.   13 Brown, *Thomas Chalmers*, pp xiv–xv.

seduce our people from a due dependence on themselves, or to a neglect of
their relative obligations[.][14]

But its true superiority, and indeed universal applicability, resided in its close approx-
imation to the providential natural laws of creation, which Chalmers, as an
evangelical Christian political economist, was convinced had been divinely ordained
for the regulation of human society. Whereas public relief to the sick, insane and incapable was legitimate and scripturally defensible, assistance to the able-bodied destitute
(or indeed to the aged, to abandoned children and even to orphans) was not, and was
likely to impede vital behavioural change by offering inducements to dependency,
wantonness or immorality.

At St John's, he continued, the Scottish system had been further perfected
through a total abandonment of charitable aid to the destitute (except for the sick
and insane, and a dying remnant of 'old' parish paupers), and the introduction of a
regime of moral inspection by the lay deacons of the parish who had distinguished
the deserving from the undeserving poor and promoted self-help among the urban
poor through advice and paternal moral care. The effect, he claimed (although this
was regularly disputed by other observers) was a sharp fall in destitution and beggary
as well as in parish expenditure on relief – allowing the transfer of resources to the
more positive agencies of moral education and church extension.

The allegedly positive response of the Irish immigrants in the parish to this
system, albeit founded on the established Church of Scotland infrastructure, had
convinced Chalmers of its transferability; indeed the absence of any pre-existing and
corrupting expectation of state relief in Ireland, and the lauded charitability of the
rural poor to each other, made this ideal. Contrariwise, the introduction of any
compulsory assessment for the poor would be disastrous, creating the false expectation of a 'right' to relief, and impeding the necessary socio-economic transition to
capitalist agriculture and industry that had been so successful in Scotland but still
faced obstacles in Ireland. If such a transition in the absence of any compulsory poor
relief might entail short-term suffering, this was preferable to the alternative of moral
abasement, which must determine the socio-economic condition of a people.
Chalmers rejected the environmental meliorism typical of many Whigs and radicals,
and replaced it with an evangelical moralism:

> The pervading fallacy in the speculations of those who advocate the estab-
> lishment of a poor rate in Ireland ... is founded on the observation of a
> connection between a high state of character and a high state of economic
> comfort ... It is often conceived that comfort is the cause, and character is the
> effect; now I hold that character is the cause, and that comfort is the effect.
> ... [I]f instead of taking hold of the man, and attempting to elevate him by

14 *Second report of the select committee on the state of the poor in Ireland,* PP 1830 (654), vii. 451,
p. 287.

the improvement of his economic condition, you take hold of the boy, and attempt to infuse into him another element, which I conceive to be the causal one, by means of education, then you will, through the medium of character, work out an improvement to his economic condition. What I should advise is, that education be made universal in Ireland, and that you should weather for a season the annoyance of Ireland's mendicity, and the annoyance of that pressure, which I conceive to be altogether temporary. This appears to me to be the only principle on which Ireland can be securely and effectually brought to a higher standard of enjoyment, and into the state of a well habited and well conditioned peasantry.[15]

Reconsidering this bleak short-term scenario, Chalmers later conceded that some temporary relief to immediate suffering through assisted emigration would be acceptable, but doubted that there was much demand for this, and demoted it from the role of panacea that some of its advocates claimed to that of a useful auxiliary to a developmental strategy based on moral rearmament rather than state intervention.

What impact did Chalmers' evidence have on Irish debates? While the Spring Rice report of 1830 declined to offer any positive recommendation on an Irish poor law, this very negativity in the face of the positive demands of Bishop Doyle and the English lobby was a de facto endorsement of Chalmers' insistence on voluntarism. It also whole-heartedly endorsed his insistence on the primacy of education, although in the highly contested Irish context it opted to recommend a national non-denominational system (subsequently enacted under Stanley in 1831) rather than that based on the Protestant church establishment which Chalmers preferred.[16]

Chalmers' evidence was also widely praised by enemies of an Irish poor law. The leading English political economist Nassau Senior urged the Scottish divine to publish it as a pamphlet, and incorporated Chalmers' evidence as an appendix to his own influential 1831 book on poor relief. Echoing the Scots divine, Senior identified the centrality of 'industry' and 'forethought' to social improvement and any real diminution of poverty; all human institutions should be judged according to their positive or (more frequently) negative impact upon these cardinal moral virtues. English and (as Chalmers had testified) recent Scottish experience had demonstrated the disastrous moral consequences of poor laws, threatening the very destruction of society if not summarily remedied. Only unmediated exposure to the direct consequences of immoral behaviour could produce behavioural improvement; universal experience 'in all ages and countries', Senior concluded, proved that 'idleness and improvidence can be prevented only be leaving them to the punishment inflicted by nature – want and degradation'.[17] This became the standard 'orthodox' text on the

---

15 Ibid., p. 315. 16 *Report of the select committee on the state of the poor in Ireland,* PP 1830 (667), vii. 1, pp 55–7. 17 Nassau W. Senior, *A letter to Lord Howick on a legal provision for the*

question, and shaped the conclusions later reached by Senior's close friend (and former tutor) Richard Whately in his Irish poor inquiry report of 1836.

Chalmers' assertion of moral certainties, as well as the deferential treatment he had received at the hands of Spring Rice's committee, drew hostile commentary from James Doyle and other commentators. *Contra* Chalmers, Doyle insisted in his evidence that the great efforts the Irish poor made in supporting their destitute family and neighbours represented, not the epitome of charitable morality, but an index of endemic immiseration. It followed that, imperfect as it was, the introduction of the current English system would be preferable to the status quo: 'We have ... a disorganized population becoming by their poverty more and more immoral, and less and less capable of providing for themselves; and we have besides that, the frightful, and awful, and terrific exhibition of human life, wasted with a rapidity and to a degree such as is not witnessed in any civilized country upon the face of the earth.' [18] Rather than offering an opportunity for the active remoralization of society through enlightened private agency, in his opinion the extremity of Irish poverty threatened social disintegration and the complete collapse of moral values into barbarism in the absence of any preventative interposition of public agency. This secular responsibility to provide a welfare entitlement was derived from the divine and natural law on which the legitimacy of any Christian state must be founded. The 'positive law of the gospel' directed that equity rather than equality be the objective of true statesmanship, but prudence indicated that this moral requirement could be met without the concession of unregulated and unlimited rights to the poor.[19] The bishop argued that the governors and elites of Ireland, and not the poor themselves, were morally responsible for the visitation of divine providence manifest in endemic poverty. Atonement could come only from the acknowledgement of state responsibility and the adoption of appropriately penitent (and socially redemptive) policies.

Bishop Doyle entered the public lists again in March 1831, with his *Letter to Thomas Spring Rice*, intended as a rebuttal to the 'leading questions' which had been put to him the previous year, the contrary evidence presented to the committee, principally by Chalmers and Bicheno, and the anodyne conclusions which its chairman had penned.[20] The pamphlet repeated much of what Doyle had already argued, but with greater coherence and framed in yet more impassioned rhetoric. He identified nine core arguments against an Irish poor law manifest in the 1830 report, and proceeded to refute them. Doyle reiterated his fundamentally moralistic case, but added a more aggressive swipe at the 'selfishness, odious alike to God and man' of those who denied its necessity out of self-interest.[21] The dogma that a poor law would drain investment capital from the wages fund he dismissed as simultaneously subverting the Gospel injunction to mercy, and ignoring the likely consequences of

Irish poor; commutation of tithes, and a provision for the Irish Roman Catholic clergy (London, 1831), p. 35. **18** *Second report of the select committee on the state of the poor in Ireland,* PP 1830 (654), vii. 451, p. 415. **19** Ibid., p. 454. **20** James W. Doyle, *Letter to Thomas Spring Rice, esq., M.P., on the establishment of a legal provision for the Irish poor* (Dublin, 1831). **21** Ibid., p. 12.

the introduction of a genuine social security: 'a Poor Rate ... would give peace to the heart of the poor – it would attach them to the laws – it would give them an interest in the property of which they shared, and teach them, not by words, but by works, that there was a government which had care of them, and a country which they could call their own.'[22]

His harshest criticisms were reserved for the hypocrisy of those who preached the moral superiority of private charity, while evading the requirements of effective relief. While refraining from mentioning Chalmers by name, Doyle denounced his doctrines and those who sought to hide behind them:

> These men abet a system which is proved in evidence to send thousands prematurely out of life – the victims of famine – the prey of disease; but they are pious withal, and are anxious that no encroachment be made on that divine commandment to which is annexed the promise of 'a long life upon the earth.' They will take care that the child honour the father, that the child may live long; but they will, should he be reduced to poverty, leave him to the care of that Providence which feeds the sparrow on the house top. He may like the lily of the field be clothed better than Solomon, but if they see him naked they will not cover him: if he be poor and a wanderer they will not take him into their house: if he be an orphan they will not break their bread to him: nor wipe away the tear from the cheek of his widowed mother ... Yes! for the first duty of a statesman is to secure the necessaries of life to the bulk of the people committed to his care, and Christianity has no characteristic, unless it be that of those who profess it loving one another, and each of them doing to the other as he would have that other do unto him.[23]

Most importantly, in his own eyes, Doyle refuted at length the argument that 'the poor have no claim founded on justice to a provision' at the expense of the propertied.[24] He had, he declared, previously reined in his opinions on this matter so as to avoid exciting uncontrollable anger on the part of the dispossessed against those who continued to deny their moral entitlement. His patience had now snapped. Far from being absolute, the rights of property (albeit necessary) were rendered by Scripture and natural justice inferior to the right to life; the state which ignored this great fact brought social anarchy upon itself. In place of Chalmers' theological defence of the primacy of private charity, Doyle offered the opposite – a social-Catholic theological justification of state relief. This sat easily with a pointed rejection of the conventional economic notion of a necessary 'transition' in Ireland towards an Anglicized future –

---

22 Ibid., p. 20.   **23** Ibid., pp 34–6. This charge was unfair to Chalmers in at least one respect; the Scots divine distinguished between famine as a product of a 'special providence', distinct from the 'normal' poverty that arose from human sin, and he adopted an interventionist line during the Great Famine in 1847, see [Thomas Chalmers], 'Political economy of a famine', *North British Review* 7 (1847), 247–90; see also Hilton, *Age of atonement,* pp 108–14.   **24** Doyle, *Letter to Spring Rice,* p. 65.

a vision which he also thought based on an un-Christian pursuit of unrestricted capital accumulation that ignored the true interests of the people and must end in revolution and social convulsion. To avoid such a disaster he would 'adopt a sump-tuary law, or a law of *ostracism*, or if not those laws, I would surely seek for a Poor Law, if for no other purpose, to check the progress of society on its "road to ruin"'.[25]

This full-blooded reaction to Chalmers was not without public effect, not least among the more radical strand in British Whiggery associated with the *Morning Chronicle*, which asked, 'Who is there of the established clergy, either of England, Ireland, or Scotland, to compare with Dr Doyle? Compare his evidence on the Poor Law Committee with that of Dr Chalmers, and his superiority appears immense.'[26] The bitter exchanges of 1830–1, when combined with the escalating tithe war and renewed threat of regional famine in summer 1831, further polarized opinion in Ireland. For supporters of a poor law, Doyle's religiously-grounded and passionate advocacy now provided a new point of reference. One Dublin pamphleteer asserted that Doyle had convincingly proved Chalmers wrong on the crucial question of the entitlement of the poor.[27] Daniel Callaghan, the Catholic MP for Cork city, declared in 1832 that he had subsequently heard nothing 'that could shake his confidence in the opinion of the view he had heard delivered ... by Dr Doyle, that the 43rd of Elizabeth, which gave a system of Poor laws to England, was the Magna Charta of the poor'. Co. Wexford's Whig-liberal MP Henry Lambert agreed that 'Doyle had so fully exposed the cant and hypocrisy of the objection to Poor laws' as to make further objection impossible.[28] The Dublin-born imperial publicist Robert Montgomery Martin also cited Doyle at length in support of his case that a poor law was essential to give justice to both Ireland and England, and to preserve the empire by under-cutting social unrest and the repeal movement it fuelled.[29]

Chalmers may, however, have had the last laugh in this clerical duel. He eventu-ally worked his evidence into his own 1832 book *On Political Economy*, a central text of evangelical economic thought and one which made a considerable (if not always acclaimed) impact on public opinion in Britain.[30] Paradoxically, however, his most important 'convert' on the poor-law question was in Ireland. Daniel O'Connell's attitude to poor laws was inconsistent and shaped by political calculation. In 1831 he had announced himself strongly persuaded by Doyle's case, but this adherence was not to last.[31] Within a year he had found a rationale for re-adopting his underlying scepticism in Chalmers' writings. While opposed to Chalmers on questions of the Union and the church establishment, O'Connell as a paternalistic (and sincere)

25 Ibid., p. 60.   26 *Morning Chronicle*, 18 Jan. 1831.   27 Anon., *The desideratum, or Ireland's only remedy; 'poor laws and education', proved on social, political and Christian principles. Addressed to the citizens of Dublin. By P.E.H.* (Dublin, 1831).   28 *Hansard*, 3rd ser., xiii, cols 858–60 [19 June 1832].   29 R. Montgomery Martin, *Poor laws for Ireland, a measure of justice to England; of humanity to the people of both islands; and of self-preservation for the empire* (London, 1833).   30 Brown, *Chalmers*, p. 192.   31 Daniel O'Connell to James Doyle, 29 Mar. 1831, cited in William John Fitzpatrick, *The life, times and correspondence of the right rev. Dr Doyle, bishop of Kildare and Leighlin* (new edn, 2 vols, Dublin, 1890), ii, 285–6.

Catholic evidently found inspiration in his idealization of the self-assistance of the working poor and emphasis on the moral responsibility of the gentry, and incorporated this into his own revived anti-poor law rhetoric.

In 1832 O'Connell proclaimed he would exert all his influence in Ireland to guard the people against the delusion that the people 'ought to rely upon the pockets of their more wealthy neighbours for support, instead of their own exertions'. Patient and minute investigation had now, he declared, disabused him of his earlier mistaken views, and convinced him that compulsory poor laws inevitably destroyed the morality of the poor, stoked class antagonisms, and distracted from the real means of improving the people. Rather than conveying natural rights, a poor law 'as implying slavery on the part of those who thus obtained relief under their provisions, was ... prejudicial to the independence of the national character'.[32]

O'Connell admitted he had been bolstered in his scepticism by encountering Thomas Chalmers' moralistic voluntarism. When Chalmers visited London in July 1833, O'Connell made the effort to meet and thank him. '[He] shook me most cordially by the hands,' Chalmers wrote to his daughter, 'complimenting me on my evidence about the Irish Poor-Laws, saying he was a disciple of mine upon that subject, and not of his own priest, Dr Doyle.'[33] This was no empty gesture. O'Connell incorporated Chalmers' vision into his parliamentary rhetoric that year. While the economic consequences of poor laws were everywhere negative, he declared, it was their moral effects that posed the greatest dangers:

> [H]e was satisfied that no laws could be devised better calculated to destroy the feelings of humanity in the breasts of the population than this system of Poor-laws. These feelings, he was happy to say, yet existed in Ireland. God had planted them deep in the hearts of the people; and the voice of revealed religion, at least told him that it was a duty to perform acts of charity – that if he expected to be rewarded hereafter, he must wipe away the tear from the eye of the widow and orphan – and that he must relieve those who were in affliction and distress.[34]

Such an overt identification with the ideas of the Scottish evangelical drew harsh criticism even from sections of the O'Connellite press in Dublin.[35] It also, rather unusually, placed O'Connell into an alliance with the mouthpiece of the Irish Conservative landed interest, which also endorsed the morally and practically superior 'Scottish system', as most applicable to Ireland.[36] While O'Connell would again,

32 *Hansard*, 3rd ser., xiii, cols 853–6 [19 June 1832].   33 Brown, *Chalmers*, pp 192–3.
34 *Hansard*, 3rd ser., xvii, cols 877–8 [2 May 1833].   35 *Freeman's Journal*, 23 Mar. 1835.
36 Anon., 'The Scottish system of poor laws', *Dublin University Magazine*, 3 (May 1834), pp 508–22. Some Scottish commentators, however, criticized O'Connell for his apparent deviation from the Scottish model in excluding the aged poor from any entitlement to relief, *The Scotsman*, 2 Mar. 1833.

for tactical reasons, backpedal on the question in 1835–6, his fundamental opposition to an Irish poor law (which he admitted placed him at odds with most of the Catholic clergy and much of his party) helped mould the negative atmosphere into which the infant Irish poor law emerged after 1838.

Chalmers' direct influence on policy can also be traced in the report of the Irish Poor Inquiry Commission of 1836.[37] This widely-misunderstood document has been (in my view wrongly) seen as offering a constructive blueprint for Irish economic development. In fact, once stripped of the accretions inserted to keep dissentient Irish members of the Commission on board (but to which 'working commissioners' and their ministerial allies had no political commitment), this document too can be seen to be stamped with the ideas of Christian political economy. This was hardly surprising, given the fact that its chair, and moving spirit, was the Anglican archbishop of Dublin, Richard Whately, himself a propagandist for and dabbler in a form of political economy that (like Chalmers, although somewhat more 'optimistically') placed moral and behavioural change at the root of economic betterment.

At the heart of the 'Whately Report' (as it became known) was an explicit endorsement of the 'Scottish System' of poor relief for Ireland. By this Whately meant poor relief (except for the special categories of sick and insane poor) principally through voluntary agency and charity, with the state restricting itself mostly to a regulatory and instigatory role. The commissioners envisaged that any public aid necessary to support the system in the first instance would gradually be reduced as the improved system of voluntarism in Ireland took hold and the relief system came progressively more into line with the Scots ideal. The view of the majority of the commissioners was that:

> although the system of providing for the poor by means of voluntary associations, aided by the public purse, and constructed upon well-digested principles, may not succeed at once in every part of the country – yet that, so far as it does succeed, it will tend to bring the population into a sound state with respect to the poor, and will we trust gradually work its way over the face of the island, and probably supersede in many places, as the Scottish system does so extensively, the necessity of a compulsory rate ... [for] although a compulsory rate might be rendered general more rapidly, and be administered by artificial means, it would every day become more difficult to manage, and tend to bring the country into a worse state than our inquiry has found it.[38]

Appendix H of the report set out a plan for a network of voluntary agencies (not, however, restricted to the established church parochial structures as Chalmers

---

37 *Third report of the commissioners for inquiring into the condition of the poorer classes in Ireland*, PP 1836 [43], xxx.1.   38 George Nicholls, *A history of the Irish poor law in connexion with the condition of the people* (London, 1856), p. 150.

favoured, but aiming to draw on the same wellsprings of religious benevolence and calculated not to discourage less structured assistance of the poor for each other). It is also true that Whately personally put greater store in assisted emigration as a first step in addressing the perceived Malthusian malaise of Ireland and stressed this as his core auxiliary in the report, but this was not wholly out of line with Chalmers' evidence in 1830, which saw the thinning of the population as a desirable (although not essential) accompaniment to the necessary remoralization of social relationships.[39]

As is well known, the Whig government in 1836 opted to reject the Whately report and instead commissioned George Nicholls to prepare a blueprint for the extension of a form of the amended English poor law to Ireland. The reasons for this decision lie outside the scope of this paper, although (among others) the view that a poor law should contribute to the governing strategy of 'justice to Ireland' in the later 1830s should not be discounted.[40] The Scottish model, with its marginalization of the state and emphasis on voluntarism, offered no place for the state (outside education and perhaps some assisted emigration) to play a role combining meliorism with the active brokering of social relationships. The English poor law offered a mechanism for doing both: the former through, as G.C. Lewis argued, facilitating economic transition, or, as others emphasized, coercing the landed class into investment and employment activity through the threat of heavy poor-rates to support the able-bodied destitute; the latter through the provision (however hedged in the 1838 legislation and restricted by the stress on less-eligibility) of a minimum entitlement to welfare provision on need (the state of destitution) rather than social category.[41] It was this idea of a poor law, rather than the patently inadequate instalment on offer in 1838, that inclined many Irish and British radicals, including Smith O'Brien and Poulett Scrope, and liberal Catholic clergymen, such as the indefatigable Fr Thaddeus O'Malley, to support the measure rather than the alternatives of a Scottish-style model (still being pressed by Whately, Senior and their allies) or nothing at all.[42]

Ironically, the Irish poor law debates sparked intense debate within Scotland itself over Chalmers' representation of the 'Scottish model' and the 'purified' form he had

39 *Poor inquiry (Ireland). Appendix (H), Part I: containing reasons for recommending voluntary associations for the relief of the poor and reasons for dissenting from the principle of raising funds for the relief of the poor by the voluntary system, as recommended in the report,* PP 1836 [41], xxxiv. 643. Part 2 of this appendix comprised J.E. Bicheno's personal rationale for supporting the report, expressed in the language of evangelical Christian economics. 40 See Peter Gray, *Famine, land and politics: British government and Irish society, 1843–1850* (Dublin, 1999), pp 31–5. The subject is dealt with at length in Peter Gray, *The making of the Irish poor law* (Manchester, 2009). 41 These ideas were most forcefully stated, albeit with different points of emphasis, in George Cornewall Lewis, *On local disturbances in Ireland; and on the Irish church question* (London, 1836), John Revans, *Evils of the state of Ireland: their causes and their remedy – A poor law* (2nd edn, London, 1837), and G. Poulett Scrope, *Plan of a poor-law for Ireland, with a review of the arguments for and against it* (2nd edn, London, 1834). 42 For O'Malley's radical development of Doyle's position, see Thaddeus O'Malley, *An idea of a poor law for Ireland* (2nd edn, London, 1837).

created at St John's. William Alison, professor of medicine at Edinburgh University, was at that time becoming engaged in a struggle for reform of the Scottish poor laws with the aim of granting a legal entitlement to the destitute poor and a more generous provision of relief, and soon crossed swords with Thomas Chalmers on the optimum mode of poor relief and the underlying question of the applicability of Malthusian doctrine to social policy.[43] In 1836 Alison made the case that the essence of 'justice to Ireland' should lie in a good poor law. In his opinion, Irish demographic history clearly proved that 'below a certain grade of poverty the [Malthusian] preventive check has no power'; in Ireland population had grown most rapidly in the poorest regions, whereas such an excess had been checked in England by the minimum entitlement existing under the law that had created the taste for 'artificial wants' that stimulated reproductive self-restraint. Chalmers' case for the moral and practical superiority of voluntary charity, which had previously proved so influential in Ireland, did not stand up to empirical scrutiny:

> The idea that the sensibility of the rich to the miseries of the poor is weakened by a system of poor laws, is, a mere speculative delusion, the very reverse of the fact. The truth is, that when the poor are left, in a complex state of society, to voluntary charity, they are miserably neglected; great numbers of them sink into abject destitution; the rich have continually before their eyes examples of poverty and wretchedness, such as are almost unknown in a country where the poor are under the protection of the law; this sight gradually becomes habitual to them, they comfort themselves with the reflection, that many beggars are impostors; and too often 'indulge in unhallowed pleasantry in the sacred presence of misery'.[44]

Such was now the case in Ireland, and would remain so, he concluded, if the Whately report was adopted. Ireland, like Scotland, needed only to grant a right to relief to the able-bodied poor within the workhouse (the infirm and helpless poor 'of good character' were best relieved in their own homes) to raise its standard of civilization and create the social security that would underpin rapid economic growth. The socio-economic crisis that engulfed Scotland in the early 1840s would see public support in Scotland shift from Chalmers to Alison and ultimately pave the way for the partial Anglicization of Scottish Poor Law in 1845 (although Chalmersian ideas of moral inspection and differentiation of the 'deserving' and 'undeserving' would long persist north of the border).

---

43 For a summary of Alison's views on this, see his *Observations on the management of the poor in Scotland; and its effects on the health of the great towns* (2nd edn, Edinburgh, 1840), and Mitchison, *The old poor law in Scotland*, pp 173–5. **44** [William P. Alison], 'Evils of the state of Ireland', *Blackwood's Edinburgh Magazine*, 40 (Oct. 1836), p. 503. See also [William P. Alison], 'Justice to Ireland – a poor law', *Blackwood's Edinburgh Magazine*, 40 (Dec. 1836), pp 812–31.

Despite the general defeat of the policy ideas espoused by Chalmers in both Ireland and Scotland, his arguments appear to have made a particular impact on one part of Ireland. Not surprisingly, this was in north-east Ulster. In 1837–8 many of Belfast's Presbyterian clerical and lay elite were strongly attached to the Chalmersian ideals of voluntary charity and moral improvement, and voiced these in protest meetings held to oppose the government's bill. The Revd R.J. Bryce, principal of Belfast Academy, quoted Chalmers extensively and praised the successful experiment in parochial voluntarism he had initiated at St John's, Glasgow. Whatever their differences on doctrinal matters, the leaders of the two principal wings of Irish Presbyterianism, Henry Cooke and Henry Montgomery, were agreed in vigorously upholding these localist and voluntarist principles and rejecting any centralized and compulsory measure. A list of extensive resolutions were agreed at a meeting in April 1837, with Cooke's preference for 'an optional Poor Law, of which they could [only] avail them-selves in times of trial and scarcity' gaining majority support.[45] In 1838 a baronial assembly at Randalstown, Co. Antrim, passed resolutions deprecating the unneces-sary costs of workhouse provision and urging an alternative of 'enabling the people to assess themselves at vestries, by parishes, half baronies, or such other unions as may be agreed on, for the support of our *Local Poor* alone'.[46] Similar points were made by local parochial meetings, such as that at Connor, Co. Antrim (where – in ideal Chalmersian form – the local 'Sabbath day collections' for food, seed and clothing were praised as already providing what was necessary by means of charitable relief).[47] The existing 'Scotch system' of voluntary relief in Ulster was lauded in parliament by Lord Castlereagh as a viable alternative to the government's scheme.[48] This was insuf-ficient to prevent the passage of the 1838 bill, but helped form a negative attitude towards the consequent relief system in Ulster and shape the minimalist attitude towards working the law that was long to distinguish that province.

In conclusion, Thomas Chalmers' ideas of welfare (and the Scottish model they idealized) appear to have been comprehensively defeated. In this respect, at least, Ireland would follow an English rather than a Scots institutional model. But the ideas that morality was causally anterior to economic condition, and that voluntary assis-tance was ethically superior to state provision, were powerful ones, and continued to have some play in Ireland and in British thinking about Ireland long after 1838. Although Chalmers had rejected (and continued to oppose) the Irish poor law, his behaviourist preoccupations informed the thinking of many during the Famine (especially key figures such as Charles Trevelyan), who sought to turn the poor law from a social safety net into a machine for the moral transformation of the Irish (pauper and landowner alike) and the forcible promotion of self-help.[49] Chalmers'

45 *Belfast News-Letter,* 18 Apr. 1837.   **46** *Belfast News-Letter,* 16 Feb. 1828; 27 Feb. 1838.
47 Ibid., 27 Feb. 1838.   **48** *Hansard,* 3rd ser., xlii, col. 718 [30 Apr. 1838].   **49** Trevelyan endorsed the evangelical reading of the situation, but tended (contrary to Chalmers himself) to see the continuing Irish crisis as more the consequence of a 'general' rather than a 'special' act of providence, see Gray, *Famine, land and politics,* pp 252, 286, and 'National humiliation and the Great Hunger: fast and famine in 1847', *Irish Historical Studies,* 32:126 (2000), pp 193–

ideas were regularly revived through the nineteenth century by many individuals –
such as the poor law 'crusaders' of the 1860s–70s and the later Irish viceroy Earl
Spencer – seeking to ratchet back what they saw as the slippage of the poor laws of
the three kingdoms towards a more extensive form of welfare provision and the
concession of welfare rights to the poor.[50] The shadow of Thomas Chalmers proved
to be a long one, and even today – when neo-liberal social doctrine appears to favour
voluntarist 'faith-based initiatives' over rights-based welfarism – it has not wholly
dissipated.

216.   **50** See Elizabeth T. Hurren, *Protesting about pauperism: poverty, politics and poor relief in late-Victorian England, 1870–1900* (Woodbridge, 2007).

The urban local state in Scotland and Ireland to 1900: parallels and contrasts

MATTHEW POTTER

A comparative study of the history of urban local government in the neighbouring countries of Scotland and Ireland indicates that there were many parallels from its origins in the twelfth century until the present day.[1] While such convergence is not surprising in the period 1801 to 1922, when both formed part of a United Kingdom dominated by their larger and wealthier neighbour England, it might seem somewhat more unexpected in the centuries before the respective Acts of Union of 1707 and 1800, and particularly before the union of the crowns in the person of James VI and I in 1603. After all, Scotland had been an independent kingdom for several hundred years before 1603, and throughout these centuries had been strongly influenced by French as well as by English models, particularly during the period of the Auld Alliance (1295–1560).[2] By contrast, Ireland's destiny was continuously and inextricably linked with that of England from 1169 onwards, and her political and administrative institutions were inevitably to take their form and character from those of its invaders.

The solution to this paradox (which is aptly symbolized by the distinctive spelling 'burgh' used in Scotland instead of the English and Irish usage 'borough' although the pronunciation remains the same) can be located in the common origins of the urban local state in the two countries. In both cases, it was an import from France and England and was but one aspect of the great expansion of the Normans in the eleventh, twelfth and thirteenth centuries. While Scotland did not experience an actual Norman invasion like England and Ireland, it did undergo a process of more gradual colonization and settlement by Norman barons and knights introduced by King David I and his successors, a process typified by the establishment of municipal corporations.[3]

---

1 For the local state in Scotland and Ireland see Mabel Atkinson, *Local government in Scotland*, (Edinburgh, 1904) and Desmond Roche, *Local government in Ireland* (Dublin, 1982). For a full account of the experience of a single urban area in each country see E. Patricia Dennison, David Ditchburn & Michael Lynch (eds), *Aberdeen before 1800: a new history* (East Linton, East Lothian, 2002); W. Hamish Fraser & Clive H. Lee (eds), *Aberdeen, 1800–2000: a new history* (East Linton, East Lothian, 2000) and Matthew Potter, *The government and the people of Limerick: the history of Limerick Corporation/ City Council 1197–2006* (Limerick, 2006). 2 Norman MacDougall, *An antidote to the English: the auld alliance, 1295–1560* (Phantassie, East Lothian, 2001). 3 A.A.M. Duncan, *The Edinburgh history of Scotland, Vol 1. Scotland: the making of the kingdom* (Edinburgh, 1978), pp 133–215. See also Seán Duffy, 'The Anglo-

Indeed the specific development of urban self-government in medieval Scotland and Ireland must be framed by the general development of such institutions throughout Western Christendom, in the economically and intellectually buoyant twelfth and thirteenth centuries.[4] Population grew rapidly, with a consequent expansion of agriculture and trade. Towns and cities were among the main beneficiaries of this astonishing growth and multiplied rapidly both in numbers and in size. New towns were founded particularly in frontier regions, like Eastern Europe, Scotland and Ireland.[5] The achievement of municipal autonomy was a Europe-wide trend which resulted from this urban revolution. The increasingly large, prosperous and confident urban areas wanted self-government both to have their property rights guaranteed and to gain control over their local economy. The movement for urban autonomy was very successful, and cities and towns all over Europe received varying degrees of self-government (usually by means of a charter) in the period 1150 to 1300.[6] Charters were documents issued to an urban area by a monarch, feudal lord or churchman, granting it a measure of self-rule and its citizens certain rights and freedoms. As part of this trend, the office of mayor and the institution of town council were imported from France into England and later to both Scotland and Ireland.[7]

Broadly speaking, the municipal history of Scotland and Ireland can be divided into two periods, the medieval and the modern, with the division between them marked by the reforming legislation of the 1830s.[8] The first Scottish burghs, Berwick and Roxburgh, were founded before 1124. Urban areas in receipt of a charter from the crown were known as royal burghs.[9] The origins of Ireland's boroughs can be traced to the Norman invasion that commenced in 1169. King Henry II of England granted the first Irish borough charter to Dublin in 1171–2 and Cork (1185), Waterford (1195) and Limerick (1197) followed soon after.[10]

In both countries, many towns were dependant on a great lord rather than on the crown directly. In Scotland these were known as burghs of regality and burghs of barony and numbered over 300 by the time of the Act of Union of 1707 although many were just tiny villages. By way of comparison, there were a mere seventy royal

Norman era in Scotland: convergence and divergence', in T.M. Devine & J.F. McMillan (eds), *Celebrating Columba: Irish-Scottish connections, 597–1997* (Edinburgh, 1999), pp 15–34. **4** These developments are described in David Abulafia (ed.), *The new Cambridge medieval history. Volume 5, c1198–c1300* (Cambridge, 1998). **5** See David Nicholas, *The growth of the medieval city from late antiquity to the early fourteenth century* (London, 1997) and David Nicholas, *The late medieval city, 1300–1500* (London, 1997). **6** Nicholas, *Growth of the medieval city*, pp 141–68, 228–321. **7** Ibid., pp 146–52, 230–34, and 290–93. **8** These 'two ages' of the urban local state were first distinguished by Matthew Potter in *The government and the people of Limerick,* pp 12–15. **9** For the origins of Scotland's burghs, see Duncan, *Scotland: the making of the kingdom,* pp 463–501. **10** John J. Webb, *Municipal government in Ireland: medieval and modern* (Dublin, 1918), pp 1–21.

burghs in 1707 of which four were ineffective.[11] In Ireland some 330 settlements had
been granted an urban constitution by 1300 and there were many later additions.[12]
However only 117 boroughs were still in existence by 1800 and the first Report of
the Commissioners appointed to inquire into the Municipal Corporations in Ireland
of 1835 found evidence of another twenty-five.[13] Nevertheless, there were also
dozens of towns and villages in existence that had no form of urban self-government
and can thus be classified as 'non-municipal'. In both countries, another classification
used was that of parliamentary borough and non-parliamentary borough. In
Scotland, only the sixty-six effective royal burghs were represented in parliament.
After the 1707 Act of Union, they returned fifteen MPs to the British parliament and
were grouped together in districts of four or five burghs each.[14] The 300-odd
boroughs of barony and of regality were non-parliamentary. In eighteenth-century
Ireland, the 117 parliamentary boroughs each returned two MPs to the Irish parliament and there was no longer any such category as a non-parliamentary borough.
Non-parliamentary was thus equivalent to non-municipal. After the 1800 Act of
Union, eighty-four of the 117 lost their status as parliamentary boroughs and only
thirty-three were empowered to return MPs to the Imperial parliament. Forty-nine
out of the eighty-four non-parliamentary boroughs became extinct after 1800 and
by the 1830s only sixty of the Irish boroughs in total were described as 'effectively
existing' and a further eight had a sort of residual existence.[15] In summary, by the
1830s, Scotland had sixty-six and Ireland had sixty-eight significant functioning
urban authorities.

    In both countries the government of the towns was vested in a mayor (or provost
as he was usually known in Scotland, although this title was sometimes used in
Ireland also) and a council, both of which were nearly always controlled by a small
group of propertied and intermarried merchants and craftsmen. In 1469, an act of the
Scottish parliament stipulated that the incoming town council should be elected by
the outgoing one and that the two councils together should elect the officers (provost
etc.) with the assistance of representatives from the guilds. In 1504, another act stipulated that the offices could only be held for a year and that only merchants could
hold office.[16] In Ireland many of the smaller boroughs were under the control of one
powerful family and even major cities like Limerick, Galway and Waterford were
governed by small and powerful oligarchies, related by blood and marriage.[17]

11 For a comprehensive account of the Scottish burghs see *Reports of the commissioners appointed to inquire into municipal corporations in Scotland*, H.C. 1835 (29). 12 B.J. Graham, 'The High Middle Ages: c. 1100 to c. 1350', in B.J. Graham & L.J. Proudfoot (eds), *An historical geography of Ireland* (London & San Diego, 1993), pp 82–84 and Brian Graham, 'Urbanisation in Ireland during the High Middle Ages, c. 1100 to c. 1350', in Terry Barry (ed.), *A history of settlement in Ireland* (London & New York, 2000), pp 131–5. 13 For the Irish boroughs see *Reports of the commissioners appointed to inquire into municipal corporations in Ireland*, H.C. 1835 (27). 14 T.M. Devine, *The Scottish nation, 1700–2000* (London, 2000), pp 196–7. 15 *Reports of the commissioners appointed to inquire into municipal corporations in Ireland*, H.C. 1835 (27), pp 4–11. 16 J.D. Mackie, *A history of Scotland* (London, 1964), pp 107–8. 17 For the famous example of Galway, see M.D. O'Sullivan, *Old Galway: the history of a*

In the Middle Ages and the early modern period, Scotland and Ireland, in common with the rest of Western Europe had a highly decentralized administrative system and consequently the municipal authorities provided the towns with a complete range of government services. Among their functions were the organisation of the town's defence (including the building and maintenance of the walls and the embodiment of a local militia); control and regulation of the local economy (including fairs and markets); administration of most of the legal system; law and order (including crime and punishment and the police); the building and maintenance of infrastructure, such as roads, bridges and quays; and protection of the environment (including fire safety and regulation of refuse disposal and wandering animals).[18]

The Reformation in Scotland and Ireland resulted in the emergence of the parish as a significant local authority and service provider, although this was to some degree a continuation of the activities of the Catholic church in the Middle Ages. After all, the distinction between the civil and religious functions of the established church had always been very blurred and unclear, both before and after the Reformation. In Scotland, what T. M. Devine has called the 'parish state' had a greater impact on the general populace that any other public or private body in the long eighteenth century.[19] The Presbyterian kirk provided a remarkably comprehensive and precocious system of near-universal education, organized poor relief, provided the lowest rung in the court system, and sternly administered the rules governing marriage and public morality.[20] In Ireland, the Highways Act of 1614 marked the real emergence of the parish as a civil local authority, involved in the building and maintenance of roads, poor relief, care of orphans, street lighting, police and fire prevention. These activities were funded by a rate called parish cess. Each parish was under the control of the Church of Ireland and was administered by a vestry or assembly consisting of all Anglican ratepayers.[21]

The eight Irish cities and towns that were administrative counties in their own right (Dublin, Cork, Waterford, Limerick, Galway, Kilkenny, Drogheda and Carrickfergus) each had their own grand jury. The grand jury consisted of twenty-three individuals chosen by the sheriffs to appear at the law courts to determine if there were sufficient grounds to proceed with a prosecution. However, in the early seventeenth century, the grand juries began to acquire administrative functions and in the eighteenth and nineteenth centuries evolved into local authorities in their own right, whose principal activity was the provision and maintenance of infrastructure such as bridges, roads and quays.[22]

Norman colony in Ireland (Cambridge, 1942).   **18** For Ireland see Gearóid MacNiocaill, *Na Buirgeisi, XII–XIV aois*, 2 vols (Charraig Dhubh, 1964). For Scotland, see Michael Lynch, Michael Spearman & Geoffrey Stell (eds), *The Scottish medieval town* (Edinburgh, 1988). **19** Devine, *The Scottish nation*, pp 84–102. **20** Ibid. **21** Elizabeth Fitzpatrick & Raymond Gillespie (eds), *The parish in medieval and early modern Ireland: community, territory and building* (Dublin, 2006), pp 228–41; 277–324. **22** Joseph Byrne, *Byrne's dictionary of Irish local history* (Cork, 2004), p. 138.

The long eighteenth century, which in the case of urban government in both Scotland and Ireland can be held to extend from the Glorious Revolution to the Whig 'decade of reform' (1830–41), was characterized by the decay of the medieval local state and the beginnings of widespread and increasingly vociferous demands for municipal reform.[23] There were four main problems affecting the municipal author-ities of this period in both countries, as well as their counterparts in England and Wales. Firstly, they became increasingly oligarchic, and often ceased to represent the interests of even the wealthy citizens of the towns. In both countries the councils were virtually always self-selecting, there were no local elections and members served for life. In Ireland, the Penal Laws enacted between 1695 and 1727 excluded Catholics from local government, and even though many of these restrictions were removed in the late eighteenth century, few Catholics were admitted to the local political system until after 1841. In addition, the borough corporations ceased to represent the interests even of the Protestant citizens of the towns, as power tended to become increasingly concentrated in the hands of a single family and their supporters. One of the most conspicuous examples was the ascendancy of the Smyths and the Verekers in Limerick city between 1776 and 1841.[24] Similarly in Scotland, 'the great majority of the merchants, manufacturers and professionals ... were ... effectively excluded from any role in urban government'.[25] Secondly, municipal governments devoted themselves more and more to political activities. In many of the smaller boroughs, their only function was to return members to parlia-ment and the purely political role of the governing body took more and more precedence over the provision of services for the population. Thirdly, this in turn resulted in the boroughs abandoning many of their functions as local regulators and service providers. Fourthly, corruption of all kinds flourished and usually included the following practices: the appointment of unfit persons to municipal office; manip-ulation of the voting system in order to control the parliamentary franchise; the appropriation of municipal lands, properties and revenues by members of the ruling cliques; and the imposition of unfair and illegal tolls and rates.[26]

However, Rosemary Sweet has recently advanced a counter-argument in her study of English towns in the long eighteenth century, which may have equal validity for Scottish and Irish urban areas. In her book *The English Town 1680–1840: Government, Society and Culture* she suggests that the apparent decay of English borough governments in this period was in fact caused by the unprecedented demands made on them as a result of rapidly increasing population, the beginnings of the Industrial Revolution and the rising expectations of a much larger, better educated and more politically aware general public. English towns underwent an 'urban renaissance' in the long eighteenth century and outgrew their medieval

23 For the Irish urban local state at this period, see Kenneth Milne, 'The Irish municipal corporations in the eighteenth century' (PhD, TCD, 1962).   24 Potter, *The government and the people of Limerick*, pp 183–282.   25 Devine, *The Scottish nation*, p. 202.   26 For detailed accounts of these abuses, see the respective *Reports of the commissioners appointed to inquire into municipal corporations in Ireland* and *Scotland*, passim.

constitutions and administrative machinery, which had never been intended to cope with such unprecedented demands and duties. Scotland underwent both the Industrial revolution and an urban renaissance in the long eighteenth century. With the significant exception of North-East Ulster, Ireland did not undergo an industrial revolution but she did experience significant urban growth amounting to an 'urban renaissance.' Rosemary Sweet also argues that much of the contemporary evidence detailing the activities of the borough corporations comes from biased and hostile sources, such as radical reformers and opponents of the urban elites, anxious to paint the blackest picture possible.[27]

Also, while the abuses of the period were undoubtedly serious and were possibly more flagrant than they had been in previous centuries, they received a particular notoriety at this time because the eighteenth and early nineteenth centuries were an age of Enlightenment, of reform and of revolution. Age-old institutions such as monarchical government, the aristocracy, the churches and the prevailing social and economic system were subject to intense scrutiny and criticism. Abuses, corruption and incompetence that would have been tolerated in earlier centuries were now judged in a much harsher and more sceptical climate of opinion.

Nevertheless, there was a marked reluctance in the long eighteenth century to enact reforms of existing institutions such as parliament, local government and the legal system particularly in Ireland where the Protestant elite feared that reform might empower the Catholic majority.[28] Instead, the decline in the role of borough corporations as local authorities resulted in emergence of a number of new service providers to remedy their deficiencies. Some of these were existing institutions, such as the parishes and the grand juries. Others were new statutory authorities with powers of borrowing and/or levying local taxation, established to provide a range of services either abandoned by the traditional local bodies, or never provided by them in the first place. These alternative local authorities were termed 'statutory bodies for special purposes' by Sidney and Beatrice Webb and could either be appointed or elected. They included stand-alone statutory bodies such as turnpike trusts, corporations of the poor and improvement commissions. In addition, local legislation was often enacted to provide for the construction of a major piece of infrastructure, or to provide grant aid in connection with it. Such local acts sometimes established improvement commissions to oversee the project.[29]

Improvement commissions proliferated in eighteenth century Britain and Ireland.[30] In Scotland these bodies were usually called police commissioners and the

27 Rosemary Sweet, *The English town, 1680–1840: government, society and culture* (Harlow, 1999), pp 141–50. For England's urban renaissance see Peter Borsay, *The English urban renaissance: culture and society in the provincial town, 1660–1770* (Oxford, 1989).   **28** For an example of this, see Potter, *The government and the people of Limerick,* pp 259–61.   **29** For a definitive account of alternative local bodies in England at this time see Sidney & Beatrice Webb, *Statutory bodies for special purposes* (London, 1922). See also Sweet, *The English town,* pp 44–56.   **30** See Joanna Innes, 'The local acts of a national parliament: parliament's role in sanctioning local action in eighteenth-century Britain', *Parliamentary History* 17:1 (1998),

legislation governing them called police acts (although this term was sometimes used in Ireland and England as well). The term 'police' had a much wider significance in Scottish than in English or Irish public affairs. Mabel Atkinson has written that 'besides the management of the constabulary, it comprises drainage, in some cases water supply, street cleaning, public health, lighting, provision of fire engines, etc.'[31] The most important police acts were those of Aberdeen (1795), Glasgow (1800) and Edinburgh (1805). Indeed, Glasgow has claimed that its 1800 Police Act established the first precocious professional police force in these islands. Among the best-known examples in Ireland were the Wide Streets Commission of Dublin, established in 1757, the Wide Street Commissioners established by the Waterford Police Act of 1784 and the Commissioners of St Michael's Parish which were established in 1807 to administer the Georgian Newtown Pery area of Limerick. In both countries, these commissions concentrated on paving and cleaning streets, water supply, lighting, and police and night watch.

In both Scotland and Ireland, the demand for reform was driven by two main trends. First, there was the phenomenal growth of cities and towns, similar to and contemporary with the English urban renaissance described by Peter Borsay. In 1750, 9.2 per cent of the population of Scotland were living in urban areas with over 10,000 inhabitants, but this proportion had increased to 32 per cent by 1850. In Ireland, the corresponding increase was from 5 per cent in 1750 to 10.2 per cent in 1850.[32] This resulted in the creation of a vastly increased, wealthy and increasingly self-confident bourgeoisie. Secondly the movement for administrative and political reform was driven by a major intellectual revolution, composed of three elements: liberalism whose proponents wanted to extend civil and religious rights to a larger proportion of the population by giving the vote to more people, ending religious discrimination and generally reforming the political and administrative systems; utilitarianism, whose followers believed that all human institutions should serve 'the greatest good of the greatest number'; and classical economics which advocated the theory of *laissez-faire*, that is, government should have a limited role in economic life. All three stressed the necessity for all institutions, including parliament, the central and local government systems, the legal system and the churches to be examined and reformed in order to make them more efficient, effective and economical. Sir David Keir wrote of the reformers of the period 1782–1867 (the high point of all three intellectual movements) that they believed that 'the administrative system needed to be overhauled and stripped of its antiquated survivals and useless accretions'.[33]

Paradoxically, the exclusive and corrupt regime in the urban local state of both Scotland and Ireland culminated at the same time that these trends took hold. In Scotland the widespread demands for burgh reform in the 1780s and 1790s coincided with and were partially a reaction to the Dundas Despotism, the political machine

23–47. **31** Mabel Atkinson, 'The organisation of local government in Scotland' in *Political Science Quarterly* 18:1 (1903), 70. **32** J. de Vries, *European urbanisation, 1500–1850* (London, 1984), pp 39–48, cited in Devine, *The Scottish nation*, pp 152–5. **33** Sir David Lindsay Keir, *The constitutional history of modern Britain since 1485* (9th edition, London, 1968), p. 369.

built by Henry Dundas, first Viscount Melville, which dominated Scotland between 1784 and 1827 and at its peak, controlled an incredible thirty-four of the forty-five Scottish MPs. This reform agitation was crushed in 1790s as a result of the reaction brought about by the French Revolution, though it revived in 1810s.[34] In Ireland the oligarchic regimes reached their peak in the municipal boroughs around 1800 and local reform movements in Limerick and elsewhere failed to dislodge them.[35] In both countries, the Tory party that emerged as part of the new two-party system of the late eighteenth and early nineteenth centuries controlled virtually all of the boroughs.

The various agitations for municipal reform ended in failure and it was the Whig triumph in the 1830s and the resultant decade of reform which led to the complete transformation of the urban local state throughout the United Kingdom.[36] This represented the most radical reform that the borough corporations had ever undergone since their establishment and was regarded as a corollary to parliamentary reform. In Ireland, the demand for municipal reform formed part of O'Connell's campaign for civil and religious equality for Catholics and in all three kingdoms, liberalism, utilitarianism and classical economics provided an ideological framework. In 1833 royal commissions were established to examine borough corporations in the whole United Kingdom and their respective reports provided the background to the municipal reform programme enacted in Scotland in 1833, in England and Wales in 1835 and in Ireland in 1840.

In Scotland, the reform package, collectively known as the Burgh Reform Acts, consisted of three separate acts that became law in 1833. The Royal Burghs (Scotland) Act extended the local franchise to all who owned or occupied property within the burgh worth £10 or more per year (the parliamentary franchise had been granted to the same categories of person in the Scottish Reform Act of 1832). In addition, eligible women were also given the local vote (something that was not to happen in Ireland until 1899). Annual elections were to be held every November and one third of the town council was to retire each year. The provost was to be elected by the councillors from among their own ranks and would hold office for three years.[37] The Burgh Police (Scotland) Act extended the scope of the existing local police acts, by enabling all royal burghs, burghs of regality and burghs of barony adopt police powers, including the paving and cleaning of streets, lighting, water supply and night watch. If three-quarters of qualified voters in a burgh declared themselves to be in favour, the act came into force and a body of elected police commissioners were to be elected annually to administer and provide these services.[38] The Parliamentary

34 Devine, *The Scottish nation*, pp 197–209; William Ferguson, *The Edinburgh history of Scotland, Vol. 4, Scotland 1689 to the present* (Edinburgh, 1978), pp 236–62 and Bruce P. Lenman, 'From the Union of 1707 to the franchise reform of 1832', in R.A. Houston & W.W. J. Knox (eds), *The new Penguin history of Scotland: from the earliest times to the present day* (London, 2002), pp 324–25. **35** Potter, *The government and the people of Limerick*, pp 249–82. **36** See Alexander Llewellyn, *The decade of reform: the 1830s* (New York, 1971). **37** 3 & 4 Wm IV, c.76. **38** 3 & 4 Wm IV, c.46.

Burghs (Scotland) Act extended the provisions of the other two acts to twelve newly created parliamentary boroughs.[39] The right to form a police burgh was extended to all towns with a population exceeding 1,200 in 1850 and to all towns exceeding 700 persons in 1862.[40] In many urban areas, a dual system of town council and police commission functioned side by side, often composed of the same membership until the Burgh Police Act of 1892 fused the two bodies into one municipal council.[41]

Borough reform in Ireland was carried our in two stages, of which the Municipal Corporations (Ireland) Act of 1840 was the first.[42] In contrast to both Scotland and England, where all of the existing urban bodies had been retained, fifty-eight of the surviving sixty-eight Irish boroughs were abolished. The remaining ten were given a similar system to the Scottish burghs; an electorate consisting of £10 householders, annual elections each November and provision for one third of the council to retire annually. However, the mayor was to elected for one year, not three and women were not given the vote. Also the powers given to the new corporations were very limited and consisted chiefly of the authority to make by-laws and to suppress dangerous or insanitary buildings or places. The second programme of borough reform in Ireland was enacted between 1849 and 1854. While there was no equivalent of the Burgh Police Act of 1833, similar provisions were already available to Irish urban areas under the Lighting of Towns Act (1828) which conferred powers to elect commissioners with powers equivalent to the Scottish police commissioners. Such powers were separately conferred on their respective borough corporations by local acts for Dublin (1849), Cork (1852) and Limerick (1853). The Town Improvement (Ireland) Act of 1854 updated the 1828 Act and provided similar machinery to that in the Scottish Police Burgh Acts, allowing non-municipal urban areas to establish their own local authority structures.[43]

In the 1830s, municipal reform in both Scotland and Ireland resulted in the overthrow of the long-established Tory oligarchies and the establishment of the rule of the urban bourgeoisie. In Scotland, Liberal elites assumed power in the burghs, while in Ireland the Catholic middle classes took control of the towns and cities outside North-East Ulster. Efficiency, effectiveness, accountability and economy were to be the watchwords of the new corporations. While not democratic, they at least reflected the wishes of a larger section of the population than had previously been the case. They were to demonstrate a willingness to tackle a wide range of problems, including the provision of infrastructure, lighting, night watch, water and sewerage systems, gas and social housing which had been largely ignored by their predecessors. Some sixty years later, the respective Acts that established elected county councils in Scotland in 1890 and in Ireland in 1899 also provided for the introduction of a householder franchise in the municipal boroughs. In consequence, the vote was given to such a large proportion of the adult population that in both countries one can date the beginnings of democracy in the urban local state from this time.[44]

39 3 & 4 Wm IV, c.77.   **40** 13 & 14 Vict. c. 33 and 25 & 26 Vict. c. 101.   **41** 55 & 56 Vict.c. 55.   **42** 3 & 4 Vict. c. 108.   **43** For a discussion of these developments, see Roche, *Local government*, pp 33–5.   **44** 52 & 53 Vict. c. 50 and 61 & 62 Vict. c. 37.

However, the local government systems in Scotland and Ireland also diverged considerably from the 1830s onwards. A number of Scottish historians have emphasized that while at the level of parliamentary and central government, Scotland was assimilated into the United Kingdom after 1707 and despite the absence of Scottish home rule, Scottish control was paramount in the local state, which was the level that mattered to the Scots themselves.[45] The poor law, prisons, public health, police, lunatic asylums and education were under the control of either town councils or supervisory boards based in Scotland and staffed by Scots. Britain was probably one of the most decentralized countries in Europe for most of the nineteenth century and local government provided most of the day-to-day administration.

By contrast, in Ireland significant areas of service provision were centralized under bodies with a nationwide remit. The primary school system, set up in 1831, was administered by the Commissioners of National Education, while control of the police was removed from local authorities in 1836. Irish central government also intervened in the fields of economic development, prisons and public health on a scale that was unknown in Britain. The Board of Works was established in 1831, and built roads, ports and other infrastructure all over the country. The provision of hospitals for the mentally ill was placed in the hands of lunatic asylum districts in 1817, under the control of a national Board for the General Control of District Asylums, which was superseded in 1843 by the Board of Works. Both mental hospitals and prisons were supervised by national inspectorates and in 1877 the prisons were entirely removed from local authority control and placed under a Central Prisons Board.[46]

Thus, the role of Irish local authorities became much more marginal than that of their counterparts in Scotland. There were a number of reasons for this. Firstly, the Irish elite was small in numbers and dispersed by comparison with that of Britain. Second, the rise of Catholic nationalism from the 1820s onwards made successive British governments wary of strengthening local authorities, which might become centres of agitation, disaffection or even rebellion. Thirdly, Irish Protestants often preferred centralization to rule by local Catholic elites. Fourthly, Irish nationalists regarded local government as a stepping-stone to the attainment of national self-rule, not as having much value in itself. Fifthly, Irish poverty and unrest meant that local authorities did not possess adequate financial resources, or ability to main order in their areas of responsibility.[47]

The sense of grievance and exclusion felt by the Catholic population and the consequent development of political nationalism in their ranks resulted in a significant

45 Devine, *The Scottish nation*, pp 287–89; Graeme Morton & R.J. Morris, 'Civil society, governance and nation, 1832–1914' , in Houston and Knox, *New Penguin history of Scotland*, pp 377–80. **46** R. B. McDowell, *The Irish administration, 1801–1914* (London, 1964), passim. **47** Potter, *The government and the people of Limerick,* pp 298–300.

cleavage existing between them and the Irish administrative system that went by the generic term 'Dublin Castle'. This was the case even with Irish-based bodies such as the Commissioners of National Education and the Local Government Board and persisted even though increasingly large numbers of Catholics came to be employed in such bodies as the nineteenth century progressed. From the 1870s onwards the demand for home rule dominated Irish political discourse and meant that the granting of significant local government reforms, such as the establishment of the county councils in 1899 did not create the sense of ownership of the administrative system felt by the Scots.[48] Ironically, a similar process was to occur in Scotland in the late twentieth century when increasing centralisation and reduction of the authority of the local state was to help fuel the demand for home rule.[49]

48 See McBride, Lawrence W., *The greening of Dublin Castle: the transformation of bureaucratic and judicial personnel in Ireland, 1892–1922* (Washington, DC, 1991).   **49** For the background to the restoration of the Scottish parliament in 1999, see Devine, *The Scottish nation*, pp 574–617.

Tuberculosis cures used in Ireland, 1700–1950[1]

SUSAN KELLY

Scientific treatments for tuberculosis were first introduced to Ireland as a result of Koch's discovery of the infectivity of the mycobacterium tuberculosis in 1882. This discovery led to the knowledge of the disease's infectivity and a 'scientific' regime of treatment, the most prominent feature being fresh air treatment in the many new sanatoria. During the following century, drugs, such as sanocrysin and Ruppel's serum, for which clinical trials were conducted in Ireland as well as many other countries, were developed, though ultimately unsuccessfully. Many treatments were tried before the discovery of successful anti-tuberculosis drugs in the late 1940s. However, there is also a parallel history of folk treatment of tuberculosis which has been largely ignored by this scientific narrative. There is a long history of self-medication in the case of 'consumption' or 'phthisis' as tuberculosis was known. Sufferers often did not make any distinction regarding the source of their cure. Indeed, they combined advice from their doctor with advice from a neighbour, remedies from the oral tradition, old written advice and also patent medicines. Patients were willing to try practically anything to cure tuberculosis and whilst few of those mentioned would restore a tuberculosis patient to health, many brought comfort or had a placebo effect and held out hope of a total cure.

This chapter considers tuberculosis cures used in Ireland from the eighteenth through to the twentieth centuries and compares them to those used in Scotland in the same period. Given this focus, what follows draws heavily upon recent oral history research into childhood tuberculosis in the north of Ireland. The specific cures considered are those taken by mouth, both ingested and inhaled, though the chapter also touches on skin preparations and the 'strokers' (or healers) who treated 'King's Evil'. It argues, firstly, that while there were similarities between Irish and Scottish folk cures, there was also a high degree of regionalism within Ireland. Secondly, that, notwithstanding the development of medical treatments for TB during the nineteenth century, folk cures remained popular, widely used and in some cases commercialized well into the twentieth century. Finally, this chapter argues that the relationship between medicine and folk cures remained much more porous than had been previously thought.

1 This article benefited from discussion with Professor Greta Jones and Dr Leanne McCormick, at the Centre for History of Medicine in Ireland, University of Ulster.

Historically, tuberculosis has been endemic in Ireland. The first written evidence is in the Dublin bills of mortality of the seventeenth century.[2] However, the disease only became epidemic in the 1860s, with mortality rates in Ireland rising steeply to a peak around the turn of the century. It was nearly ninety years into the Irish epidemic before anti-tuberculosis drugs were developed. As a result, self-medication and home remedies were common in Ireland. Most patients with tuberculosis in these years would have been nursed at home. Even with the advent of the voluntary hospitals in the eighteenth century, the poor law dispensary doctors of the nineteenth century and finally the easier access to doctors via socialized medicine, many families looked after their ill at home and self-medicated. Up to the eighteenth century this involved home diagnosis, and brewing treatment recipes. By the eighteenth century, however, patent medicines could be bought and illnesses treated, often again without reference to a doctor. However, as access to doctors became more common, a mixture of home cures and patent medicines were often used to complement those prescribed by the doctor. This was particularly so with a disease like tuberculosis as it was often of long duration and of a capricious nature. Sufferers were, therefore, likely to try a variety of cures.

In Scotland the epidemic followed a different pattern with numbers rising steeply earlier than in Ireland and peaking in the 1870s.[3] As in Ireland, however, the disease had been endemic for centuries. Therefore Scotland also had a lengthy period before the discovery of successful anti-tuberculosis chemotherapy when folk medicine and home cures were used. In Ireland, however more is known about this as between 1935 and 1970 the Irish Folklore Commission gathered one of the world's largest folklore collections. It was set up to collect, classify and study aspects of Irish folk tradition including cures. Folk records in Scotland, in contrast to Ireland, are fragmentary.[4]

Families in the seventeenth century had to be medically self-sufficient, with the mistress of the house providing resources to cope with every ailment. The family recipe book provided instructions to make both meals and medicines. These listed concoctions to treat a full range of illnesses often identified by the part of the body rather than the disease. Many of these recipes required elaborate apparatus and a full herb garden.[5] This would have likely been beyond the resources of the poor. For those who did not have the facilities to make their own medicines, an abundance of patent medicines were available by the middle of the eighteenth century. These medicines, however, were often expensive. Viper drops for improving the circulation, restoring youthful bloom and curing both 'barrenness' and impotency cost £1 3s. for a large bottle, at a time when a housekeeper earned £25 a year.[6] In addition, there would have been patent cures for each income bracket.

2 James Deeny, *Tuberculosis in Ireland: national tuberculosis survey* (Dublin, 1954), p. 14. 3 Jacqueline Jenkinson, *Scotland's health 1919–1948* (Oxford, 2002), p. 273. 4 Niall Ó Ciosáin, 'Approaching a folklore archive: the Irish Folklore Commission and the memory of the Great Famine', *Folk-Lore*, 115:2 (2004), 222–32. 5 Tony Farmar, *Patients, potions and physicians: a social history of medicine in Ireland* (Dublin, 2004), pp 22–3. 6 Ibid., p. 48.

Medical self-help books became more common during the eighteenth century; for example, George Cheyne's *Essay on Health and Long Life*, was published in 1724.[7] John Wesley's 1747 *Primitive Physick* was aimed at the poor who lived in the countryside where physicians were scarce.[8] *Domestic Medicine* by William Buchan was published in Dublin in 1774 and suggested various special diets for consumptive patients, along with syrup recipes and plant infusions for the cough.[9] The increased circulation of this type of book expanded the trade of countryside herb gathering as apothecaries and druggists in the cities required more ingredients to satisfy public demand.[10] This was an early example of the commercialism that would increasingly influence the use of 'cures'. These medical books would have been expensive and poorer homes may not have been able to afford them, relying instead on a cheaper almanac, which contained some medical advice. Both medical books and almanacs had an impact for many years after they were first published as they could remain on family bookshelves for successive generations.

Scrofula was the name given to tuberculosis of the glands. These glands sometimes suppurated to the skin leaving an unsightly raw area. In the seventeenth century this disease was known in Scotland as 'the cruells'.[11] It was also known as 'Kings Evil' or 'Queen's Evil' as it was believed a monarch laying hands on it could affect a cure. Monarchs, such as James I, Charles I and Charles II, undertook this practice, and though William III was sceptical of the practice his wife Anne performed the ceremony. The service was only removed from the Book of Common Prayer in the eighteenth century. It would have been difficult for many Scottish and Irish sufferers to benefit from this cure but other healers were available to offer the same service. The most famous seventeenth-century healer was Valentine Greatrakes, an Irish man who had served under Oliver Cromwell. He 'cured' many Irish patients of scrofula in the years after 1660 but failed in a demonstration before King Charles II in 1666. Robert Kirk, a Scottish clergyman, described the treatment in his book of 1691 entitled *The Secret Commonwealth of Elves, Fauns and Fairies*. He described how cures were carried out by

> ... such as Master Great-rake, the Irish stroker, seventh sons and others that cure the King's Evil, and chase away disease and pains, with only stroking of the affected part; which (if it be not the relics of miraculous operations, or some secret virtue in the womb of the parent, which increaseth until seventh-sons be born, and decreaseth by the same degree afterwards) proceeds only from the sensitive balsam of their healthful constitutions; virtue going out from them by spirituous effluxes unto the patient.[12]

---

7 Ibid., p. 49. **8** David E. Allen & Gabrielle Hatfield, *Medicinal plants in folk tradition: an ethnobotany of Britain and Ireland* (Portland, 2004), p. 24. **9** William Buchan, *Domestic medicine: or a treatise on the prevention and cure of disease by regimen and simple medicines* (Dublin, 1774), pp 149–150. **10** Allen & Hatfield, *Medicinal plants*, p. 24. **11** John Comrie, *History of Scottish medicine* (London, 1932), p. 226. **12** Robert Kirk, *The secret commonwealth of elves, fauns and fairies*, intr. Marina Warner (1661, repr. New York, 2005), p. 24.

Valentine Greatrakes, however, did not claim to have magical powers believing instead his cures stemmed from natural sources.[13] Kirk writes elsewhere of 'the seventh son in Scotland' who also cured.[14] Healers, both religious and secular continued to treat tuberculosis in Scotland and Ireland while the disease remained a widespread problem. Laurence M. Geary gives a detailed account of miraculous healing in early nineteenth-century Ireland in *Medicine, Disease and the State in Ireland, 1650–1940*.[15] Interestingly another cure for 'King's Evil' used in Ireland developed simply from the name. Dr Eileen Hickey writing in 1938 in the *Ulster Medical Journal* of 'Medical Superstitions Used in Ireland' mentioned 'an ancient cure for scrofula was the application of the blood of nine or twelve young wrens, i.e. King's blood as the wren is the king of the birds.'[16]

The thinking behind pre-twentieth-century cures is often unknown. They could develop from medical thinking that had become out of date or from family recipes that gained a wider popularity. Since a successful medical treatment for tuberculosis was not available until the 1940s home cures continued to be tried in desperation. Many of these may well have been similar to those used in the home a hundred years before. Patrick Logan describes two undated cures he collected in recent times in Dublin for tuberculosis. 'One is that the patient must drink four teaspoons of paraffin oil daily … the other is a sandwich of bread and butter with a filling of fresh dandelion leaves.' Garlic and 'Carrigeen to which nasturtium seed have been added … boiled and drunk' were also treatments he mentions.[17] Simon Guest quotes from one Dublin woman, recalling a time between 1932 and 1957, who stated, 'You'd get all those cures down the country.'[18] She implied presumably that they were not favoured as much by those living in urban areas. A Belfast lady, however, when asked about home cures for tuberculosis remembered they were certainly tried in her city in the 1930s.

13 J.P. Sommerville, 'Magic and medicine', history.wisc.edu/sommerville/367/367–101.htm accessed 28 May 2008.   14 Robert Kirk, 'Diary', quoted by Marina Warner in the introduction to *The secret commonwealth*, p. xiv.   15 Laurence M. Geary, 'Prince Hohenlohe, Signor Pastorini and miraculous healing in early nineteenth-century Ireland', in Elizabeth Malcolm & Greta Jones (eds), *Medicine, disease and the state in Ireland, 1650–1940* (Cork, 1999), pp 4–58.   16 Eileen M. Hickey, 'Medical superstitions in Ireland', *Ulster Medical Journal* 7, 4 (Oct. 1938), 268–70.   17 Patrick Logan, *Irish country cures* (Belfast, 1981), pp 22–23. Patrick Logan's information was collected in the thirty years prior to publication. The Dublin cures were contributed by the staff and patients of the Dublin Regional Chest Hospital, p. 4. It is not possible, therefore, with the information given to date the cures. Carragheen (Carrigeen) and Dandelion are confirmed as medicinal plants in folk tradition in Ireland in David E. Allen, Gabrielle Hatfield, *Medicinal plants in folk tradition: an ethnobotany of Britain and Ireland* (Portland, 2004), pp 44 and 287. Though dandelion has many medicinal uses throughout the British Isles, all those for consumption are from Ireland: Allen & Hatfield, p. 287.   18 Simon Guest, 'Cure, superstition, infection and reaction: tuberculosis in Ireland, 1932–1957', *Oral History*, 32:2 (Autumn 2004), 66. Interview with BR, Dublin, recorded by Simon Guest, 16 Sept. 1999. Interviewees describing their experiences with tuberculosis in Ireland in the 1930s, 1940s and 1950s.

They tried, yes there was. Yes, that was one thing they did try, you take this an' you take the other thing, you know. And lemons, oh God lemons, they always wanted you to … 'Now lemons would help clear the child', all the lemons grown would never clear that dear. But that was one thing, everybody came an' rapped the door and maybe give you a couple of lemons. 'Try that', you know. But as I say, lemons would have never done anything for TB.[19]

She was not sure what they were actually supposed to do with the lemons or whether her aunt had tried this remedy on her young cousin. Other Belfast residents brought their country remedies to the city. One lady remembered the treatment her father gave to her brother and herself when they suffered from tuberculosis in 1926.

So my father came from the farming country out at Kilwater [a village in Co. Antrim in the North of Ireland], he decided to take it into his own hands to cure my brother. Because the doctor had said, 'I don't think this boy will make, I don't think he'll make grey hairs,' you know whatever term they used. Old bones I think he said. 'They will never make old bones.' So my father went out to the country and picked from the surrounding countryside stuff called bogbean. Ever heard of it? … It's a bit like, you know the shape of bamboo. Eh, although it's quite short, and sort of wiry, bendable, flexible. My father used to come home with a great bunch of this, and he had other people collecting it as well. And he cooked it on the range and he put it in a big pot and covered it, presumably with water. And cooked it night, for two or three nights it sat on the hob. Simmered away and the smell was awful. It was black and horrible. And when it was cooked he fed my brother, what he called a wineglass full, every morning before we went to school … he was brought up in that county. That was where he was a boy. And bogbean was an old-fashioned, one of these old remedies, you know that go out of fashion because they bring in, eh they bring in drugs don't they? … Well, it was a cure. He thought. Bogbean, it was called. So my brother got better [and he died aged 84] … My father used to give me the odd glass just to keep me going you know. Ewh. But my brother stoically took this and we all believe that bogbean cured him.[20]

Bogbean was traditionally used in Ulster for blood disorders rather than for pulmonary tuberculosis though this use was favoured in the Highlands of Scotland.[21] Allen and Hatfield list fourteen folk herbal cures used in regions of Ireland for tuberculosis. Those mentioned earlier are dandelion, caragheen and bogbean. Great mullein will be discussed later. The others are knapweed, ox-eye daisy, honeysuckle, crows-foot, gorse, valerian, heart's ease, fig-wort, house leek and marsh pennywort.

19 Oral History 18, recorded by the author 19 Apr. 2004. **20** Oral History 17, recorded by the author on 9 Apr. 2004. **21** Allen & Hatfield, *Medicinal plants*, p. 202.

The use of hemlock has been described in a pill form for scrofula, used from the early nineteenth century until the early twentieth century, by the Cooke family of Co. Cavan for themselves and local people. 'Great care was taken not to over-do the dose.'[22] This oral use of a most poisonous plant is not listed in Allen and Hatfield though a type of hemlock was used as a poultice for scrofula in the Aran Islands.[23] Most of these remedies were used in specific regions of Ireland and in general different plants were used in the rest of the British Isles, though there was some overlap.[24]

Hatfield and Allen in their study of medicinal plants used in folk tradition found that Ireland had many more plant uses in common with Scotland than with the rest of Britain. This was due partly to environmental affinities but also cultural links. None of the plant uses they list in common refer to cures for tuberculosis however. Bogbean as mentioned above is listed as a cure for tuberculosis in Scotland rather than Ulster where it had other uses. The Ulster oral history interviewee refers to it as an 'old fashioned cure'. Whether it had a regional tradition in a small part of Ulster that Hatfield and Allen were unaware of, or whether it came to Kilwater directly to the interviewee's family from a Scottish connection is not known.

John Comrie describes, in his *History of Scottish Medicine*, seventeenth-century Highlanders using holy wells for cure of consumption.[25] Whilst on the Isle of Skye during the same period they used hartstongue and maidenhair boiled in ale.[26] V.G. Hatfield writing of eighteenth-century Scotland states the 'population at large relied on traditional herbal remedies, derived from ancient and medieval herbals and traditional medical practices, which were communicated by word of mouth, through ballads and songs, and in writing, in family manuscripts and increasingly in print.'[27] David Rorie described as the 'first folklorist in Scotland' who 'occupies an important ... place in the history of medical folklore study', wrote between 1902 and 1937.[28] Curiously, though, phthisis is described as one of the 'commoner complaints' he mentions very few cures for its treatment. One that is included is the *lapis hectius* stone 'for consumption in man or beast'. The stone was made red hot, cooled in water or milk and the liquid given to the patient to drink.[29] Also used was the earth cure, where 'a patient was made to lie [*sic*] face downwards over a hole in which a black cock had been placed. A handful of earth was thrown in and the patient inhaled

22 L.L., 'Notes: Cures and charms', *Ulster Folklife*, 6 (1960), 65–7.   23 Allen & Hatfield, *Medicinal plants*, p. 187.   24 Ibid. Allen and Hatfield list forty plants used for pulmonary tuberculosis in the British Isles, p. 406.   25 Comrie, *History of Scottish medicine*, p. 236. 26 Ibid., p. 238.   27 V.G. Hatfield, 'Domestic medicine in eighteenth-century Scotland' (PhD, University of Edinburgh, 1980) quoted by Dr James Kelly in his paper 'Self medication as a feature of medical care in late early- modern Ireland' given on 26 Apr., at a symposium 'Ireland and Medicine in the Seventeenth and Eighteenth Centuries' at Queen's University Belfast, 25–26 Apr. 2008.   28 David Buchan, professor of Folklore at Memorial University of Newfoundland, writing of David Rorie in the introduction to, *Folk tradition and folk medicine in Scotland: the writings of David Rorie* (Edinburgh, 1994), pp 11 and 13.   29 Ibid., p. 50

the earth stirred by the fluttering of the bird's wings.' Rorie also described how seventeenth-century consumptives in Moray, Scotland would be passed three times through a wreath of woodbine.[30] The final cure for consumption that Rorie described is 'the oil of white slugs … used as a cure for consumption. They are placed in a jelly-bag with salt, and the oil dripping out is collected.'[31] The use of snails and slugs as cures for consumption seems to have been popular in both Ireland and Scotland.[32] Whilst most of these cures would not directly cause harm to the patient the belief that an older person could 'draw strength oot o' the younger' could cause great harm if a youngster was to sleep in the same bed as an older consumptive.[33] Rorie did not give any indication of whether these 'cures' were still being used at the time of his writing or were memories from previous generations.

Other cures for tuberculosis could fall into a modern-day category described as 'building-up agents'. Tuberculosis was often accompanied by weight loss as the name consumption implies; the body literally being consumed by the disease. Therefore, weight gain gave the appearance of health. In fact, food did offer a form of protection as if a person's diet was deficient in fat or protein they were more susceptible to tuberculosis and less able to recover. A Co. Leitrim cure 'consisted of two raw eggs beaten up with sugar and a little whiskey'.[34] Whiskey was also believed to cure tuberculosis in Belfast. An 83-year old lady remembered the suggestions made to help her 14-year-old cousin who had tuberculosis in the 1930s:

> I laughed one day, one woman said, when she heard him out on the, now she was actually standing speaking on the street and she heard him [coughing]. And she said, 'If he had 'a been a wee bit older you could have given him a drop of whiskey.' Would have cleared him. Imagine whiskey! [Incredulous tone of voice]. If he had 'a been a wee bit older you could have given him a drop of whiskey. [35]

The addition of whiskey or other alcohol may have been as a simple appetite stimulant to enable the patient to achieve the desired weight gain. A little pre-dinner sherry was often prescribed for elderly people in hospital with appetite loss.[36] Logan notes that raw eggs were used in many sanatoria.[37] Eggs were also the only article of diet that relatives were allowed to bring into Belfast Municipal Sanatoria (Whiteabbey) in 1916.[38] In pre-streptomycin days fresh air and good food were the only treatment and certain foods, which 'built up', became associated with a cure.

---

30 Ibid., p. 127. **31** Ibid., p. 245. **32** Dr James Kelly, '*Self medication as a feature* …', describes three Irish collections of personal recipes, dating from the seventeenth century onwards, which include the use of snails to treat consumption. **33** David Buchan, *Folk tradition,* p. 99. **34** Eggs and whiskey were also advocated by many doctors of the late eighteenth and early nineteenth century see Logan, *Irish country cures,* p. 22. **35** Oral History 18, recorded by the author on 19 Apr., 2004. **36** Personal experience of the author in the 1980s. **37** Logan, *Irish country cures,* p. 22. **38** Minute Book of the Tuberculosis Committee, Belfast Corporation Papers, PRONI, LA7/9AE/2.

Raw eggs would appear to fit into this category. Another Belfast lady remembered
that when she was recovering from tuberculosis as a 10-year-old in the late 1940s she
was fed every morning,

> raw eggs ..., and the cream of the milk and a whiskey in it ... I used to give
> my breakfast to the cat. You know I was so fed up ... food was supposed to
> protect you and make you well. So I was kind of faced with that.[39]

Eggs may also be a throw-back to the humouric medical tradition prevalent in the
seventeenth and eighteenth centuries. Physicians used both drugs and diet to
improve the humours. Certain foods were prescribed as 'cooling or heating' and eggs
were frequently used. Sir William Whitla, professor of Materia Medica at Queen's
University, Belfast, who will be discussed later, prescribed both eggs and whiskey for
phthisis in his 1884 *Dictionary of Treatment*. He stated that 'food is of far more importance than medicine' for phthisis and 'at five in the afternoon ... the yolk of an egg
beaten up with a little brandy and water' could be taken. He also suggested that
'where softening of the lung has occurred whiskey may be allowed in fair quantity
and if mixed with the patient's milk any reasonable amount may be allowed without
danger of doing harm.' He was, however, referring to cases, which expected a fatal
outcome. Therefore there could be no 'moral objection to creating an alcohol
habit.'[40] Eggs were, however, regarded as good invalid food for many conditions and
were promoted as such by the esteemed Victorian ladies Mrs Beeton and Florence
Nightingale. Even in 1941 a doctor felt compelled to write to the *British Medical
Journal*, 'Sir, I am concerned about the country's production ... of that outstanding
article of an invalid's diet – the egg.'[41] The use of eggs for the tuberculous may partly
have been as food for an invalid but there does seem to have been a particularly
strong association with the disease.

An elderly man from Newry remembered an unusual treatment for tuberculosis
in his area.

> There was a clinic down in Water Street, tuberculosis, and they would send
> people down to the abattoir ... for blood ... aye the abattoir was just at the
> start of the Warrenpoint Road ... and any patients that went round to the
> clinic in Water Street, they would send them down to the slaughter house to
> get lambs blood to drink it.[42]

The speaker remembered this as a supplement to treatment in the days 'before streptomycin and penicillin'.[43] Cow's blood was still used by one surgeon in the Royal

39 Oral History 46, recorded by the author on 18 June 2004.   40 Whitla, *A dictionary of
treatment* (London, 1894), p. 640.   41 Richard Bell, 'Invalid diet and the egg shortage',
British Medical Journal (22 Mar. 1941).   42 Oral History B (Newry), recorded by Connor
Rafferty, Oct./Nov. 2004.   43 Ibid.

Victoria Hospital Belfast throughout the 1920s. It was as a protection against septi-caemia, however, rather than a treatment for tuberculosis. His patients and junior staff were made to drink this 'objectionable fluid' until he devised a method to convert the blood into tablets.[44] The milk of goats and Kerry cows, which have a high resist-ance to tuberculosis, were supposed to have special value.[45] It is unclear from Logan's report, however, whether this was as protection or cure, or both.

Another remedy for tuberculosis and other chest complaints was to take the sufferer to the Belfast gas works. 'It was believed the coal gas fumes helped to clear the chest'.[46] This was mentioned by a couple of elderly ladies in Belfast in relation to tuberculosis.[47] It is not known when this cure originated but the building of the gasworks in Belfast began in 1822 so it would have to have been after this year. This may have been the poor man's version of the inhalation of iodine treatment, which was popular in Dublin medical circles in the 1830s.[48] Sir Charles Scudamore, a London physician, moved to Dublin in 1829.[49] He published a paper in 1834 about the inhalation of iodine and conium in tubercular phthisis.[50] This was in a widely read publication and may have contributed to the popularity of inhalation cures for phthisis in Ireland.[51] It was, however, read further afield also and was quoted by H.J. Bigelow writing in the *Boston Medical Surgical Journal* in 1846. He stated, 'Sir Charles Scudamore has advocated the inhalation of iodine and conium in phthisis, and the vapor of tar has been often inhaled in the same disease.'[52] By 1899 there were over 100 gasworks in the area that later became Northern Ireland. Brian McKee, of the Gasworks Museum of Ireland, has observed,

> with regard to breathing in the fumes, this was quite a common occurrence and I have heard it stated for Belfast, Carrickfergus and Dublin. It is probably for other gasworks as well. The fumes were usually from the tar tank. It is not clear how effective these were.[53]

Another Belfast woman remembered a family who lived near her during the war, taking her children to the local gasworks in Coleraine, to ease their whooping cough.[54] It seems, therefore that this practice may have been carried out all over Ireland. Rorie, writing in 1914 of taking the air near gas-works in Fife, Scotland,

44 Ian Frazer, *Looking back* (Privately published, 1993), p. 33. **45** Logan, *Irish country cures*, p. 22. **46** Simon Guest, 'Cure', p. 67. **47** Personal conversation with the author on 18 and 22 March 2004. **48** Greta Jones, 'Women and tuberculosis in Ireland', forthcoming article, University of Syracuse Press. **49** *Oxford dictionary of national biography* (Oxford, 2004), xlix, 577. **50** Sir Charles Scudamore & Lord Percival Barton, On the inhalation of Iodine and Conium in tubercular phthisis', *The Athenaeum* (22 Mar. 1834) 334. **51** *The Athenaeum*, a weekly literary review particularly successful under editorship of Charles Ewentworth Dilke (1830–1846). **52** H.J. Bigelow, 'Insensibility during surgical operations produced by inhalation', *Boston Medicine and Surgery Journal*, 35 (1846), 310. http://www.general-anaesthesia.com/bigelow.html, accessed 23 June 2006. **53** Personal communication with the author, 7 June 2005. **54** Personal conversation with the author, 17 June 2006.

claimed 'the air in and near a gas-works contains pyridin, which acts as an antiseptic and a germicide'.[55] Also in Scotland, when roads were being tarred in the 1950s children with chest problems were brought to breath in the tar fumes.[56] This process became more commercialized, as sufferers who were unable to visit gasworks in 1927 were able to purchase from Boots a 'Vaporizer and Coal Tar inhalant'. This was advertised as being 'most effective in the treatment of whooping cough, croup, asthma, bronchitis, influenza and all diseases of the respiratory organs'.[57] Boots' brands were not available in Ireland until 1966 but local chemists would have marketed their own brands if there was a demand.

Another example of the commercialization of an old cure is the use of Mullein. Mullein was widely cultivated in Ireland as a cure for tuberculosis. Described by Allen and Hatfield as 'the favourite remedy for pulmonary tuberculosis in Ireland throughout recorded history', this 'heavy Irish use is not matched in the records from else where in the British Isles ... and would appear not even to have been a member at all of the Welsh or Scottish folk repertories'.[58] It is a dramatic biennial herb of the Scropulariaceae family. It was so valued that it was grown in many Irish cottage gardens and advertisements offering it for sale were placed in newspapers and it was sold in chemists in Dublin.[59] The family name may have developed from the word 'scrofula' one of the types of tuberculosis it was used to treat. It grows on both sides of the Atlantic and Native American Indians smoked dried mullein and coltsfoot cigarettes as a remedy for asthma and bronchitis. An enterprising Belfast tobacconist in the late nineteenth century reputedly sold Mullein cigarettes either for the prevention or cure of tuberculosis. Whether he got the idea of smoking mullein from across the Atlantic or simply combined the Irish use of Mullein for tuberculosis and the idea of inhalation we can only surmise.

The commercialization of folk remedies became particularly common in the nineteenth century. For example, the German Madaus ethnobotanical industry started in the late nineteenth century when Magdalene Madaus started selling kits of her homeopathic remedies.[60] The firm attracted notoriety in the 1940s as the work of

55 Buchan, *Folk tradition*, p. 243. **56** Information obtained from the audience when a version of this chapter was presented at 'Across the Water: Ireland and Scotland in the Nineteenth Century', at University of Ulster, Magee Campus, 17 June 2006. **57** *Nursing Times*, 30 July 1927. Boots' brands were not available in Ireland until 1966 when their first Irish branch opened. Local chemists may have stocked their own coal-tar inhalants. **58** A few examples are to be found of great mullein being used in the south east of England but none are listed for the Welsh or Scottish repertories, Allen & Hatfield, *Medicinal plants*, p. 250. **59** Ibid., p. 251. **60** The beginnings of the Madaus industry were discussed in a paper given by Dr Carsten Timmerman (University of Manchester), 'Scaling up tradition: folk medicine, science and industry in early twentieth-century Germany', at a one-day workshop, 'The medical marketplace and medical tradition: interfaces between orthodox, alternative and folk practice in the nineteenth and twentieth centuries', Centre for the History of Medicine in Ireland, University College Dublin, 1 Feb. 2008.

Magdalene's son Gerhard Madaus, on medicinal sterilization, interested the Nazi eugenicists. They survived this brief scandal, however, and are still in business today.[61] Mullein cigarettes did not, however, become a big seller, though mullein tea and tincture are still for sale on both sides of the Atlantic. Mullein tea is recommended by current herbalists to relieve chest congestion and dry bronchial coughs. Oral History interviews comment on the role the more prosaic nicotine cigarettes played in a desire to prevent tuberculosis. A 15-year-old in 1951 remembers of her contemporaries that 'some refused to come near me. Others smoked in my presence saying that the smoke would kill my germs.'[62]

Patent medicines were available from the eighteenth century but their use accelerated from the late nineteenth century, for a number of reasons. Firstly, many doctors turned away from the poly-pharmacy that had been advocated in previous years as the chemical properties of ingredients were isolated and described.[63] Secondly, mass marketing and mass advertising created increased demand for these new products. These products were often used in conjunction with orthodox medicine. Patrick Logan, writing about the late 1940s describes a situation when

> the patients in an Irish Sanatorium used to go regularly to a folk curer who lived about ten miles away ... About the same time, the Minister for health was asked in the *Dail* if he would make a widely advertised cure for tuberculosis available to Irish patients.[64]

Patients saw a role in their treatment for patent medicines, orthodox treatment and old-style folk medicine. While no medical cure was available sufferers were very vulnerable to the claims of unscrupulous advertisers.

Tony Farmar has highlighted one such advertisement headed 'Consumption can be cured'. The 'specialist discoverer' of this remarkable cure for consumption was originally a vet. When the *British Medical Association* analysed his cure, it was 'mostly glycerine, colouring, flavouring and water'. In an analysis of the advertisements in the *Weekly Freeman's Journal*, January 1905, Farmar found twenty-one for proprietary medicines.[65] Of these, six might have appealed to consumptives; Angier's Emulsion 'for lung troubles', Congreve's Elixir for consumption, Veno's Lightning Cough Cure 'to nip consumption in the bud', Keating's Lozenges which 'easily cure the worst cough', Scott's Emulsion as a 'great thrower out of disease', and Mother Seigel's Syrup which made the interesting claim that 'Half dead people gain new life'. In 1909, the British Medical Association found it cost one third of a penny to make but was sold for 2s. 6d.[66] As much as three quarters of the advertising space of the *Weekly Freeman's*

61 Michael G. Kenny, 'A darker shade of green: medical botany, homeopathy, and cultural politics in interwar Germany', *Social History of Medicine*, 15:3 (2002), 481–504. **62** OH50 interviewed by the author on 11 Sept. 2004. **63** Farmar, *Patients, potions and physicians*, p. 124, 'From the 1830s alkaloids and other chemical substances were described'. **64** Logan, *Irish country cures*, p. 21. **65** Farmar, *Patients, potions and physicians*, p. 127. **66** Leo Knowles & Leo Harris, 'The golden days of Dr Quack', *History of Medicine*, 6:3 (1975), 81.

Journal was taken up by proprietary medicines. This paper though printed in Dublin
also had an extensive rural readership.[67] It is easy to see how hope of a cure could
make people part with large sums of money and fortunes were accumulated by
manufacturers.

Guest mentions that in Dublin some patients bought by post, from Manchester,
a costly prescription called 'Umkalubo'.[68] Patients were known to take this in the
sanatorium alongside their prescribed treatment. It was confiscated by staff if found.
The touch of exoticism is echoed in Newry, pre 1948, where cures were sold for
'chest complaints' by the 'black men ... in the markets selling rubs. They also went
door-to-door selling cures.' The same person remembers 'Dr Severn brown paper'
being put on a sickly chest 'to keep the heat in.'[69] This is echoed by a young girl in
Belfast who had pleurisy each winter, in the late 1930s, which later turned out to be
tubercular. She had a vest made out of 'anti-figestine' (spelt phonetically).[70] She
recalled that,

> it was like orange cotton wool and you had a vest made of that for the heat
> ... and then there was a poultice you used to buy, I can't remember the name
> of it, in a tin. And it was heated till it was very hot and then tied to cloths and
> that was put on your lungs ... to loosen it and also to give, the pain was
> horrendous. You know the pain with pleurisy is horrendous. It was
> comforting, very comforting.[71]

Anti-phlogestine was actually the poultice used. It may not have helped to heal the
tuberculosis, but the heat eased painful lungs.

What were the medical establishment prescribing for patients in the north of Ireland
in the early years of the epidemic? The Medical Officer's register for Omagh Union,
1894–7, provides some details. In 1895 Alex Robinson, age 14, who was suffering
from tuberculosis of the glands, known as Scrofula, was prescribed *ol morphu, mist
quin*, and ungt acid carbolic.[72] According to Whitla's *Materia Medica* of 1882, *ol morhu*
was cod liver oil used as a nutritive tonic. *Mist Quin* was short for mixture of *Quiniae
Sulphate*.[73] Sir William Whitla, in 1915 described this as 'one of the most frequently
prescribed drugs in the pharmacopoeia'.[74] It was made from the bark of the

67 Louis Cullen quoted in Farmar, *Patients, potions and physicians*, p.125.   68 Guest, 'Cure',
p. 67.   69 Oral History C (Newry), recorded by Gerard Smith, 28 Sept. 2004.   70 Oral
History 35, recorded by the author on 26 May 2004. This is likely to be antiphlogistine. 'A
proprietary preparation containing kaolin, glycerine, antiseptic and aromatic substances. It is
used for poultices, acting as an antiseptic, analgesic and counterirritant in cases of deep-
seated inflammation', *Churchill Livingston pocket medical dictionary* (Edinburgh, 1978), p. 23.
71 Oral History 35, recorded by the author 26 May 2004.   72 PRONI, BG26/JA/1
(papers of the Boards of Guardians).   73 William Whitla, *Elements of pharmacy, materia
medica and therapeutics* (London, 1882), pp 171, 190, 230.   74 Whitla, *Elements of pharmacy,*

Cinchona tree and was a bitter tonic and anti periodic.[75] An anti periodic was any agent that prevented the periodic return of a disease, such as the use of quinine to prevent malaria. *Ungt Acid Carbolic* was a cream of carbolic acid. This was applied to the skin if the tuberculosis gland had suppurated to the surface. It was, as Whitla states, 'a powerful antiseptic, destroying minute forms of animal and vegetable life'.[76] It would have had deodorant qualities as well. For tuberculosis of the lungs, or phthisis, Whitla states that the treatment by drugs 'is one of ceaseless activity, and of incessant changes'.[77] He advocated the use of cod-liver oil but admitted if it was regarded as a medicine 'butter has … quite as much a right to rank as a medicine'.[78]

Whitla, in 1894, felt that creosote tablets 'relieved cough, lessened expectoration, lowered fever heat, checked night-sweats, and improved the appetite', but he could not 'speak definitely about its specific or curative properties'.[79] (Creosote is a product distilled from coal tar, an echo once more of the coal tar at the gas works.) He mentioned many other treatments recommended by various physicians and suggested some combinations, which might bring comfort to a patient with a troublesome cough.

Two of these involved lemon juice, the first as an expectorant when mixed with potassium. The second remedy mixed *sal volatile* and a sixteenth of a grain of morphine with the lemon.[80] Morphine would have acted as a cough suppressant. The use of lemons was omitted from Whitla's 1912 *Dictionary of Treatment*. But Whitla was a Belfastman and the use of lemons in the 1894 version of his dictionary in some treatments of tuberculosis could have contributed to the faith some Belfast inhabitants still had in the 1940s for their curative powers. Interestingly, the *Nursing Times* of September 1925 printed a page about the use of 'Lemons in the Sickroom' due to their ability to increase the 'alkaline character of the blood', aid digestion and 'cool … in fever cases'.[81] This language takes us right back to the humouric medical traditions of the seventeenth and eighteenth centuries.

Advertisements for patent medicines also continued to advocate the power of lemon juice. An advertisement for Robeline published in 1928 did not mention any particular disease but suggested that, when taking it, 'Shallow chests grow deep. Narrow shoulders broaden. … [a] builder of bone'.[82] These claims appealed to parents eager to prevent or cure tuberculosis in their children. Lemon juice is claimed to be a 'builder of bone'.[83] Lemons had been discovered to cure and prevent scurvy by James Lind in 1753.[84] It was, however, not until the 1930s that the curative element Vitamin C was isolated.[85] This meant that for about 180 years lemons were known

materia medica and therapeutics (London, 1915), p. 15. **75** Whitla, *Elements of pharmacy*, p. 190. **76** Ibid., p. 230. **77** William Whitla, *A dictionary of treatment* (London, 1894), p. 646. **78** Ibid., p. 645. **79** Ibid., p. 647. **80** Ibid., p. 656. **81** *Nursing Times*, 5 Sept. 1925. **82** *An Ulster Garland, 1928: an occasional publication in aid of the hospital for sick children Belfast* (Belfast, 1928), 5. **83** Ibid. **84** James Lind, 'A Treatise of the Scurvy' (London, 1753). Transcribed by Lars Bruzelius http://www.bruzelius.info/Nautica/Medicine/Lind(1753).html, accessed 23 June 2006. **85** Linus Pauling Institute at Oregon State University, http://lpi.oregonstate.edu/infocenter/vitamins/vitaminC/, accessed 23 June

to cure scurvy, but the mechanism was not fully understood. It seems likely that this contributed to the faith some people placed in lemons as a cure for diseases other than scurvy.

This chapter has described the cures used in Ireland by people suffering from tuberculosis during the eighteenth, nineteenth and early twentieth centuries, with reference to similar treatments in Scotland. More work is needed to untangle the origins of much of this information. We have no means of knowing how rapidly in the past use of specific herbs could spread from one area to another. Hatfield and Allen demonstrate some sharing of cures between Scotland and Ireland though at what period the exchange of information occurred is unknown. Bogbean would appear to be one such case. As was said earlier, a doctor, keen to ensure he mentioned all possible hopes for a cure might have included folk recipes he knew from the community he lived in. These folk recipes, which had previously passed purely by word of mouth, would now enter the written medical canon. The interest of the medical community in folk cures increased when the Apothecaries' Act of 1815 meant that medical students wishing to be licensed to practise in England and Wales had to pass an exam in herbal knowledge. The influence was felt in Ireland and Scotland too. The increased knowledge of botany led to a re-examination of the local plant remedies that were used in the area around them.[86] The discovery in the late eighteenth century by botanists of the medicinal properties of willow and foxglove led to the sale of aspirin in 1885 and eventually to the extensive twentieth-century use of digitalis for heart failure. These discoveries increased the fashionable interest in botany.[87] Many doctors incorporated local botanical cures into their publications along with a wide variety of other possible cures in the hope that one of them would work. Whitla wrote in 1894, 'drugs play a very minor part in the treatment of phthisis', a tribute to the influence of the revolution in the treatment of tuberculosis brought about by Koch's discovery.[88] However, Whitla still devoted sixteen pages to the subject.

There was also a flow of information in the opposite direction. Publishers of home almanacs could read the scientific journals and copy treatments for popular use. As the written evidence was lost sight of, confusion arose as to the source of the information: was a particular cure from the oral or folk tradition or a popularized medical cure? One such example of this process was the use of milk in which snails had been boiled, as a cure for consumption, as mentioned earlier. This was mentioned in Edward Barry's *Treatise on Consumption of the Lungs* (1776), intended to be an exemplar of the latest scientific medicine. Dr H.S. Purdon, in 1904, wrote of this as 'an old north of Ireland cure' for consumption, as told to him by his gardener. Purdon's gardener may, however, have acquired the information indirectly from

2006. **86** Allen & Hatfield, *Medicinal plants*, p. 21. **87** Ibid., p. 20. **88** Whitla, *Dictionary of treatment*, p. 636.

Barry's work possibly via an almanac rather than from an unbroken oral tradition.[89] Conversely Barry might very well have taken the cure himself from folk tradition but thought it worth his while to include it.

The process, by which sufferers acquired information, regarding the treatment of tuberculosis, was therefore complex. The mother, or member of the family treating a sufferer, could have formed their ideas on advice from a qualified medical practitioner, from their network of friends and colleagues, from any books that they had access to, or from advertisements directly aimed at encouraging the purchase of branded products. Whatever the source of the cure, whether a pharmaceutical treatment provided by doctors, one created at home or bought over the counter, they often provided comfort and hope for the patient rather than a cure for the disease. While tuberculosis continued to visit the population, killing or maiming some victims, leaving some unscathed and avoiding some altogether, 'cures' offered hope to a mystified public. Effective anti-tuberculosis drugs streptomycin, para-aminosalicyclic acid and isoniazid were eventually developed between 1945 and 1952. With them the numbers of tuberculosis patients gradually declined and the use of all other cures became part of folk-memory.

89 Jones, 'Women and tuberculosis in Ireland'.

St Patrick's Day in Dundee, c.1850–1900: a contested Irish institution in a Scottish context

RICHARD B. McCREADY

This chapter looks at the contest between the competing claims of Catholicism and Irish nationalism in the Irish Catholic community in Dundee in the latter half of the nineteenth century. The main focus is the celebrations surrounding St Patrick's Day in the city of Dundee. By way of comparison it also considers other events such as elections and the celebrations of the centenary of the birth of Daniel O'Connell. While the majority of Irish migrants to Dundee in the nineteenth century were Roman Catholics, it is clear that a considerable number were not Roman Catholics, and the existence of the Orange order in the city is evidence of the presence of Irish Protestants in Dundee. This chapter suggests some ideas about the nature of the Irish diaspora and the place of the Irish in Scotland, and in Dundee in particular.

In nineteenth-century Scotland large-scale Irish migration came about for a variety of reasons. There were job opportunities in Scotland – for example in Dundee's textile industry – as well as economic and social problems in Ireland, the most extreme of which was the Famine. As a result, Dundee in the first half of the century was a rapidly expanding town. Dundee recorded remarkable rises in its population between the decennial censuses. For example, between 1821 and 1831 the population rose by 48 per cent and between 1831 and 1841 it rose by a further 38 per cent.

The Irish made up a significant part of Dundee's population; in 1841 9 per cent of the population of the city had been born in Ireland and by 1851 this percentage had risen to 19 per cent. Moreover, the Irish community was larger than these figures suggest, due to the children of Irish immigrants considering themselves to be Irish. In Scotland as a whole, the Irish formed a proportionately significant element in the population. The Irish in Scotland, though numerically smaller, made up a proportionately larger section of the community than the Irish in England. Within that community there were places, like Dundee, where the Irish were far more concentrated than elsewhere.[1]

In the popular imagination, Irish emigration is believed to be a result of the Great

---

1 J.F. McCaffrey, 'Roman Catholics in Scotland in the 19th and 20th centuries', *Records of the Scottish Church History Society*, 21 (1983), 276.

Famine of 1845–9. However, even by 1841 there was a large Irish community in Dundee, forming at least 9 per cent of the total population. The Catholic church in Dundee had been built to accommodate over one thousand people in 1836. In 1847 it was claimed that the number of Catholics in Dundee was between nine and ten thousand.[2] Therefore it is clear that in terms of Catholics, the majority of whom would have been Irish, there was a significant number present in Dundee before the Famine.

St Patrick's Day is not an uncontentious event, even in modern Scotland. After witnessing the 2006 celebrations of St Patrick's day in Dundee, one local resident wrote to the *Dundee Evening Telegraph* to say: 'Can anyone please tell me why this country goes mad on St Patrick's Day? Bars are packed with people off their work. When do you ever see the same happen on St Andrew's Day?'[3] The tradition of celebrating St Patrick in this manner is of fairly recent vintage. In the nineteenth century there were other ways of celebrating the day; however, many of them were equally recent inventions. The fact that celebrations were recently invented does not make these celebrations meaningless.[4] Eric Hobsbawn has commented on the fact that the changes that came about as a result of industrialization in the nineteenth century led to what he called the 'invention' of tradition at this time. Industrialization was the specific factor which led to many Irish people and people of Irish descent finding themselves in Dundee in the second half of the century.[5] Benedict Anderson has described the nation as an 'imagined community';[6] it is a community where it is not possible to know everyone or all of the area of the nation. It can be seen that an immigrant community, which proclaims a national identity for a country that few of the community's members have actually visited, must in a very real sense be imagined and invented.

Another aspect of industrialization was the increasing 'Anglicization' of Irish culture. Events like St Patrick's Day allowed the Irish either in Ireland or in the Diaspora to stress their Irish identity. Often this was a romanticized view of Irish identity which stressed its ancient culture and nationalist tone, and it was in contrast to the reality of the industrialized Anglicized society in which many of the Irish, even in Ireland, found themselves. For the migrant Irish it was often a chance to proclaim their distinctiveness in places like America and Australia, and in Britain in places like Dundee.[7] This distinctiveness was often imagined, as traditions allegedly from Ireland were followed with a fervour largely unknown in Ireland. It has been argued that amongst the diaspora the tradition of St Patrick's Day was '(re)discovered and shaped anew'.[8]

2 *Catholic directory for Scotland 1847* (Aberdeen, 1847), p. 80. **3** *Dundee Evening Telegraph,* 27 Mar. 2006. **4** B. Walker, *Dancing to history's tune: history, myth and politics in Ireland* (Belfast, 1997), p. 109. **5** Ibid., p. 7; E. Hobsbawn, 'Mass producing traditions: Europe, 1870–1914', in E. Hobsbawn & T. Ranger (eds), *The invention of tradition* (Cambridge, 1983), pp 263–307. **6** B. Anderson, *Imagined communities: reflections on the origin and spread of nationalism* (London, 1991). **7** M. Cronin & D. Adair, *The wearing of the green: a history of St Patrick's day* (London, 2002), p. 59. **8** Ibid., xxi.

In popular perceptions and in popular culture in Scotland today, the link between Catholicism and Irishness is firmly established.[9] The reality of the situation in the nineteenth century was, of course, not quite as straightforward. For example, in Scotland the leadership of the Catholic church at that time was almost exclusively Scottish, with Archbishop Eyre of Glasgow being a notable English exception. There was only one Irish-born bishop in Scotland. This situation in Scotland was somewhat different to that in other parts of the Irish diaspora. It has been suggested that the lack of Irish priests in leadership positions demonstrated that the Irish in Scotland were 'second-class Catholics'.[10] Over time, this led to an ongoing tension between Irishness and Catholicism.

Despite this, to outside observers, Catholicism and Irishness were often seen as inexorably linked. For example, the *Dundee Advertiser* in 1900 carried a report of a Catholic celebration of St Patrick's Day under the headline 'Blending of Religion and Patriotism'.[11] Many commentators have highlighted attempts by the hierarchy of the Catholic church to 'mollify' the Irish and their celebrations of their nationality and their patron saint. Often the leadership of the Catholic church took pains to stress the religious nature of St Patrick's Day and to emphasize the common Catholic cause which in turn deflected the focus from any nationalistic elements that might otherwise have become central to the celebration.[12] Speaking in Dundee, Monsignor Robert Clapperton said that their St Patrick's Day meeting was a 'grand and noble Catholic meeting – like so many others throughout the length and breadth of the world, to honour St Patrick, for the Catholic Church was spread all over the world, and so were the children of St Patrick. (Cheers)'. The clear implication of Clapperton's words are that St Patrick's Day was a celebration only for Catholics. At the same meeting, another priest, Fr Harris, moved a motion in reference to St Patrick which stated that those assembled would remain 'steadfast to the teachings and practices which as an inheritance of priceless worth our fathers received from the great apostle, have faithfully guarded, and in unsullied purity handed down to our keeping'.[13] The Irish in Dundee may not have occupied the highest social positions but in this priest's view they did have access to something which was priceless, namely, their Catholic faith. An Irish priest, Fr Michael Lavelle, speaking in Dundee on St Patrick's Day in 1893 commented on the relationship between the clergy and the people of Ireland and presumably the relationship between the clergy and the people of the diaspora, 'from the time of St Patrick down to the present day the Irish Bishops and priests had stood by their people and their people had stood by them'.[14] The agreement of the Irish present at the meeting was signified by their applause. It

9 B. Aspinwall, 'Faith of our fathers living still … Time warp or Woof! Woof!', in T. M. Devine (ed.), *Scotland's shame: bigotry and sectarianism in modern Scotland* (Edinburgh, 2000), p. 106. 10 J. Quinn, 'The mission of the churches to the Irish in Dundee, 1846–1886' (M.Litt., Stirling, 1993), p. 66. 11 D[undee] A[dvertiser], 20 Mar. 1900. 12 S. Fielding, *Class and ethnicity: Irish Catholics in England, 1880–1939* (Buckingham, 1993), p. 42. 13 *DA*, 18 Mar. 1890. 14 *DA*, 18 Mar. 1893.

is interesting to note that these sentiments can also be seen as an indirect criticism of the Scottish Catholic church.

Patrick's position as a symbol of Roman Catholicism and of Irish nationalism was not undisputed. There were many who claimed that Patrick was not a Roman Catholic and that he had belonged to a Celtic church. The Celtic church has been claimed as a precursor of the Reformed tradition, whilst at the same time as many people have highlighted its close links to Rome. It is clear that Patrick or rather a series of 'Patricks' were claimed by both Protestants and Roman Catholics during much of the nineteenth century. In the early part of the nineteenth century celebrations of St Patrick had been shared, at least in the sense that both Catholics and Protestants could enjoy them. As a result of the political and religious changes which took place in Ireland during the century, Patrick was claimed almost exclusively by the Catholics and the nationalists.[15]

The Roman Catholic hierarchy was restored in Scotland in 1878, and Dundee became part of a restored diocese of Dunkeld. The first bishop of this diocese, George Rigg, was of Scottish stock, and while his pro-cathedral was in Dundee, the biggest Catholic centre of his diocese, he chose to live in Perth. There is no evidence of his celebrating St Patrick's Day. His successor was James Smith, who went on to be archbishop of St Andrews and Edinburgh; Bishop Smith was a regular attendee at St Patrick's Day celebrations in Dundee. In 1900 he told the Dundee gathering that there were only two points to be celebrated: 'faith and fatherland'.[16] Some commentators have seen evidence of this attitude in the Catholic hierarchy in Ireland. The attachment to 'faith and fatherland' is said to be the work of Cardinal Paul Cullen.[17] It is rather ironic that the Scottish church had tried so hard to ensure that Cullen had little or no influence in Scotland. In 1895 the Catholic St Patrick's Day celebration in Dundee heard a speech from Fr Michael Phelan, an Irish priest working in Dundee, on 'Our Faith and Fatherland'. Phelan's speech called for peace and unity among the Irish and claimed that this would bring about the prosperity in Ireland which they all wanted.[18]

The links between faith, fatherland and St Patrick have not gone uncontested. Since the sixteenth century there have been many who have tried to claim Patrick for their own versions of Christianity. He has been called 'one of the most popular and most contested figures in Irish history'.[19] However, he has also been claimed by just about every Irish Christian group, with each group claiming that his teachings corresponded with their own.[20]

A St Patrick's Day speech in 1885 in Dundee created a sectarian disagreement. Fr

15 Cronin & Adair, *The wearing of the green*, p. 26. 16 *DA*, 20 Mar. 1900. 17 C.C. O'Brien, *Ancestral voices: religion and nationalism in Ireland* (Dublin, 1994), p. 22. 18 *DA*, 19 Mar. 1895. 19 Walker, *Dancing to history's tune*, p. 77. 20 Cronin & Adair, *The wearing of the green*, xxviii

Joseph Holder, a senior priest in the city, spoke on the subject of 'Modern Attempts at Ireland's Perversion'. The 'perversion' being attempts to convert the Irish to Protestantism.[21] This provoked a correspondent to the *Dundee Courier* named 'Patriot' to respond that Patrick was not a 'Papist', that Patrick's father was a deacon and his grandfather a priest and also to say that there was no celibacy in the early Irish church.[22] 'Patriot' is attempting to make the point that the true inheritors of St Patrick's legacy were the Protestants of Ireland.

The political statements of the Catholic clergy at St Patrick's Day events caused many people to question the role of the clergy in politics. The clergy could take quite partisan positions in defending themselves. Fr Michael Lavelle in Dundee said in response that if the priests were promoting the 'Tory Party' there would be no controversy about their political views. He was keen to point out that bishops and priests in Ireland were 'well-educated' and had a right to be heard. To the acclaim of his audience he said that he had never heard anyone say that there should be 'no ministers in politics.'[23] Lavelle's speech brought a stinging response from the more conservative *Dundee Courier*. It was claimed that his speech was 'another illustration of the overwhelming zeal of the Roman Catholic priesthood to exercise political influence'. The *Courier* was happy that this 'zeal' did not normally exhibit itself in Scotland and that 'clerical intimidation' was unknown in Scotland. However, it was concerned that Fr Lavelle and others wanted to import this sort of behaviour from Ireland.[24] In 1886 Monsignor Clapperton told the St Patrick's Day meeting that their demonstrations were getting 'grander and grander' just as the church was 'progressing' every year.[25] Over the years, green favours were said to be seen in many parts of Dundee and special services were held in the Catholic churches across the city.[26]

There were times however when the Catholic church's political concerns were different from the political concerns of Ireland. Although home rule was mentioned in 1885 at the Catholic celebration in Dundee, there was also a political speech on the topic of education.[27] Indeed, the Catholic hierarchies in Britain were very concerned that home rule would virtually eliminate Catholic MPs from the house of commons and were active in promoting the retention of Irish MPs at Westminster even after the devolution which they apparently supported.[28] The bishops based in Britain were concerned that there would be no one to promote the interests of Catholic schools in Britain if there were no Irish Catholic MPs in the house of commons.

There were those who suggested that the Catholic church was not really a friend of home rule. It was reported in the Dundee press that Dr MacEvilly, the Catholic archbishop of Tuam, had said that Pope Leo XIII was a friend of the Irish people and that the pope would 'never turn against the legitimate aspirations of the people of Ireland'.[29] The pope was also a popular topic at St Patrick's Day celebrations. On St

21 D[undee] C[ourier], 18 Mar. 1885. 22 DC, 21 Mar. 1885. 23 DA, 18 Mar. 1893.
24 DC, 18 Mar. 1893. 25 DA, 18 Mar. 1886. 26 DA, 18 Mar. 1895. 27 DA, 18 Mar.
1885. 28 DA, 25 May 1886. 29 DA, 8 Feb. 1888.

Patrick's Day in 1880 Leo XIII was described as the 'greatest King on the earth, with 200,000,000 subjects who were ready to cheer him and face all the enemies of the world'.[30] This statement was greeted with loud applause. The Catholic St Patrick's Day celebration in Dundee in 1878 was treated to speeches about the then recently elected Pope Leo XIII; in 1899 a similar gathering was informed that he was 'one of the greatest and best of men'.[31]

On some occasions in Dundee the St Patrick's Day celebrations were used as an opportunity to make charitable collections. It appears that this might have been seen as a compromise solution to bring both the political and religious elements of the celebration together.[32] It was claimed that the St Patrick's Day celebration was held for the benefit of the Society of St Vincent de Paul to collect funds for a children's charity. This claim made by the *Dundee Catholic Herald* would appear to be open to challenge over time. Throughout the second half of the nineteenth century it appears that most St Patrick's Day events in Dundee had a religious or political tone rather than a charitable one.

On St Patrick's Day 1874 there was a meeting which was chaired by Fr MacManus and on the same evening the 'Home Rulers' held a festival and ball.[33] This highlights the church's 'ambiguous' position with regard to the political aspira- tions of the Irish.[34] Political meetings appeared to be popular among the Irish diaspora in Britain, for example in Hamilton and in Cumbria.[35] On some occasions in Dundee there were overtly Irish political aspects to the St Patrick's Day celebra- tions. In 1890 the 'Catholic people of Dundee' recorded their 'unswerving fidelity to the cause of Home Rule'; they also recognized the 'evils of foreign mis-government' and hailed with delight the 'coming triumph' of home rule in a motion which was passed. The same meeting also expressed its 'unabated confidence' in Charles Stewart Parnell. The meeting had opened with the singing of the nationalist song 'The Wearing of the Green'.[36] In 1893 a pro-Liberal party speech was made, which stated that helping the Liberal Party was the 'duty' of Irishmen.[37]

At times the home rulers met in more select groups. In 1880 between thirty and fifty members of the Dundee Home Rule Club celebrated St Patrick's Day with a dinner in the Queen's Hotel. A 'pleasant' evening was spent and the toasts give some indication of the priorities of the members and also their wish for respectability. They toasted 'Pope Leo XIII', 'The Sovereign, Lords and Commons of Ireland', 'The Irish Home Rule Parliamentary Party', 'The Day we celebrate', 'The Irish National Land League', and the 'Dundee Home Rule Club'.[38] In 1875 those present at a meeting in Dundee were told how to vote at the next general election by Mr J.P. McAllister,

30 *DA*, 18 Mar. 1880. 31 *DA*, 19 Mar. 1878; 18 Mar. 1899. 32 *Dundee Catholic Herald*, 24 Mar. 1899. 33 *DA*, 20 Mar. 1874. 34 D.M. MacRaild, *Irish migrants in modern Britain, 1750–1922* (Basingstoke, 1999), p. 97. 35 M.J. Mitchell, 'The Catholic community in Hamilton, *c*. 1800–1914', in T.M. Devine (ed.), *St Mary's Hamilton: a social history 1846–1996* (Edinburgh, 1995), pp 53–4; D.M. MacRaild, *Culture, conflict and migration: the Irish in Victorian Cumbria* (Liverpool, 1998), p. 114. 36 *DA*, 18 Mar. 1890. 37 *DA*, 18 Mar. 1893. 38 *DA*, 19 Mar. 1880.

a delegate of the Home Rule League in Dublin. Dundee's two MPs had pledged to vote for home rule at the 1874 general election. One of them had not voted as he said he would, and McAllister thus encouraged the Irish to remember this and 'to throw him out, to kick him out of Parliament the first opportunity they had'.[39] A nationalist meeting in 1878 was informed that 'St Patrick taught them that their first duty was to love their God, and their second duty to defend their country from foreign foes and internal traitors.'[40] Therefore it is clear that there were many instances when the interests of the Irish nationalists and of the Catholics in Dundee were compatible.

The Irish parading tradition was often problematic for the authorities, and the practice of having parades on St Patrick's Day was a concern to the authorities.[41] T.G. Fraser has highlighted that tensions over parades came about as a result of five key factors – 'territory, tradition, cultural identity, civil rights and politics.'[42] He argues that the most contentious of these was territory; despite many local myths there were very few places in nineteenth-century Scotland where there were Orange or Green ghettos. Claims, therefore, of ownership of any 'territory' were problematic. In Scotland all Irish parades were treated with 'even-handed distaste' and suffered from 'official and popular disapproval'.[43] Parades often formed a prelude to the main St Patrick's Day celebration in Dundee with parades coming from various parts of the town to a hall in the town centre. The parades in Dundee appear to have been attractive to young people who sang songs 'some appropriate, and others not'.[44] On occasion these parades in Dundee could attract 'considerable attention' and present a 'splendid appearance'.[45] These parades in Dundee seem to generally have passed off peacefully despite the enthusiasm of some of those taking part.[46]

In other areas it would appear that 'Donnybrook fair' was the order of the day on St Patrick's Day.[47] A polemical anti-Irish book published in 1927 claimed that it was impossible for the Scots and Irish to live peacefully together because 'Donnybrook is an institution that the Irish take about with them as the Jews did the Ark of the Covenant.'[48] Even when those taking part in the St Patrick's Day parades in Dundee were armed with sticks, they were 'intended to give a bellicose colouring to the demonstration; but it was only a colouring, for although they indulged in a lot of noise and singing they were otherwise peaceful and harmless'.[49] A similar display in 1895 was also described as 'harmless' and in 1899 it was very orderly.[50] Despite this

39 *DA,* 19 Mar. 1875.   **40** *DA,* 19 Mar. 1878.   **41** Cronin & Adair, *The wearing of the green,* p. 57.   **42** T.G. Fraser, 'Introduction', in T.G. Fraser (ed.), *The Irish parading tradition: following the drum* (London, 2000), p. 6.   **43** E. McFarland, 'Marching from the margins: Twelfth July parades in Scotland, 1820–1914', in Fraser (ed.), *Irish parading tradition,* pp 65–6.   **44** *DA,* 18 Mar. 1899.   **45** *DA,* 18 Mar. 1893; 18 Mar. 1890.   **46** *DA,* 18 Mar. 1886.   **47** MacRaild, *Culture, conflict and migration,* p. 115.   **48** G.M. Thomson, *Caledonia or the future of the Scots* (London, 1927), p.14.   **49** *DA,* 18 Mar. 1893.   **50** *DA,* 19 Mar. 1895; 18 Mar. 1899.

there were occasions when some of those either watching or taking part in the parades found themselves in trouble with the law.

At the end of the period under consideration in this chapter the contribution of the Irish to the British efforts in the Boer War led to a widespread celebration of St Patrick's Day among the Irish and the non-Irish in Dundee and elsewhere. Queen Victoria allowed soldiers in Irish regiments to wear shamrocks on St Patrick's Day in 1900. This started the long-standing tradition of a member of the royal family presenting soldiers in Irish regiments with shamrocks on the day.[51] In Dundee it was claimed that the queen's 'dispensation' had brought the shamrock 'more into prominence this year than usual, and large numbers of persons not directly connected with the Irish nationality wore buttonholes formed of it'. A Free Church of Scotland bazaar was being held in Dundee on St Patrick's Day in 1900, and among other goods it also sold shamrocks.[52]

Irish support for the Boer War was not universal, for example, in Lurgan there was a pro-Boer demonstration on St Patrick's Day in 1900. However, in Dundee the local leader of the United Irish League, J. O'Donnell Derrick, asked how 'Britain had found that Irishmen could well manage the affairs of Britain in South Africa, and why should Britain deny Irishmen at home the right to manage their own affairs'.[53]

The nature of the Catholic church in Ireland and the Catholic church in Scotland in the nineteenth century was quite different. Scottish priests often found themselves in conflict with their Irish parishioners. The conflicts revolved around differing attitudes to religion and nationality and in particular to the relative weight given to one or other of these important markers of identity.[54] Tension between Catholicism and nationalism came about because religion also claimed to 'transcend secular politics'.[55] The attitude of the Scottish clergy to those Irish who supported Irish nationalism is best summed up in the words of Bishop Murdoch, vicar apostolic of the Western District, when he said that the best solution to the Young Ireland movement in 1848 was a 'skinful of bullets'.[56] A Scottish priest wrote to his bishop that 'Irish ignorance and unwillingness to learn were astonishing'.[57] Over time the attitudes of the Catholic clergy in Scotland can be seen to have changed as did their ethnic make-up.

The differences between the Irish and the Scottish clergy and the lay faithful were exposed in the controversy which surrounded the politics and attitude of the *Glasgow Free Press*. Although clearly from its title the *Free Press* was published in Glasgow, it

51 Walker, *Dancing to history's tune*, p. 79.   52 *DA*, 19 Mar. 1900.   53 *DA*, 20 Mar. 1900. 54 B. Aspinwall & J.F. McCaffrey, 'A comparative view of the Irish in Edinburgh in the nineteenth century', in R. Swift & S. Gilley (eds), *The Irish in the Victorian city* (London, 1985), p. 140.   55 J.F. McCaffrey, 'Irish issues in the nineteenth and twentieth century: radicalism in a Scottish context', in T.M. Devine (ed.), *Irish immigrants and Scottish society in the nineteenth and twentieth centuries* (Edinburgh, 1991), p. 116.   56 Aspinwall & McCaffrey, 'A comparative view of the Irish in Edinburgh', p. 135.   57 Ibid., pp 136–7.

was certainly read in Dundee. The *Free Press* controversy resulted in numerous pamphlets being written.[58] The controversy revolved around the alleged anti-Irish bias of the leadership of the Catholic church in Scotland. On the Scottish side they beseeched and implored 'as you value your immortal souls and the peace and welfare of your families – as you love truth and your holy faith, and wish for the freedom and happiness of your native land – cease to support the *Free Press*'.[59] Bishop Murdoch of the Western District described the work of A.H. Keane, the editor of the *Free Press*, as 'calculated to uproot from their bosoms all confidence in and respect for their Scotch pastors, whom with few, perhaps I should say scarce any exceptions he represents as being hostile to the Irish race'. Keane on the other hand believed that 'no more unhappy fate' had ever befallen human beings as the fate of the Irish in Scotland.[60] The controversy over the *Free Press* was indicative of the tensions within the Catholic and Irish communities in the 1860s and 1870s.[61]

A different Irish saint was celebrated by the Scottish hierarchy and the Catholic Church in 1888. This was the occasion of a national pilgrimage to Iona to celebrate the rededication of the diocese of Argyll and the Isles to St Columba.[62] About 100 pilgrims left from Dundee for this event and they were told by the *Dundee Advertiser* that Columba was more like a Protestant minister than a Roman Catholic prelate.[63] There is no evidence that such organized pilgrimages were made to sites associated with St Patrick. This is despite the fact that some of these sites allegedly associated with St Patrick were in the more easily accessible county of Dunbartonshire. The town on Old Kilpatrick, which local tradition claims as the birthplace of Patrick, is only around ten miles from the centre of Glasgow.

The conflicts and controversies around St Patrick's Day were reflected in other aspects of the history of the Irish in Dundee. Two examples include the election campaign of 1874 and the centennial celebrations of Daniel O'Connell's birth. For the 1874 general election the Home Rule Association in Dundee was more organized than it had been at previous elections. The actions of the home rulers would have long lasting consequences amongst the Irish Catholic community in the town. The Home Rule Association issued a questionnaire to the candidates. This covered seven issues ranging from the political to the religious.[64] One of Dundee's sitting MPs, James Yeaman, replied in terms which encouraged the Irish to support him and see him as being a supporter of many of their causes. A meeting of the Irish electors gave Yeaman their undivided support.[65]

58 For example, J. Doud, *The 'Free Press', Keane and the Keanites* (Glasgow, 1863); A.H. Keane, *The case of the Irish Catholics in Scotland stated* (Glasgow, 1864); *The school for scandal no. 1 'Free Press' portraits* (Dublin, 1864); *Address to the Irish Catholics residing in Scotland* (no place or date of publication)   **59** *Address to the Irish Catholics residing in Scotland* (no place or date of publication), p. 8.   **60** A.H. Keane, *The case of the Irish Catholics in Scotland stated: being a memorial on the present state of the Catholic church in Scotland addressed to his eminence Cardinal Alex. Barnabo* (Glasgow, 1864), iii.   **61** McCaffrey, 'Roman Catholics in Scotland in the 19th and 20th centuries', p. 278.   **62** St Columba is known as St Columcille in Ireland.   **63** *DA*, 12 June 1888; 13 June 1888.   **64** *DA*, 4 Feb. 1874.   **65** *DA*, 5 Feb. 1874.

As seen elsewhere, there was often scope for conflict in the Irish community over politics. There was a major division in 1874 between what could be called the Catholic faction and what could be called the national faction. This revolved around who had the right to direct the Catholic vote, the Home Rule Association or the clergy. Indeed, the issue was whether the vote being debated was an Irish vote or a Catholic vote. Fr James McGinnes claimed that the meeting which had plumped for Yeaman was purely a Catholic meeting and was not a home rule meeting.[66] The home rulers replied that if they wanted to set questions for candidates they could do so. The 'Officebearers of the Home Rule Confederation, Dundee' asked what would be left of the Catholic body if home rulers were subtracted. The answer they came up with was that all that would be left was the 'denationalised Irish in a miserably insignificant minority'. Fr McGinnes was attacked by the home rulers; they would not be led by him 'or his anti-Irish club'.[67] This division could not be politically advantageous to either party. The ill-will between McGinnes and the home rulers was seen again during the celebrations of Daniel O'Connell's centenary in 1875.

The celebrations which took place in 1875 to mark the centenary of Daniel O'Connell's birth illustrated many of the tensions prevalent within the Irish Catholic community in Dundee. The *Advertiser* told the Irish they were 'bound to honour the memory of Daniel O'Connell'.[68] The same article then went on to criticize the ultramontanes in the Catholic church and to say that though 'an ardent and devout Catholic' O'Connell would have opposed the current ultramontane party. The *Courier* claimed that O'Connell had been successful until he suggested repeal of the Union.[69] Those wishing to celebrate had great difficulty in reconciling the two aspects of his career; the first as the gainer of civil rights for Catholics and the second as the advocate of repeal of the Union.

Cardinal Cullen issued a pastoral letter praising the Catholic aspect of O'Connell's career. The main celebration of the centenary in Dublin was Catholic in nature rather than 'nationalist'.[70] This was also the situation in Dundee. 'Garry Owen' in a letter to the *Advertiser* complained that the proposed commemoration in Dundee was organized by those who sought 'to dissuade their countrymen from being national.'[71] In reply, 'Connaught' claimed that the national movement did not wish to clash with these 'obscure parties.' The home rulers were sending fifteen delegates to Dublin and did not wish to compete with the 'anti-Irish party' who were in charge of the Dundee celebrations.[72] This shows a lack of organization on the Dundee home rulers' part. Going to Dublin may have been a more attractive prospect to the committee members than organizing a meeting in Dundee. Subsequently, the main Dundee celebration was a Catholic one, with several priests on the platform. The lay members on the platform were leading Catholics rather than Irish nationalists. Speeches at this meeting laid more emphasis on Catholic emancipation than on the later nationalist part of O'Connell's career.

66 *DC*, 5 Feb. 1874. **67** *DC*, 7 Feb. 1874. **68** *DA*, 6 Aug. 1875. **69** *DC*, 6 Aug. 1875. **70** David Thornley, *Isaac Butt and home rule* (London, 1964), p. 265. **71** *DA*, 3 Aug. 1875. **72** *DA*, 6 Aug. 1875.

In the Partick area of Glasgow, the O'Connell celebrations led to an outbreak of serious rioting.[73] The riots have been variously described as 'the worst spasm of sectarian rioting ever seen in Victorian Scotland' and 'the last major anti-Catholic riot in greater Glasgow'.[74] The Partick home rulers were attacked on their return from the O'Connell celebrations in Glasgow by Orangemen, and this caused sporadic violence for several days. The Riot Act was read, and the Volunteers were needed to restore order. The *Courier* commented on the fact that Dundee had been spared this violence. The Dundee Irish were not 'in the habit of troubling the peace of the town'; even as early as 1875 it was claimed that the sectarian situation was 'different in the west of Scotland.'[75] It is also worth noting that in August 1875 there was a major strike in the Dundee jute industry; thus there were plenty of people with free time if they wished to riot. However, it appears that workers' solidarity was more important than sectarian strife.[76]

Along with Irish Catholics, there were also a number of Irish Protestant migrants in Dundee, and they too brought their distinctive traditions to the city. It is often stated that for the Orange Order to be vibrant there needs to be a strong Irish Protestant immigrant community.[77] It has been claimed that in Dundee there was little or no Orange presence. Walker claims that there was 'no effective Orange outpost in Dundee'.[78] McFarland has followed Walker's analysis; she also accepts Walker's assertion that the Dundee Irish were predominantly Roman Catholic. Recent research has questioned this analysis. John Quinn has pointed out that the Dundee Irish were predominantly from Ulster. The counties with the highest representation in the Dundee Irish were Cavan and Monaghan, and although Ulster counties were predominantly Catholic, Fermanagh and Tyrone were also well represented and all these counties had relatively large Protestant populations.[79]

It is clear that Walker has underestimated the strength of Orangeism in Dundee. As early as 1845, 150 Orangemen celebrated the anniversary of the victory at the Boyne.[80] There is no evidence of the Dundee Orangemen having taken part in Orange parades or other outdoor demonstrations in Dundee. However, there were Dundee contingents at some of the major Orange demonstrations in Glasgow and the west of Scotland.[81] Dundee opinion seems to have been against party processions.

73 *DA*, 10 Aug. 1875.   74 I.S. Wood, 'Irish nationalism and radical politics in Scotland 1880–1906', *Journal of the Scottish Labour History Society*, 9 (1975), 21; J. Smith, 'Class, skill and sectarianism in Glasgow and Liverpool 1880–1914', in R.J. Morris (ed.), *Class, power and structure in British nineteenth-century towns* (Leicester, 1986), p. 192.   75 *DC*, 11 Aug. 1875.   76 *DC*, 13 July 1875; 3 Aug. 1875; *DA*, 10 Aug. 1875.   77 E. McFarland, *Protestants first: Orangeism in nineteenth century Scotland* (Edinburgh, 1990) p. 103.   78 W.M. Walker, *Juteopolis: Dundee and its textile workers 1885–1923* (Edinburgh, 1979), pp 120–1.   79 Quinn, 'The mission of the churches to the Irish in Dundee', p. 42; R.B. McCready, 'The social and political impact of the Irish in Dundee, *c*. 1845–1922' (PhD, University of Dundee, 2002), pp 91–5.   80 *Dundee, Perth and Cupar Advertiser*, 18 July 1845.   81 *DA*, 13 July 1878.

The *Advertiser* called them a 'dangerous force'.[82] The Dundee Orangemen may have bowed to local opposition or they may have shown their relative weakness. It has been argued that processions were used to mark out territory. As Hempton has argued, 'where you could "walk" you could control'.[83] Although it cannot be argued that Dundee was controlled by Orangemen they were certainly a presence in the city. The Orange walk could also been seen as a reflection of the anxiety of the Orange population or even as an attempt to gain control of certain areas, neither of these manifested itself in Dundee.

When looking at reports in Dundee newspapers of Orange activity elsewhere, it seems clear that the Dundee Orangemen were more peaceable than their brethren in some other places. Reports in the run up to the Twelfth of July often reported expectation of disturbances, but trouble was never anticipated in Dundee. There is evidence of high levels of Orange membership in the Scottish Episcopal church in Dundee. Irish Protestant migrants in Dundee who were members of the Orange Order have left their mark. There were many Protestant migrants who were not members of the Orange Order; they present a problem to historians in tracing them. The Episcopal mission of St Mary Magdalene had a largely Orange Irish congregation. This was a difficult situation as the incumbent was William Humphrey, a ritualist who would eventually become a Jesuit. In 1867 he irritated his congregation when on Sunday 12 July he followed Catholic practice for 'ordinary Sundays' and dressed the altar in green frontals.[84] Many of these Orange Anglicans found their home in St John's Church of England in Dundee, which was an evangelical congregation. Orange reaction to ritualism in Anglican churches was important elsewhere, for example, in Liverpool, and Orangeism contributed to the formation of a strong working-class Conservative movement there.[85] This was not the case in Dundee, where no effective working-class Tory movement ever developed. In part this was due to the different ecclesiastical settlement in Scotland.

As the Orange vote was closely associated with the Conservatives and Dundee was famous for being a 'Liberal toun', it can be concluded that the political impact of Orangeism was slight in Dundee. The Orange element, on the whole, received favourable coverage in the *Courier.* In the 1870s this newspaper was broadly Liberal, though not so radical as its competitor the *Advertiser.* The *Courier* probably set the political line of the Dundee Orangemen. It is difficult to assess the political strength of Dundee Orangeism. 'A Professional Man' in a letter to the *Courier* in 1880 stated, 'My information convinces me that the Orangemen of Dundee have more votes all told than the whole Catholic community.'[86] It is difficult to agree with this assessment as there are no known cases of politicians in Dundee appealing to the Orange vote, whilst there are many cases of the cultivation of the Irish Catholic vote.

82 *DA*, 23 Aug. 1872.   **83** D. Hempton, 'Belfast: the unique city?', in H. McLeod (ed.), *European religion in the age of the great cities* (London, 1995), p. 152.   **84** R. Strong, *Alexander Forbes of Brechin: the first tractarian bishop* (Oxford, 1995), p. 86.   **85** See F. Neal, *Sectarian violence: the Liverpool experience, 1819–1914* (Manchester, 1988) passim.   **86** *DC*, 24 Mar. 1880.

The Orange Order in Dundee was certainly more powerful than has been previously claimed. Its political impact may have been muted by the overwhelming Liberalism of the town. It may be the case that the major impact of Orangeism in Dundee was to keep the Catholic community in the city organized and much more aware of its Irishness.[87] Like the Catholic Irish who have dominated the historical debate of the Irish in Scotland it is clear that the Protestant Irish brought with them (and even invented) Protestant, Irish and British identities which set out to mark the distinctiveness of their community. To a certain extent, the identities which marked people out were part of the 'cultural baggage' exported from Ireland, but they were also constructed in Scotland to emphasize that the Protestant Irish were different from the Catholic Irish and often that they were more respectable.

This chapter has argued that the celebration of St Patrick's Day in Dundee in the later nineteenth century was not without controversy. The anniversary often demonstrated the tensions within the Irish Catholic community in the city and elsewhere in Scotland. There were those who promoted the claims of the Catholic church and there were those who promoted the claims of Irish nationalism. Within both these groups there could often be even further divisions, for example between the indigenous Catholic church and the ultramontane piety of the post-Famine Irish or between home rulers and Fenians among those promoting Irish nationalism. Often these groups could find a common cause but at other times there were conflicts and tensions. The nature of St Patrick's Day was frequently contested in nineteenth century Dundee. The identity of the Irish community in Dundee was made up of many varied and sometimes conflicting features. These tensions witnessed in Dundee and elsewhere in Scotland demonstrated the rivalry between clergymen and the lay leadership of the community. The celebrations of St Patrick's Day highlighted many of the fractures within the Irish community in Dundee, it would appear that similar fractures were replicated in other areas with an immigrant Irish population. The historian is forced to deal in generalities but must always remember that beneath these generalities a much more complicated picture exists. The Irish in Scotland were not universally devout Catholics in the thrall of their clergy neither were they always united in their political views, even among those who supported a change in Ireland's position within the United Kingdom. Understanding that the Irish in Dundee, like the Irish in Scotland as a whole and across the wider Irish diaspora, were not a homogeneous group, can only add to our overall understanding of the Irish in Scotland and of the Irish abroad.

87 S. Gilley, 'The Roman Catholic church and the nineteenth century Irish diaspora', *Journal of Ecclesiastical History*, 35 (1984), 193.

'All Irishmen of good character': the Hibernian Society of Glasgow, 1792–1824[1]

AMY O'REILLY

During the late eighteenth and early nineteenth centuries, the friendly society move-ment performed an important function as a safety net for many members of the working-class population throughout the British Isles. Especially popular in areas of growing industrialization, these societies, though occasionally viewed with scepti-cism, were increasingly seen by social reformers and the government as a positive venue for self-help amongst the working class (though they were not restricted to such) and as a means of reducing the overall cost of poor relief.[2] In exchange for a small entrance fee and a regular contribution, friendly societies provided for a number of needs and offered a range of services, among them giving members the ability to take some precautionary steps against temporary loss of income and the means to ensure a dignified burial for themselves and their immediate family. Additionally, many friendly societies acted as a means of drawing together members of ethnic or religious communities, or individuals with a particular political bent or social outlook. Building on the earlier work of P.H.J.H. Gosden, a number of recent studies have addressed various aspects of the friendly society movement in England and Wales, but less interest has been shown in the role of friendly societies in Irish or Scottish society, the exception being the well-deserved and growing attention that is being paid to the Orange and Ribbon movements in both countries.[3] Lack of atten-tion should not, however, be interpreted as an indication of the absence of friendly societies from these areas, and as much can be learned from in-depth analyses of Scottish or Irish societies as can be learned from studies of their admittedly more numerous English and Welsh counterparts.

1 Partial funding for research was provided by the Stuart Fund of the Department of History at the University of New Brunswick. 2 P.H. J.H. Gosden, *The friendly societies in England, 1815–1875* (Manchester, 1961), p. 2; Eric Hopkins, *Working class self-help in nineteenth century England* (Birmingham, 1995), pp 4, 10, 14, 25. 3 On friendly societies in Ireland, see A.D. Buckley, 'On the club: friendly societies in Ireland', *Irish Economic and Social History*, 14 (1987), 39–58. See also Máirtín Ó Catháin, 'Bullet moulders and blackthorn men: a comparative study of Irish nationalist secret society culture in mid-nineteenth century Scotland and Ulster', in R.J. Morris & Liam Kennedy (eds), *Ireland and Scotland: order and disorder, 1600–2000* (Edinburgh, 2005), pp 157–8; Elaine McFarland, *Protestants first: Orangeism in 19th century Scotland* (Edinburgh, 1990).

By the late eighteenth century, a number of friendly societies could be found in the city of Glasgow and its environs, ranging from occupationally based groups such as the Calton Weavers' Society to ethnic support organizations such as the Glasgow Highland Association.[4] Though few of Glasgow's friendly societies were restricted to the Irish themselves or to those with ties to Ireland, many were assumed (rightly) to contain a majority Irish membership. Loyal Orange Lodges, which often provided a number of the same benefits as friendly societies, and other specifically Orange-associated funeral and benefit societies were the most notable of these. The Glasgow Orange Union Funeral Society, for example, provided benefits for members around Calton and Mile End in the city.[5] Parallel Catholic funeral and benefit societies also existed in Glasgow and were more numerous after the completion of St Andrew's Cathedral in 1816 and the subsequent growth of an established Catholic presence in the city. Though the Irish were largely absent from the Catholic church's hierarchical authority in the early decades of the century, the large and growing proportion of the Irish among Glasgow's Catholic population practically ensured their participation, and the Catholic church's support of these societies was in no small part a direct result of its desire to refocus the attention of immigrant Irishmen from Ribbon societies and the pub culture that accompanied them, and which, as Anna Clark has shown, played an important role in the life of the working man.[6] Though not as immediately visible as the Orange presence in the city, there was nonetheless a documented and established Ribbon network in Glasgow in the first half of the nineteenth century.[7] Like the Orange Lodges, Ribbonism was a direct import from Ireland.

The Hibernian Society of Glasgow is a fascinating example of one of the many friendly societies existing in the city at the time, and one of the few outside of the religious or sectarian milieu that primarily served the Irish immigrant community. Like many societies it was relatively short-lived, though it did survive longer than some. And though a smaller friendly society movement open to women did exist in some parts of Britain, the Glasgow society was, like the majority of societies, open only to men. As well, it faced a number of financial setbacks over the years; this was a typical problem facing smaller friendly societies at the time.[8] In the thirty-two documented years of its existence, however, the Hibernian Society provides an espe-

4 On the Highland Society, see Charles W.J. Withers, 'Kirk, club and culture change: Gaelic chapels, Highland societies and the urban Gaelic subculture in eighteenth-century Scotland', *Social History*, 4:1 (1985), 171–92. 5 McFarland, *Protestants first*, p. 50. See also, Glasgow Orange Union Funeral Society Articles, 1841 N[ational] A[rchives of] S[cotland], FS1/16/108. 6 See Anna Clark, *The struggle for the breeches: gender and the making of the British working class* (Berkeley & London, 1995). See also the Airdrie St Patrick Catholic Friendly Society Records, NAS, FS1/16/11); Glasgow St Andrew Catholic Society Records, NAS FS1/16/116; and Glasgow St John's Catholic Friendly Society Records, NAS FS1/16/117. 7 Ó Catháin, 'Bullet moulders', 157. 8 On problems of sustainability for small friendly societies, see, for example, Audrey Fisk, 'The friendly societies and local history', *Local Historian* 29:2 (1999), 92.

cially welcome insight into the lives of a particularly understudied segment of the Irish diaspora population, the Protestant Irish immigrant community in Scotland. The society itself was established with a minimum of fanfare, and an analysis of the entries in its minute book, which survives and contains documentation of regular meetings, elections, and other society business conducted between the years 1792 and 1824, reveals a number of general trends about the community that both ties its experience to that of the larger Irish immigrant one as well as shows an option for the expression of an Irish identity of a more modest and non-political sort.

On 16 June 1792, a group of Glasgow merchants, artisans and tradesmen met at the home of changekeeper Andrew Menzies to promote 'the continual society for the benefit of all Irishmen whose character entitles them ... also Scotch men and others who have been three full years in Ireland or such as are married to an Irishman's widow or daughter'.[9] Sixteen men, including Menzies, signed the charter, the entry fee was set at 3s. with dues of 4s. 4d. payable in quarterly increments, and £26 12d. was collected to begin the work of the society.[10] A few weeks later, on 30 June, the group met at Lemuel Wiers' home in the Saltmarket and on 31 August in Bridgeton, to look over and discuss the orders and articles of other friendly societies upon which they might base their regulations. By 14September, the core group were ready to advertise for members in the *Glasgow Mercury Journal* and the *Glasgow Advertiser* and soon after, the society began meeting semi-monthly to elect officers, discuss group business and most significantly, lend sums of money to members in good standing who were able to provide guarantors. Except in times of low funds, the Society was able to extend a number of these loans, usually averaging about £20. In at least three cases between 1792 and 1824, however, the society had sufficient capital to grant loan requests of £80 to £100, and these were given in exchange for property bonds as surety. In 1811 the society advanced loans of £15 each to three other friendly societies, the Gorbals, Drygate Toll and Rottenrow Board of Union Societies, enabling them to continue in their own interests.[11] Aside from this, the society maintained funds to a level enabling it to continue its main stated purposes – the distribution of monies for the funeral expenses of members and their immediate families and the payment of 'bedfast" and 'walking' aliment to those members in need of support in times of incapacity.

Unlike the Orange, Ribbon, or religious societies, the Hibernian Society seems not to have existed to serve either religious or ethnic community exclusively. While a man was required to be judged of 'good moral character' to be admitted, none of the thirteen articles describing terms of membership mention religious affiliation of

9 H[ibernian] S[ociety of] G[lasgow] M[inute] B[ook], (1792–1824), 16 June 1792. Glasgow City Archives, Mitchell Library, TD200/7. Note also the term 'changekeeper', a denotation of an inn-keeper. 10 HSMB, Membership article 9, 'Terms of Entry and Quarter Accounts'. 11 HSMB, 25 Nov. 1812.

any type. Rather, ethnic identity and financial standing took priority. In addition to being in 'a visible way of supporting himself and any family if he has any', a potential member was required to be 'an Irishman born, and Irishman or [Irish]woman's son, a members' son, or one who has been three full years in Ireland, or is married to an Irishman's widow or daughter'.[12] The significance of a specific Irish affiliation being upheld, it was some aspect of a self-professed Irish identity that led a man to join this particular society, for as has been stated, there existed no dearth of other options from which he might choose.

A perusal of the names of Hibernian Society officers and benefit recipients in the early days following its establishment tends to reflect families of primarily Scottish or British ancestry –Menzies, Hunter, Craig, Montgomery, McEwan, Donaldson, Agnew, Campbell, names also traditionally associated with the Protestants of Ireland – yet the minute book, concurrent with the development of the society, increasingly suggests a more diverse population. One begins to see with regularity names more traditionally associated with the Catholic Irish – Devlin, McMullen, Quin, Kelly, O'Brien, O'Rourke, Doherty, Docherty. Although it is impossible to definitively declare the religious affiliation of a single individual based on surname, the growing appearance of ethnically diverse names, especially when seen in conjunction with other evidence, such as occasional requests from the society for proof of infirmity from a parish priest, may be indicative of cross-community participation.[13] Even if a number of these individuals were members of the established church, it remains likely that a number of them may have been Catholic. It is in the predominance of apparently Protestant and ethnically Scottish names, however, that much of the significance of the Hibernian Society for the purpose of this study lies. For it is these men who on the surface seemed least likely to choose a specifically Irish-associated organization in which to invest their money and time whilst living in a Scottish environment.

Many aspects of the Protestant Irish immigrant experience mirrored that of the Catholic Irish immigrant, and data gleaned from the Hibernian Society minute book reflects some of these commonalities. The fact that the majority of Catholic Irish immigrants to Glasgow were from the counties of Ulster quite probably played a role in this commonality, though, as will be shown later, it could also imply a certain amount of animosity between the two.[14] In the case of the individuals who joined

---

12 HSMB, Membership Article 2, 'The persons entitled to be entered members'. Membership was extended to the son of an Irishwoman on 18 Sept. 1807. See HSMB, 18 Sept. 1807. **13** There has, however, been at least one attempt to categorize immigrants in order to first name. See for example, John Foster, Muir Houston & Chris Madigan, 'Distinguishing Catholics and Protestants among Irish immigrants to Clydeside: a new approach to immigration and ethnicity in Victorian Britain', *Irish Studies Review*, 10:2 (2002), 171–192. **14** See, for example, the *Royal commission on the condition of the poorer classes in Ireland. Appendix G – report on the state of the Irish poor in Great Britain*, 1835, evidence of Mr George Burns, part owner and agent of the Belfast and Glasgow Steam-boat Company, p. 103; evidence of John Cameron, agent of the Londonderry Steam Packet Company, p. 104; evidence of Revd Andrew Scott, Roman Catholic bishop of Glasgow, p. 105; evidence

the Hibernian Society, however, it is important to recognize that the trends reflected were those typical of the lifestyle of the Irish immigrant who was sufficiently solvent to have the means to join a society, at least at the time of his initial entrance. Occupationally, membership of the society largely consisted of the ranks of somewhat better off artisans or more skilled workers, though only a very small number were successful enough to merit listings in the *Glasgow Directory*, a compilation of the city's businesses, businessmen and notables, a fact which points to a rather low to modest level of class rank among the society's membership. However, the requirements of admission included the purchase of a copy of the articles of membership, in order that a member may not 'pretend ignorance' to the rules of aliment, other benefit, or the system of fines. Such a requirement implied that members were of a class wherein at least a minimal education, in this case the ability to both read and comprehend the articles as written, was expected.[15]

Throughout the period covered by the minute book, approximately 400 individuals are mentioned by name. Of these, eighty-six names appear in conjunction with a specific occupation and/or location of residence. Most of these members were listed as requestors of loans or aliment, guarantors for loans, or as executive members of the society in whose homes meetings were occasionally held. When viewed together, the occupational and residential data are reflective of the wider community. An analysis of the locations of residence mentioned in association with these names reveals a clear correlation with those areas traditionally associated with a high concentration of Irish settlement – thirty-seven individuals, or a little less than half, were listed in conjunction with the areas of Bridgeton, Calton, and Anderston.[16] By 1825, these three districts comprised the highest concentration of textile manufacture in the city, and the large population of Irish there reflected the importance of the textile industry for the immigrant community.[17] Although occupational demographics of this group did not reflect an exclusively textile-industry orientation, many of the listed occupations would have functioned in support of the basic industrial and residential makeup of their respective districts. In Bridgeton, for example, nine of the twenty-one occupation-mentioned individuals were identified as weavers and six as either changekeepers or innkeepers. Of the remaining six, there were three grocers, a vintner, a mason, and a smith. In Calton, changekeepers dominated, comprising half of the fourteen total occupationally identified members in that district. An additional thirty-two individuals, slightly more than a third of the total, were listed as being residents of the city of Glasgow, indicating the city centre rather than one of Glasgow's outlying districts. Some individuals listed as residing in the city

of Mr David McCulloch, agent to Robert Walker's weaving house in Glasgow, p. 151; and evidence of the Rev. Richard Sinott, priest, p. 152. **15** HSMB Article 9, 'The Terms of Entry, and Quarter Accounts.' **16** Data compiled from the HSMB. Specific occupational breakdown for these districts: Bridgeton: Weaver – 9; Changekeeper – 5; Grocer – 3; 1 each of Innkeeper, Vintner, Mason, Smith. Calton: Changekeeper – 7, Wright – 2, Grocer – 2; 1 each of Vintner, Portioner, Surgeon. Anderston – 1 each of Wright, Weaver. **17** Michael Pacione, *Glasgow: the socio-spatial development of the city* (Chichester, 1995), p. 68.

itself were more specifically placed in Banns Wynd, Kirk Street, Bells Street, the Trongate, Gallowgate, and the Saltmarket. Samuel Weir, in whose home meetings were occasionally held, was identified as being a changekeeper located 'above the Cross of Glasgow'.[18] Despite the concentration of these specifically mentioned members on the north side of the Clyde, several felt close enough ties to the society to travel across the river from Tradeston and the Gorbals in order to participate in the Society's proceedings, with the listed occupations of these men including a spirit dealer, a cabinetmaker, and a surgeon. In later years, these areas south of the Clyde would take over as centres for new immigrants, of whom the Irish continued to form the largest percentage. Within the city's central districts, general occupational distribution was wider, though a full half of the total consisted of men identified as either vintners or owners of public houses.[19]

The homes of a number of vintners and changekeepers served as meeting places for the society, and these men often served as president or in some other executive office. At other times the society paid for venues, particularly at the larger quarterly meetings where dues were collected. Such a practice indicates not only a certain level of solvency, but also the need for space for a greater membership than the core group indicated by name in the minute book might otherwise indicate. Over the years, the society paid for meeting space at the Burgher Meeting House on Campbell Street, the Kirk Street Session House, and the North Albion Street Session House, all of which were located in areas with large Irish-born populations. In 1806, a quarterly meeting, apparently well attended, was held at the Barony Church in the city.[20] That the Barony Church, at which worshipped members of the High Kirk, acted as a meeting locale can perhaps be interpreted as further proof of the overall Protestant nature of the society in its early years.

For those able to satisfy the requirements of membership, keeping their dues out of arrears and following the stipulated procedures of application, the benefits could be immense. Private loans and aliment benefits could have, in certain circumstances, proven to be life-changing sums, allowing the member to speculate in business, save a troubled enterprise, or stave off insolvency at times of unexpected illness or disability. The Hibernian Society provided a level of sickness benefit comparable to that of other friendly societies of the time, and made relief available to eligible members incapacitated by 'sickness, lameness, old age or indisposition of body or mind'.[21] A 'distressed member confined to his bed' received 5s. per week, while one able to walk about, but still unable to work, received 3s. per week.[22] Allotted benefit

18 HSMB, 27 Dec. 1793. 19 The specific occupational breakdown for the city of Glasgow consisted of: vintner – 15; changekeeper – 5; weaver – 4; tailor – 2; and 1 each of: portioner, merchant, stationer, public house owner, grocer, brocker. 20 HSMB, 19 Sept. 1806. 21 See, for example, Norman Murray, *The Scottish handloom weavers, 1790–1850: a social history* (Edinburgh, 1978), pp 141–2. 22 Occasionally when the society was low in funds, these amounts were somewhat reduced. See for example, HSMB, 17 Sept. 1824. At

could be continued for a year, at which point a member still unable to work was to be placed on a superannuated list and receive 1*s.* per week throughout the duration of his incapacity. After recovering, a member was again eligible for full benefits following a year of paying regular dues, a responsibility suspended at the time of his illness.[23]

Checks were in place to ensure the appropriateness of applications and officers of the society made regular visits to members collecting aliment to access their eligibility. Aliment recipients living outside of the realm of an easy visit, described in the articles as being in the districts of Bridgeton, Rutherglen, Calton, Glasgow city, Anderston, Gorbals, Tradeston, or Camlachie, were required to provide a statement of their condition given by a minister and a parish elder along with their request. Though it was not the norm, it was not altogether uncommon for the visiting committee to find a man faking his condition, at which point he faced a fine, usually of 6*s.*, and repayment of the disability benefits that he had already received.[24] Mostly these transgressions involved being found to be 'walking about' whilst technically on bedfast aliment, but on at least two occasions members were found to be in their workshops, and for one member, continuing 'proof' of his incapacity to work being given by his inability to 'see some horse races as he intended', was apparently not sufficient for the continuation of benefits.[25] In the vast majority of cases, it appears that the fine was collected and the aliment money repaid with little resistance. Occasionally the offending member was punished merely by having his previously approved bedfast aliment reduced to the lower 'walking about' aliment.[26] Accusations of fraudulent collection were taken seriously, and false accusations discouraged.

Maintaining a sense of personal honour within the society was a required part of sustaining the respectability of the society itself. The membership seemed to be supportive of this system of discipline and this surely played some role in the fairly willing acceptance of punishment, or at least the general lack of recorded resistance to it. Some members went out of their way to maintain their good standing with the society even when they found themselves in a spot of trouble otherwise. One of the more interesting anecdotes to be found in the minutes is the case of society president Thomas Douglas, who in April 1804 had the forethought to call several of the society's managing officers to his home to 'Remove the Society's Box as he was Badly and [since] Some other Occurences ... [were] likely to take place, they judged it prudent to comply'.[27] They collected the box, taking it to the home of the collector, and upon making an immediate accounting of its contents, found all the money to be in place. Douglas made no appeal for aliment for 'being badly' and the 'other occurrences' were not explained at the time. A replacement president was

this time, the executive committee voted, based on lack of funds, to temporarily reduce available aliment to 4*s.* bedfast and 2*s. 6d.* walking aliment. **23** HSMB, Membership Article 10, 'Subsistence, how, and to whom to be given'. **24** Ibid. **25** HSMB, 13 Oct. 1794; 3 Mar. 1803; 13 Apr. 1808; 15 Sept. 1808; 28 Jan. 1812; 16 Apr. 1812; 19 Mar. 1813. **26** HSMB, 3 Mar. 1803. **27** HSMB, 5 Apr. 1804.

quickly elected though after missing a number of meetings, Douglas began to reappear with regularity in the minute book.

All of this might be easily dismissed if one did not notice a later entry, in 1816. Normally an active member, Douglas again disappears temporarily from the book. Soon, the committee began to discuss a bond the society held on the property of 'Thomas Douglas, at present confined on a charge of forgery'.[28] Perhaps Douglas had already had encounters with the authorities before? At the very least, it is of anecdotal interest that one man had such a dedicated sense of responsibility to the society. On the other hand, on at least one occasion a treasurer was found guilty of mishandling the monies in the box, though he promptly repaid.

Overall, proper deportment at meetings was emphasized, and the membership articles outlined fines for any individual found to be drunk, swearing or using abusive language toward another member in a meeting.[29] No one was exempt, at least from the latter. On 27 October 1808, during an emergency meeting called to elect a new collector, Peter Cook was fined 2*d.* for swearing the oath 'Devil a bit', on 17 June 1814, Evans Hunter, who had been active in the society since its inception and had previously held several offices, was fined 5*s.* for 'swearing five times in the name of God' during a meeting to elect new officers, and on 1 August 1816, then president John McLean was fined 2*s.* for 'abusive language' towards committee member Duncan McCormack, when the validity of the president's calling of the meeting was questioned.[30] Whilst no incidents of drunkenness in meetings appear in the minute book, one John Boone, who at the time was living in Ireland, was fined and removed from the benefit roll 'in consequences of a strong report [that he had] been engaged in Illegal Distillation in the month of December 1814 while receiving aliment'.[31] That said, the society was not particularly interested in promoting temperance. More then once, meetings were followed by the executive committee and, at times, a number of the membership retiring to a public house or other abode for suitable refreshment, a practice that was at least once claimed by the officers to be a necessary expense to be covered by the society's coffers.[32] Since most friendly societies met in pubs or other venues where alcohol flowed freely, a fact which was a source of contention for many of their critics, this practice was not particularly unusual. And, even in John Boone's case, it is unclear whether the society perceived his greater crime to be the illicit distillation, or being found to be 'working' at some activity whilst receiving aliment. The idea of friendly societies meeting in pubs and involving any aspect of a drink culture grew increasingly contentious from the onset of the nineteenth century, when 'respectability' began to be more and more tied to middle-class ideas of proper deportment, including the middle-class belief that pub culture should be eradicated from working class life.[33]

28 HSMB, 1 Aug. 1816; 22 Oct. 1816. 29 HSMB, Membership Article 13, 'Disorderly and obstinate Members [*sic*] to be fined'. 30 HSMB, 27 Oct. 1808; 17 June 1814; 1 Aug. 1816. 31 HSMB, 30 Apr. 1816. 32 HSMB, 17 Mar. 1809. 33 See Fisk, p. 93 and Elizabeth Kowalski Wallace, 'The needs of strangers: friendly societies and insurance societies in late eighteenth-century England', *Eighteenth Century Life*, 24 (2000), 62. On the friendly society

Proper deportment at meetings was an expectation, but just as in any group where a number may gather, the society was immune neither to petty squabbles nor to personality conflicts. The case of Hugh O'Rourke provides a rather colourful example of conflict that escalated beyond the level of minor disagreement. In 1812, O'Rourke petitioned for aliment, which the society duly granted. O'Rourke had previously been elected an officer, in September 1811, but had been replaced for non-attendance, presumably due to his illness. When his replacement, Charles Black, and another officer, John McLean, went to visit O'Rourke, as was customary to confirm the validity of a member's petition for aliment, he refused to 'let his leg or foot be examined' by either, insisting instead on producing a note from a surgeon of his own election. This response was in direct violation of the set regulations.[34] Eventually, O'Rourke was fined 5s. for his insubordinate behaviour, ordered to reimburse the society for the aliment already paid him, and on 20 April 1813 warned to attend a meeting to mitigate his fine and to pay his quarterly accounts or be struck from the membership roll. When O'Rourke failed to appear, he was, as threatened, struck from the roll.[35]

The news of his banishment must have travelled quickly. On 30 April, the then-president, Peter McCorry, called a general meeting to announce that O'Rourke was about to enter a law plea for his failure to receive aliment and was demanding reinstatement.[36] After a debate, the executive committee decided, that in order to avoid the trouble of a lawsuit, reinstatement would be allowed, assuming that O'Rourke paid his fine. O'Rourke did not seem particularly interested in accepting the gesture. He refused to receive the letter of reinstatement sent him, and went forward with his complaint, which was served on the first of May.[37] After a series of daily meetings in which the minutes were reviewed, 'men of business' consulted, and options discussed, the executive committee finally capitulated and agreed to O'Rourke's demand, even going so far as to agree to pay for half of the expense of O'Rourke's lawyer as well as to bear all of the additional expenses incurred as a result of the suit. While the minutes do not reveal the reasoning behind the committee's collapse, other than a wish to avoid the trouble that might be involved in a lawsuit, that O'Rourke was eventually able to hold the sympathy of the majority of the voting membership of the society is clear; on 17 September 1813, he was elected president.[38]

In addition to its role in providing sickness benefit, the group also acted as a burial society, a function of utmost importance at the time. Burial societies were quite heavily relied upon by a large percentage of the working class, as little was considered so undignified as a pauper's burial.[39] A member not in arrears at the time of his

movement as a means of expression of respectability for the working class, see Evelyn Lord, 'The friendly society movement and the respectability of the rural working class', *Rural History*, 8:2 (1997), 165–173 and Simon Cordery, 'Friendly societies and the discourse of respectability in Britain, 1825–1875', *Journal of British Studies*, 34 (1995), 35–58. **34** HSMB, 20 Sept. 1811; 16 Apr. 1812. HSMB, Membership Article 10, 'Subsistence, how, and to whom to be given'. **35** HSMB, 20 Apr. 1813. **36** HSMB, 30 Apr. 1813. **37** HSMB, 1 May 1813, 3 May 1813. **38** HSMB, 4 May 1813 and 17 Sept. 1813. **39** Murray, *Scottish*

death could count on the society to provide £2 to defray the cost of his own funeral. He could also rely on the society to provide £2 for his wife's funeral and his widow remained eligible for funeral benefit after his death, as did his unmarried children.[40] If a member, or his widow, were to die with no relations, the society president was bound by the articles to arrange that they be 'decently interred' and the funeral attended both by him and by a number of the society's officers. If a family requested the presence of the president or the officers at a member's funeral, they were additionally honour-bound to attend, with any officers warned to attend a funeral and failing to do so to be fined 6*d*.[41] In the thirty-two years covered by the minute book, and the number of funerals mentioned or listed in the accounts, this particular fine was never assessed on a single president or officer. Unfortunately the minute book is uneven in its recording of the number of funerals paid for, but in some years as many as seven were noted.[42]

While there is no definitive account of the exact date of the Hibernian Society's demise, there is little evidence of its existence after the end of the minute book, at which time membership was already declining. Perhaps the society fell victim to the same fate that faced many of the independent societies toward the middle of the nineteenth century, primarily competition for membership from the much larger affiliated societies and from trade unions.[43] Indeed, in some ways it is perhaps remarkable that it was able to exist and even prosper for so long, given that so many other small societies failed during this period.

While evidence exists for cross-community participation in the Hibernian Society, it is still clear that the *majority* of the membership was either of Irish Protestant or what

handloom weavers, p. 133; *Minute book of the incorporation of weavers of Calton and Blackfauld*, Glasgow City Archives, ML T-TH5–3; *Minute Book of the Freeman Weavers of Calton 1786–1872* (ML), cited in Murray, *Scottish handloom weavers*, p. 133. See also Hopkins, *Working-class self-help*, pp 22–3.   **40** HSMB, Membership Article 11th. Members [*sic*] funerals, and sums given to the wives, their widows and children, or relations.   **41** Ibid.   **42** Identifiable burial expenses reveal the following tallies for funerals for members and their eligible family: in 1800 – 1; 1802 – 1; 1805 – 2; 1807 – 6; 1808 – 3; 1809 – 2; 1811 – 7; 1812 – 4; 1814 – 5; 1815 – 4; 1816 – 6; 1817 – 3; 1817 – 3; 1817–1818 – 9; 1819 – 4; 1820 – 7; 1821 – 4; 1822 –5; 1824 – 5, for a total of 78, including 47 members and 29 wives and 2 widows. Additional burials are known to have taken place, but names and per-burial amounts of outlay were unspecified (for example, outlays for 1801 were recorded as 'funerals now and formerly').   **43** A number of historians of the friendly society movement have discussed rise of affiliated societies and their role in usurping the primacy of smaller local friendly societies. See, for example, Fisk, p. 92, Michael Watson, 'Mutual improvement societies in nineteenth century Lancashire', *Journal of Educational Administration and History*, 22:2, 4, and Robert Humphreys, 'The development of friendly societies in nineteenth-century Surrey', *Local Historian*, 35:3 (2005), 190–2 and 198. Later in the nineteenth century, the rise of penny banks in Glasgow would further aid in the demise of the local friendly society movement there. See Duncan M. Ross, '"Penny Banks" in Glasgow, 1850–1914', *Financial History Review*, 9 (2002), 21–39.

would today be termed 'Ulster-Scots' heritage or identification. The importance of this cannot be understated, as the strong Irish quality of the society infers the presence of at least some Irish self-identification on the part of members and contradicts the assertion that Irish Protestants, especially those of an ethnically Scottish background, chose either of two venues upon 'returning' to Scotland – absorption and cultural assimilation into Scottish society or sole identification with specifically sectarian organisations or ideology.

Donald MacRaild has asserted that for both Protestant and Catholic Irish, the emigrant experience served as a seedbed for 'exaggerated senses of identity', with the creation of specific institutional outlets for this identity becoming more important in the early-to-mid nineteenth century.[44] And, in his study of Scotch-Irish identity in the American South, Kirby Miller argues that, for many of the early immigrants, Irishness was more important than Scottishness or Protestantism. He also notes that in the early nineteenth century, the most active Hibernian and Irish-American nationalist societies were usually headed by Ulster Protestant immigrants or those of Ulster Protestant ancestry.[45] That Ulster Protestants in other areas of the diaspora might have felt a similar tie to their homeland and have expressed it in a mixed venue is perhaps therefore not so surprising. Considering other historical examples of promoted Protestant/Catholic unity, in the ideology of the United Irishmen for example, it is also not unlikely that certain men within the Irish Protestant community would have felt comfortable about cross-community interaction in a friendly society, though how far this extended is debatable given that sectarianism in practice was not unknown within the United Irishmen or in any other society in which cross-community ideology was espoused. Indeed, that many Irish Protestant immigrants did carry old antipathies towards Catholics with them to Glasgow is undeniable. Preachers with strong anti-Catholic views spoke in churches, regularly gave anti-Popery sermons, and often provided sermons at Orange functions.[46] The Revd Thomas Chalmers, social advocate, founder of the Free Church of Scotland,

---

44 McFarland, *Protestants first*, p. 31, in Donald M. MacRaild (ed.), *Irish migrants in modern Britain, 1750–1922* (New York, 1999), p. 9. [?] **45** Kirby Miller, '"Scotch-Irish", "Black-Irish" and "Real Irish": emigrants and identities in the old south', in Andy Beilenberg (ed.), *The Irish diaspora* (Harlow, 2000), p. 143; M.F. Funchion, *Irish-American voluntary organizations* (Westport, CT, 1983), pp 117, 114–15, 239, in Miller, '"Scotch-Irish"', p. 143. **46** See for example, *Lectures on Popery: delivered in Glasgow, at the request of the Glasgow Protestant Association by the Rev. John Forbes, et al.* (Glasgow, 1836). The work consists of a collection of 13 sermons given in the city that year, the contents of which clearly illustrate a popular anti-popery slant. See also John Campbell Colquhoun. *Address of the Glasgow Protestant Association, to the members of the Church of Scotland* (Glasgow, 1836) and *Ireland: popery and priestcraft the cause of her misery and crime* (Glasgow, 1836); John Leech, *Irish church or report of speeches delivered in the city hall of Glasgow by Rev. William Burnside B.D. and Rev. John Flanagan, A.M. on the 2nd of November 1866 at the annual soiree of Orangemen of Glasgow* (Armagh, 1867); and, W.B. Moffatt, *A homily on Protestant unity and concord: an address delivered at the opening of the Grand Orange Lodge of Scotland at the general half-yearly meeting, on Friday, the 19th of June, 1863, in the Orange Hall, 33 Candleriggs Street* (Glasgow, 1863).

and one time minister of the Tron Church and later the large St John's parish in Glasgow, was a particularly influential public speaker and advocate of the anti-Popery movement (though he did also assert the need for a sympathetic tolerance of one's Catholic neighbours per se).[47] A strong evangelical movement and the semi-regular surges of anti-Popery sentiment that characterized the Glasgow religious and political scene would have bolstered pre-existing feelings of distrust and enmity among the Irish Protestant population of the city.

The superintendent of the Gorbals police reported to the 1835 committee investigating the Irish poor in Great Britain that 'the rows of the Irish are chiefly among themselves, betwixt the Catholics and Protestants'; yet as James Reed, a surgeon of the Kilmarnock Dispensary, noted, 'the well behaved of either sort always get out of the way when they see any dispute likely to end in a disturbance'.[48] Perhaps the Hibernians can be seen as representative of this 'well behaved' element. For many Irish Protestants, so often associated primarily with the disturbances of Orange parades and other sectarian conflicts, the presence of a milder, more positive venue in which to participate provides evidence of the less obvious, of a part of the multi-faceted nature of Irish immigrant society which still remains to be explored.

As an individual society, the Hibernian Society of Glasgow performed a number of functions characteristic of friendly societies, primarily the distribution of sick and funeral benefits, while also addressing more middle to lower-middle class concerns such as the granting of business loans. As well, the society provided a means of ethnic expression and social support for its members. In contrast to membership in the Orange Order or any of the Catholic secret or church-related societies, membership in the Hibernian Society was not restricted by religious or political affiliation. The Hibernian Society opened its membership to anyone, or rather any man, with ties to Ireland by birth or blood and it provided benefits for any member with the ability to pay his dues. In this way it was ideologically more reflective of the Freemasons, who as Neil Jarman, in his study of parades and visual displays in Northern Ireland, notes were largely anti-sectarian and integrated in Ulster at the time.[49]

---

47 Both because of his large parish community and due to his public visibility, Chalmers' influence is unquestionable. His condemnation of Catholic church doctrine was aimed at showing the 'light' to the Catholic population. For an example of one such sermon, see Thomas Chalmers, *The doctrine of Christian charity applied to the case of religious difference: a sermon preached before the Auxiliary Society, Glasgow to the Hibernian Society for Establishing Schools, and Circulating the Holy Scriptures in Ireland* (Glasgow, 1818). Note that the Hibernian Society for establishing schools was a different organisation than the Hibernian Society which is the focus of this essay.   48 *Royal commission on the condition of the poorer classes in Ireland. Appendix G – report on the State of the Irish poor in Great Britain*, 1835. Evidence of Mr George Jeffrey, superintendent of the police of the Gorbals, p. 120; evidence of James Reed, M.D., p. 144.   49 Neil Jarman, *Material conflicts: parades and visual displays in Northern Ireland* (Oxford, 1997), pp 50–3.

Both the Catholic and Protestant Irish communities in Glasgow had an ability and interest in developing and maintaining a distinct sense of community and a cultural awareness that both divided and united them. Though considerably smaller and less influential than other ethnically based societies such as that formed by Scottish highlanders (in the form of the Highland Association), in theory the Hibernian Society functioned to much the same end: as a venue for ethnic expression. Though it lacked the ability to put on the large cultural displays or form the charity-base the Highland Association was able to, it nonetheless is representative of the desire of the group to bond on the basis of a common heritage. As a liberal fraternity, imbued with the self-help ethos, the Hibernian Society is further evidence of the multiple options for the expression of Irish identity which existed in late eighteenth- and early nineteenth-century Glasgow.

Michael Collins and Scotland

MÁIRTÍN Ó CATHÁIN

Michael Collins is reported to have visited Scotland but once in his life and that, significantly, was en route to England. As was probably reported in much of the emigrant press elsewhere in the Irish diaspora, at the time of his death he had been preparing a visit that would now never be made. The obligatory pathos that permeated every post-mortem analysis of Collins' career was particularly ardent among the Irish abroad, maybe because they felt that Collins was one their own. His apparent lack of interest in Scotland, however, and his transitory visit, or more especially his eventual destination of London, reflects much of the anglocentric rub of his early years as much as it poses the question of why examine Collins and Scotland at all. The former in many ways explains the latter. It was precisely because of Collins' disinterest in Scotland and the workings of his elaborate network there that many of his political and personal connections unravelled. Scotland, and Glasgow in particular, became the primary weapon against Collins in the hands of his enemies. Moreover, his standoffish relations with the more advanced elements of the Scottish nationalist movement rendered much of their ambitious planning for a Scottish uprising largely null and void.

Irish-Scotland has always played second fiddle to the wealthier and more influential Irish America and is similarly demoted by the intellectual power and networks of the Irish in England. Michael Collins understood this on two levels – firstly, as an Irishman – and perhaps as a west Cork Irishman, he recognized the importance of the Irish in the United States as pre-eminent in the diaspora – and secondly, as a young emigrant himself in the great metropolis of London to whose inhabitants Scotland appeared but a grey, desolate and cold northern 'other'. These views are apparent in his letters and although they underwent modification in the welter of combat and comradeship during the years 1916 to 1921, they remained more or less in place.

An irony of Michael Collins' career (and appellant to the 'great men' history more generally and the myths surrounding him) is that it was often largely the unacknowledged work and loyalty of his much-abused intermediaries in various locations that built his reputation. On their initiative and energy, as much as Collins' directives and orchestration, rests a good deal of the political and military success enjoyed by republican forces. His Scottish wire-pullers, Dan Branniff, Joseph Vize and Joe Furlong, among others, were not the mere automatons programmed in the Frongoch hothouse that some writers have portrayed, and while their loyalty needs to be addressed, it was their Irish Republican Brotherhood (IRB) oath as well as their friendship with Collins on which their fealty rested. Any discussion therefore about Michael Collins and Scotland should also be an analysis of the activities, ideas and impact of these men.

Unlike many leaders of Irish republicanism and Irish nationalism, Collins was not well-acquainted with Scotland. This is in contrast to many of his contemporaries: Griffith, Markievicz, Mellows and even de Valera had all visited Scotland at one time or another and spoke there.[1] Despite the presence of a handful of Corkmen among the Irish in Scotland's republican milieu, there was little or no linkage with which Collins would have been acquainted in his formative years. Even in later years, it is somewhat remarkable that fairly senior Corkonians in Glasgow's republican circles, such as Seán O'Shea and Con Phibbs escape mention in Collins' Scottish correspondence.[2] Part of this may be explicable in terms of the high mobility of the Irish in Britain generally with which Collins himself was personally familiar, but it is more obviously the result of a generally sketchy knowledge of Scotland.

It was only with the Easter Rising that Collins came into some contact with Irish republicans from Scotland in the cramped quarters of the so-called Kimmage Garrison in the grounds of the Plunketts' home that housed the 'overseas' sections of the Irish Volunteers. Most of the garrison found themselves at different outposts during the Rising and Collins was joined in the General Post Office by individuals from Scotland such as Charles Carrigan, a socialist from Denny in Stirlingshire, the Scottish nationalist Alex Carmichael, and the Dubliner Frank Scullin.[3] However, here again, Collins does not appear to have made any particular bond with those from Scotland. Perhaps given the strong Scottish nationalist sympathies of some of the Scottish Battalion they tended to see themselves as quite apart from their comrades in the 'English' sections of the Irish Volunteers. This was a nuance many historians who continue to write of the 'Irish in Britain' have missed, but even for years after partition, the veterans of the 1916 to 1923 period from Scotland organized themselves as a distinct body. Given the nature of Anglo-Irish relations it is perhaps easy to understand why Volunteers from London and Liverpool failed to assign themselves an 'English Battalion' title, even out of a sense of irony. It is possible though that Collins' sense of the refined sensibilities and urbane sophistication of the Edwardian London 'gent' and/or the cultural loci of the London Irish generally did not lend itself to a friendly bond with the rougher charms and leftist politics of the Glasgow

---

1 *Glasgow Observer*, 21 Mar. 1908; 25 Jan. 1908; 11 Dec. 1926. For de Valera and his previous visits see, statement of Patrick McCormick, N[ational] L[ibrary of] I[reland], MS. 15,337, p. 1; Pádraig Ó Baoighill, *Óglach na Rosann* (Baile Átha Cliath, 1994), p. 148.   2 *Irish Press*, 18 Oct. 1949; NLI, MS 15,337, p. 2.   3 *An tÓglach*, St Patrick's Day 1962; Easter 1963; Summer 1964; Easter 1965; Frank Gallagher Papers, NLI, MS 21,265, pp 61–5; M[ilitary] A[rchives of] I[reland], B[ureau of] M[ilitary] H[istory], Witness statements, WS/627; WS/1767, statements of Séamus Reader. Carrigan, who was also a member of the Independent Labour Party and Catholic Socialist Society, was killed in the O'Rahilly's fateful charge up Moore Street after the evacuation of the GPO.

Irish. Neverthless, the 'Scottish Brigade' as it became known, remained a coherent unit with their own identity and camaraderie, every bit as much as Scottish regiments in Flanders, though mixed among their fellow Irish exiles from England throughout the Rising and internment.[4]

Only two members of the Scottish Brigade, Patrick James Maguire and Joe Duffy, both Fermanagh men resident in Glasgow were present with Collins in Stafford and later in Frongoch. Another member, the acerbic Séamus Robinson, whose brother Joseph commanded the Brigade, spent some time in Stafford also with Collins but only one month in Frongoch. Whether he developed his disdain for Collins at this time is difficult to ascertain but his account of the camp resistance among the Kimmage men to conscription clashes quite directly with the role assigned Collins by his latest biographer. Peter Hart writes of Collins being a senior, if not the senior, voice of opposition to attempts by the British to force into the army those prisoners, like himself, who had British residency or birth. While his sources are as friendly towards Collins as Robinson was hostile, it is interesting that the latter singles out the London and Liverpool Volunteers for allowing themselves to be 'harried' in a way the 'Glasgow desperadoes' avoided by a unified stance and a declaration of their intention to shoot their officers should they be put in a British uniform.[5] As there only appears to have been a few Glasgow men in Frongoch, it is doubtful if they featured much in this argument which may have been more targeted at the English contingent, but written as it was in the 1940s and seasoned with Robinson's particular antipathy towards Collins, it falls mainly within the ambit of the 'auld enemy' Anglo-Scottish needle that the rivalry of the 'British' sections of the Volunteers rather bizarrely exhibited. Moreover, Robinson was not unused to a disingenuous or selective recollection of events as, for example, when he alleged in the famous 1922 Dáil attack on Collins' military record that he had come from London as he (Robinson) had from Glasgow in 1916, to avoid conscription. In fact, Robinson records no such reason for leaving Glasgow in his own memoir and recalls correctly that it was an IRB directive for men with engineering experience to report to Dublin that heralded his and other Glasgow Irish Volunteers' departure.[6]

One friendship made by Collins in Stafford and Frongoch that bore great fruit and not a little heartache was with a merchant seaman from Wexford named Joseph Vize (1881–1959) who became Collins' main organizer in Scotland from 1918 to 1920. Vize's father was a bank manager, and it may have been this rather than his

4 Private Papers of Éamonn Mooney, Commandant, Scottish Brigade IRA (1919–25), Minutes of Scottish Brigade, Old IRA Association (1947–55), in possession of Mrs Cathleen Knowles-McGuirk. I am grateful to Stephen Coyle and Cathleen Knowles-McGuirk for access to and use of these papers.   5 Peadar Livingstone, *The Fermanagh story* (Enniskillen, 1969), p. 280; Peter Hart, *Mick: the real Michael Collins* (London, 2006), pp 104–6; Frank Gallagher, NLI, MS 21,265, p. 65.   6 Hart, *Mick*, p.79; Tim Pat Coogan, *Michael Collins* (London, 1991), pp 305–6; NLI, Frank Gallagher Papers, MS 21,265, pp 60–1; MAI, BMH, witness statements, WS/272, statement of Daniel Branniff; WS/1767, statement of Séamus Reader.

knowledge of port and harbour controls that encouraged Collins to befriend him at this point, searching around as he was for career as well as political opportunities.[7] In the wake of internment Vize returned to the dangerous seas of the wartime Mediterranean and Collins to a position combining his financial and political talents in the National Aid and Volunteer Dependants Fund, and it was with IRB stalwart, Michael Staines that Collins first began to learn of Scottish reorganization efforts. With the notable exception then of Vize, Collins' networking skills established no connections with the Irish in Scotland, and possibly even intentionally or otherwise won enemies among them rather than friends.

With the exception of Séamus Robinson, the 1916 men from Scotland all returned to Scotland after imprisonment, a factor that may have made them exempt from much of the antipathy towards Collins' coterie of 'refugees' from England who took up residence, and their share of National Aid money, in Dublin from 1917 onwards.[8]

The IRB that re-constituted itself in 1917, and into which Michael Collins devoted increasing amounts of energy delivering a yield of contacts and supporters second to none in the separatist movement, was loved and loathed in almost equal measure. The former 'Glasgow desperado' and redoubtable rising star of the South Tipperary Volunteers, Séamus Robinson, had attended a meeting on release and did not like what he saw. He felt the organization had lost prestige in the Rising and its 'authority was moribund where not already dead'. With characteristic malice afore-thought he then walked out of the meeting disgusted with the 'Tammany Hall' attempts to capture control of the Volunteer executive, impressively, before the meeting actually even began, declaring never again to have anything to do with the 'sinister cabal', as he described it in a 1940's memoir.[9] Robinson's reaction may have been related to the particularly bad showing of the IRB in Scotland in 1916, the inquiry into which Collins, as secretary of the Brotherhood, became intimately involved with. The so-called military secretary of the Scottish IRB and a man referred to as the father of Sinn Féin in Scotland, Tom McDonnell from Tempo in Co. Fermanagh, had apparently failed to turn out for the Rising. Moreover, it was alleged he may even have been in Dublin and refused to take part, spiriting himself back to Glasgow after it ended.[10] Confused orders and police surveillance had left Scotland's IRB chief, Patrick McCormick, and his lieutenant, Daniel Branniff, chairman of the Glasgow Centres Board, marooned in Belfast while their men headed directly for Dublin. Some blamed John Mulholland, who had briefly held the

---

7 Hart, *Mick*, pp 110–11, 114. I am indebted to Major General Vize's sons, Joseph and John (also a major general, since retired), and also his grandson Joseph for their help and biographical information. **8** Hart, *Mick*, p. 145. **9** Frank Gallagher Papers, NLI, MS 21, 265, p. 18; Hart, pp 141–2. **10** John McGallogly statement, U[niversity] C[ollege] D[ublin] A[rchives], P60, p. 18; Éamonn Mooney Papers, application and statement of Thomas McDonnell, 627 Maryhill Road, Glasgow to Military Service Pensions Board, 4 July 1939; Michael Collins to Joe Vize, 3 Mar. 1920, Mulcahy Papers, UCDA, P7/A/11.

Scottish position on the Supreme Council, but resigned that position and his more
senior one as the body's President in opposition to plans to stage a rising during the
war. The immediate difficulty for Collins was to keep track of the case in the wake
of Patrick McCormick's resignation from the Council which came after, if not as a
result of, Thomas Ashe's death on hunger strike in September 1917.[11] McCormick
had not long been confirmed in the post and was obviously trusted by Collins and
his colleagues. Even so, the new IRB president, Seán McGarry, returned to Scotland
with McCormick to oversee the election that put him in post, as Collins probably
ensured his close collaborator, Michael Staines, acted as interlocutor and overseer of
the election of McCormick's replacement, Dan Branniff. Branniff, from Dromara,
Co. Down, had been in the Glasgow IRB since 1907 and also served briefly, as representative for Scotland, on the Supreme Council between 1912 and 1914. He was thus
an old hand by 1918 and remained in the job until the Treaty, which he may have
opposed, though he made clear in later years that his resignation from the Scottish
charge was a result of his taking up permanent residence in Belfast.[12]

Branniff's was not an easy task. After their release from prison, the former
dynamos of the republican movement in Glasgow, Joseph Robinson and Séamas
Reader, were involved with the two opposing factions which emerged during the
fallout over the IRB's performance in the Rising. Ironically, both men were arrested
together before the Rising and imprisoned, so neither was in a particularly good
position to know who fought and who shirked. Reader's affiliation was to those who
did not take part and his chief loyalty was to the Fianna and IRB, whereas Robinson
perhaps influenced by his brother gave his primary allegiance to the emergent Irish
Republican Army (IRA) and although he had been a member, he was wary of the
Brotherhood. It is unclear where Branniff stood in relation to this split, which
continued even after Robinson was arrested and imprisoned on gun-running
charges, but Collins certainly appears to have favoured more the Reader faction,
though he nonetheless orchestrated various informal arms smuggling operations via
individual Volunteers, IRB men, Cumann na mBan activists and even sympathetic
miners, de-mobbed soldiers and assorted civilians. Collins generally saw Scotland as
a bit of a mess. He was not in a position to do anything about it at this point, but
was clearly frustrated by the lack of clarity, validation and control. The bickering and
arrests were a familiar landscape and, indeed, Collins proved fairly adept at negoti-
ating these from a distance obviously with Branniff's help; but the relative chaos and
dearth of accountability on the chief issue of arms procurement was to a book-
keeper's mind completely unacceptable.[13]

11 McCormick statement, NLI, MS 15,337, pp 7–11; MAI, BMH, Witness statements,
WS/272, statement of Daniel Branniff, pp 2–6; WS/828, statement of James Byrne, pp 1–2;
WS/777, statement of Patrick Mills, pp 1–2. 12 McGallogly statement, UCDA, P60, pp
19–20; MAI, BMH, Witness statements, WS/272, pp 1–2. Branniff lived in Herbert Street in
Ardoyne and appears not to have involved himself in post-Treaty republicanism.
13 McGallogly statement, UCDA, P60, pp 18–19; Iain D. Patterson, 'The Activities of Irish
Republican Physical Force Organisations in Scotland, 1919–21', *Scottish Historical Review*,

Arms and ammunition did seep into Ireland from Scotland but Collins was dissat-isfied with what he regarded as the 'casual' nature of these shipments. By 1918 he was in a better position, as adjutant-general (and effective Director of Operations) firstly and then from the start of 1919 as Director of Intelligence, to take a firmer hold of events. Chance, as ever with Collins, made a timely appearance in the form of Joe Vize who had returned from the merchant marine after his ship was torpedoed and sunk by a German U-boat in June 1918. Mick's offer to his old comrade was scarcely more appealing: to go to Scotland, reign in and formalize structure and organisation, and most importantly, secure and increase the flow of arms and ammunition to Ireland. Had he been caught, as he came close to on more than one occasion, the prospect of going down with the *Clan Forbes* collier a hundred miles off the coast of Alexandria might not have seemed such a bad fate. Joe Robinson had been sentenced to ten years in Britain's most northerly prison, Peterhead, for one such shipment.[14] Vize accepted, however, and arrived in Scotland in late 1918 or early 1919, though almost certainly not in any capacity as a senior officer, as suggested by Patterson, nor with the remit apparently of sorting out the Glasgow warring factions, as Hart implies. He was certainly given the command of the Scottish Brigade (though nominally this was the responsibility of Glasgow barber, John Carney), but this seems to have come later – perhaps in 1920 – for it was primarily in an IRB capacity that Collins sent him, and it was the IRB who took for themselves the control of the supply chain of arms and ammunition.[15] A long-time colleague of Collins, Joe Furlong, who he had known since his London IRB days was also despatched to Scotland to help Vize. Together the two Wexfordmen quickly got down to business and, while Collins oversaw, much of the graft and initiative belonged to Vize. Within a year he had gone from three to twenty-one companies, recruited in the initial stages from IRB circles as probably directed by Collins, opened

72:193 (1993), 50, 56; Michael Collins to Patrick Clinton, 30 June 1920, Mulcahy papers, UCDA, P7/A/11; *An tÓglach*, Easter 1965; MAI, BMH, Witness statements, WS/627, statement of Séamas Reader, pp 11–12; *Sunday Press*, 28 Feb. 1954. The rift between Robinson and Reader was obviously healed in the post-Treaty environment when the bigger split ironically appears to have acted as a binding agent on Clydeside with both men opposed to the Treaty and Reader taking command of the Scottish Brigade and IRB after Robinson and Branniff respectively. **14** Hart, *Mick*, p. 172 & p. 203; Michael Collins to Patrick Clinton, 30 June 1920, Mulcahy papers, UCDA, P7/A/11; Michael Collins to Joseph Vize, 14 Feb. 1920, Mulcahy papers, UCDA, P7/A/11; Personal information from Vize family, Wicklow, 14 Nov. 2006. Information on sinking of the *Clan Forbes* from 'British vessels lost at sea 1914–1918' by HMSO (1919) on website http://www.naval-history.net/WW1oMSLosses1918.htm , accessed 9 May 2008; Ó Baoighill, *Óglach na Rosann*, p. 157. **15** Patterson, 'Organisations in Scotland', 41; Peter Hart, 'Operations abroad: the IRA in Britain, 1919–23', *English Historical Review*, 115:460 (2000), 73; MAI, BMH, Witness statements, WS/776, statement of Joseph Booker, p. 1; WS/828, statement of Byrne, p. 2; WS/777, Mills statement, p. 2; Piaras Beaslaí, *Michael Collins and the making of a new Ireland* (Dublin, 1926), ii, 161; C. Desmond Greaves, *Liam Mellows and the Irish revolution* (London, 1971), p. 221.

up several gun-running and ammunition streams (due partly no doubt to his maritime connections), and organized a successful raid for arms on Hamilton Barracks. Vize also counselled against deployment of the Scottish Brigade in Ireland citing the ever-authoritative 'instructions from Collins' to remain in place and concentrate on supplies, though the irresistible mobility of the Irish in Scotland (rather than impetuous rebel hearts), did lead to the odd returning émigré, as Collins himself was.[16]

Things advanced also on the political front, though this was not without its own difficulties. Seán (or Jack) O'Sheehan was sent as a Sinn Féin organizer in 1918 with one source suggesting, rather unconvincingly, by Collins personally. O'Sheehan was certainly on the Ard-Chomhairle by 1918, and may have had some influence. However, it was that executive body that would have authorized the organizer's role, not any single individual. Vize seemed unsure of him but O'Sheehan helped overhaul Sinn Féin in Scotland to a remarkable degree: from one central club in Glasgow in 1917 (merged with the remnants of the pre-Rising Éire Óg cumann) to 75 clubs in 1919. He also established, with P.J. Little, a thriving republican press in Glasgow after Little's operation came under increasing pressure in Ireland with the suppression of his *New Ireland* paper in 1919. For good measure, the Glasgow Irish press baron and owner-editor of the city's main Irish newspaper, the *Glasgow Observer*, Charles Diamond, also weighed in on the propaganda front.[17] The politicos in Sinn Féin had done much to improve their attitude to republicanism after Vize's first year in Scotland but he remained, like many of Collins' clique, deeply suspicious of their commitment. Among them he identified only Séamas O'Keeffe as a particularly good sort 'but unfortunately blind, if he had his sight he would be a marvel . . . a great speaker, and a tower of strength to the cause over here'. He was joined by another blind Sinn Féin leader, Seán O'Shea, the Scottish delegate to the party's Ard-Fheiseanna for many years who had been active in Glasgow since 1915. This Homer

16 MAI, BMH, Witness statements, WS/828, statement of Byrne, pp 2–4, WS/696, statement of Henry O'Hagan, p. 7; Hart, *Mick*, p. 65.   17 John Burrowes, *Irish: the remarkable saga of a nation and a city* (Edinburgh, 2003), p. 227; Joe Vize to Michael Collins, 24 June 1920, UCDA, Mulcahy Papers, P7/A/11; Ó Baoighill, *Óglach na Rosann*, p. 156, 165; Colin S. Johnston, *Irish political and radical newspapers of the twentieth century: A Guide* (Jordanstown, 1981), pp 20–1; James E. Handley, *The Irish in modern Scotland* (Cork, 1947), p. 298; Owen Dudley Edwards, 'The Catholic press in Scotland since the restoration of the hierarchy', in David McRoberts (ed.), *Modern Scottish Catholicism* (Glasgow, 1979), pp 169–73. For references to O'Sheehan and Sinn Féin, see Richard P. Davis, *Arthur Griffith and non-violent Sinn Féin* (Dublin, 1974). Patrick Little (1884–1963), who became Minister of Posts and Telegraphs in de Valera's 1939 government, remaining in office until 1948, had a background in law but turned to nationalist propaganda prior to the Easter Rising. After *New Ireland* was suppressed and became *Old Ireland* in Glasgow from 1919 to 1921, Little involved himself with a host of other papers including *Dark Rosaleen* edited by O'Sheehan. Little married a Gàidhlig-speaking Highlander, Seonid Ní Leoid which possibly influenced his relocation to Scotland for a few years. He also helped make Glasgow the centre of anti-Treaty propaganda, see his articles in the *Capuchin Annual* (1942).

and Tiresias of the Irish republican movement in Scotland were joined in the political work by the 1916 skiver Tom McDonnell. Collins and Vize, however, worked
hard to sideline McDonnell in IRB circles, judging him to be 'lazy and lacklustre' if
not 'sleeping' entirely, after they failed to build enough of a case (dereliction of duty?)
against him.[18]

Collins' administrative flair and Vize's energy and enthusiasm combined to tap
many sources in Scotland, some of which, like the wives of a bigamist were never to
meet each other. It is unclear why these paths were never to cross, though overall
IRB control, possible penetration by enemies and spies, and/or strategic support for
certain IRA companies over others may all have played a part in this circumspection.
Collins was always keenly aware of the dangers of an exiled support network; he
knew and understood the transitory nature, low pay and dissonance of the Irish in
Britain. He saw their vulnerabilities and thus maintained other links and sources of
information and arms. For Scotland, Derry's intelligence officer, George Armstrong
(who worked the 'Scotch boat'), combined with Collins' personal publican and land-
lord in Dublin, Liam Devlin (also from Derry originally but who had been an IRB
man in Greenock) to provide occasional back-up knowledge and expertise. He also
ensured Vize had ready replacements and deputies should arrests take place.
Interestingly, when the crackdown came Vize had already departed for greater things,
though he would later return to Scotland with not a little acrimony.[19]

Occasionally, Collins asked Vize to do some detective work on individuals who had
fled to Scotland, and responded in turn to requests from Vize to check up on some
of the Glasgow personalities. Slackers and malcontents – at one time an entire
Glasgow company of the IRA – were stood down or suspended. Vize made a few
appeals to Collins and GHQ to deal with the more irascible individuals, but mostly
acted on his own initiative on discipline matters confident that his friend and superior would back him if necessary. For his part, Collins happily obliged and, when the
proverbial storm broke over the Glasgow accounts, he allowed nothing to come back
on Vize even though a scapegoat would have conveniently fended-off the thunder-
ings of Cathal Brugha. Not that there was an actual hole in the Scottish account
books, more a virtual hole, created by the necessity of disguising the multiple supply
lines, protecting IRB channels, and ironically, but most importantly, protecting
civilian contractors.[20]

18 Patterson, 'Organisations in Scotland', 51; Joe Vize to Michael Collins, 20 Feb. 1920,
UCDA, Mulcahy Papers, P7/A/11; Joe Vize to Michael Collins, 15 Feb. 1920, UCDA,
Mulcahy Papers, P7/A/11; Michael Collins to Joe Vize, 26 Feb. 1920, UCDA, Mulcahy
Papers, P7/A/11. **19** Joe Vize to Michael Collins, 4 Mar. 1920, UCDA, Mulcahy Papers,
P7/A/11; Beaslaí, pp 37–8; Coogan, *Collins*, pp 134–5; John Cooney, 'The Irish Republican
Brotherhood in Scotland: the untold stories of Andrew Fagan and Michael O'Carroll', in
T.M. Devine (ed.), *Celebrating Columba* (Edinburgh, 1997), p. 137. **20** Michael Collins to
Joe Vize, 26 May 1920, UCDA, Mulcahy Papers, P7/A/11; Joe Vize to Michael Collins, 11

The mechanics and record of the Scottish arms smuggling operation of Collins and Vize, which contributed so centrally to the major post-Treaty rift between Brugha and Collins (as it did the widening gulf between the army and the Brotherhood), has been a contested one. The Irish in Scotland grandee, James Handley, was comprehensively challenged on his analysis by Patterson who, like Cooney, Ó Baoighill and Hart did not have access to the important Bureau of Military History witness statements when writing. Despite varying interpretations of the importance of the republican movement in Scotland among these writers, they all find common cause with the majority of Collins' biographers in delineating the contours of his Scottish operation. The agreed premise is tight IRB control of arms procurement and supply, deliberate obfuscation of the IRA, and a similar ostracisation of the Volunteers from full access to funds.[21] The truth, as acknowledged most recently by Hart, is a little more difficult and, indeed, perplexing. Certainly, Vize, no doubt on Collins' instructions, ensured IRB control of the emergent companies by recruiting them from existent circles, but he equally displaced and marginalized IRB men, such as Séamus Reader, Joseph Robinson and Liam Gribbon, who were unwilling to cooperate. There was also an outmanoeuvring of the Volunteers though this may also have been related to the penchant among some of that number to collect and send arms to the remnants of the Irish Citizen Army. Neither Vize nor Collins had serious leftist sympathies and their joint fear of communist or socialist influence (a difficulty in itself in a country where socialist ideas had growing support) may have affected their actions. The nub, however, of the problem for many in republican circles in Scotland, as well as in Dublin when it finally emerged, was Collins' sanction for the use of civilians at the heart of the Scots' arms smuggling network.[22]

Much of the strength of the Collins and Vize network rested not on the traditional centre of Glasgow (where the Scottish IRA's 1st Battalion was based), but in the 2nd (Lanarkshire) and 3rd (Edinburgh) Battalion areas. Two reasons appear to be behind this decision: firstly, the richest source of explosives and detonators lay in the Lanarkshire coalmining and steel-working districts of Hamilton, Bothwell and Motherwell (obtained as often for free, contrary to Patterson's estimation, from Volunteers and sympathizers as those that were paid for), and Edinburgh (or rather

June 1920, UCDA, Mulcahy Papers, P7/A/11; Joe Vize to Michael Collins, 26 Mar. 1920, Mulcahy Papers, P7/A/11; Joe Vize to Michael Collins, undated (received stamp, 8 Apr. 1920); Patterson, 'Organisations in Scotland', 53, 55; Beaslaí, pp 161–2; Coogan, *Collins*, p. 174; T. Ryle Dwyer, *Michael Collins* (Cork, 1990), pp 130–1; Andrew McCarthy, 'Michael Collins: Minister for Finance, 1919–22', in Gabriel Doherty & Dermot Keogh (eds), *Michael Collins and the making of the Irish Free State* (Cork, 1998), pp 60–1; Rex Taylor, *Michael Collins* (London, 1958), pp 108–9; Leon Ó Broin, *Michael Collins* (Dublin, 1980), p. 90; Frank O'Connor, *The big fellow* (New York), pp 139–40. **21** Handley, *Irish in modern Scotland*, p. 299; Patterson, 'Organisations in Scotland', 58–9; Cooney, *Irish Republican Brotherhood*, pp 137–8; Ó Baoighill, *Óglach na Rosann*, pp 154–7; Hart, 'Operations Abroad', 73–4. **22** Hart, 'Operations abroad', 80; Patterson, 'Organisations in Scotland', 44, 50; Greaves, *Liam Mellows*, pp 224–5.

Leith), which was the entrepôt for Vize's Hamburg contacts for guns; secondly, the strength and influence of the recalcitrant 'A' company in the Glasgow 1st Battalion and in particular their socialist and even Scots' nationalist entanglements and intriguing dissuaded Collins and Vize from using them. Instead, they employed the services of two businessmen with no connection or membership of any republican body, a Derry coal merchant named James Chambers and another Glasgow provisions merchant, Bernard McCabe. In Edinburgh, they had a similarly inconspicuous and unaffiliated shopkeeper named Gordon and his wife to deal with the Hamburg guns arriving up from Leith (where Connolly had enjoyed a strong influence and where a unit of the Irish Citizen Army was based). These individuals appear to have been brought onto the Purchasing Committee (Gordon even paid off the dealers and collected the arms) in a move that was to prove immensely unpopular, probably in contravention of standing orders, and ultimately would lead to court martials, resignations and splits that reached the ear of Brugha himself.[23] There are several ironies in this even though it might be expected that Collins, the accountant, and Vize, the bank manager's son, would have considerable respect for and trust in men of commerce. Chiefly, it is in contradistinction to the oft-repeated charge of only dealing through IRB channels, and even ensuring those Volunteers involved in the arms trade were sworn in as members of the Organization, if they were not already so. Moreover, although buying guns was tricky and normal rules rarely applied, their almost total abandonment in Scotland – use of civilians, high spending sprees and (in spite of Hart's doubts) holding weapons back in Scottish dumps – all challenge the notion of Collins' normally tight control, his judicious sense of fiscal propriety and probity, and his scrupulous sense of security and fear of penetration.[24] It would be easy to admit, as Lee points out, that Collins was a 'cluster of personality types' and thus prone like most complex individuals to apparently conflicting behaviour, or to embrace the popular myth of the big fellow who broke even his own rules to get the job done and that was all that mattered. In reality there was a wider phenomenon at play here and it is one suggested not just by the morass that the Scottish operation

23 MAI, BMH, Witness statements, WS/776, statement of Booker, pp 1–2; WS/828, statement of Byrne, pp 2–7; WS/696, statement of O'Hagan, pp 4–7; WS/777, statement of Mills, p. 2, 5–7; Cooney, *Irish Republican Brotherhood*, p. 143; Michael Collins to Richard Mulcahy, 9 Apr. 1922, N[ational] A[rchives] of I[reland], Dáil Éireann Papers, DE/2/435, correspondence mainly between Collins and Art O'Brien concerning links between Irish republicans and Scottish nationalists; Vize to Collins, 20 Feb. & 15 May 1920, UCDA, Mulcahy Papers, P7/A/11; John Carney to Cathal Brugha, 7 Dec. 1921 and 21 Feb. 1922, NLI, Seán O'Mahony Papers, MS.24, 474. 24 Hart, *Mick*, p. 263; Joe Vize to Michael Collins, 21 Feb. 1920, UCDA, Mulcahy Papers, P7/A/11; Michael Collins to Joe Vize, 4 Mar. 1920, UCDA, Mulcahy Papers, P7/A/11; Michael Collins to Joe Vize, 9 Apr. 1920, UCDA, Mulcahy Papers, P7/A/11; Joe Vize to Michael Collins, 26 Mar. 1920, UCDA, Mulcahy Papers, P7/A/11; ; Joe Vize to Michael Collins, 25 June. 1920, UCDA, Mulcahy Papers, P7/A/11; Joe Vize to Michael Collins, 3 July 1920, UCDA, Mulcahy Papers, P7/A/11; MAI, BMH, Witness statements, WS/828, statement of Byrne, p. 6; WS/777, statement of Mills, p. 3, 5.

became but by the fact that the English one did not become the same. This was Collins' continuing sense of nonchalance about Scotland, his instinctive anglocentric view which was the product as much of his formative experience in the London civil service as it was in his war with the British. Interestingly, this was in spite of his knowledge of Scottish nationalists whose ministrations he had been in receipt of since 1919.[25]

Scottish nationalist interest in the Irish national movement had strong roots in fin-de-siècle pan-Celticism, though the tributaries of the 'New Departure' had included an American Fenian-Scottish nationalist-Irish Land League axis for a brief period. Scots filtered in and out of the early Sinn Féiners in Glasgow and London (with its large exiled Scots community many of who were wealthy, thrifty and lonely in the metropolis and so welcoming of an appropriate socio-political and cultural set), and a few even took part in the Easter Rising. How aware Collins was of this is difficult to say, but Art O'Brien in London quickly became his advisor and their (the Scots nationalists') advocate.[26] As early as 1919 his contacts with the dynamo of Scottish Gaelic nationalism, Ruairidh Erskine of Mar (1869–1960), arranged a meeting between the latter's Parisian supporter and the Irish Versailles delegation. Since launching the *Guth na Bliadhna* newspaper in 1904, Erskine had been a strong supporter of a pan-Celtic approach to language revival and independence in both countries. His 1919 appeal drew little support for the Scottish nationalist claims, but aided by another London-based Scot, William Gillies (Liam Mac Giolla Íosa), who was an active Gaelic Leaguer and friend of Art O'Brien, they eventually dipped into Collins' war chest. This was initially with the modest goal of supporting a joint Hiberno-Caledonian propaganda paper named *Liberty*, though it rapidly developed into a quest for arms. The support for an independent Scottish worker's republic from the increasingly Connollyite Glasgow Marxist, John Maclean (and Erskine and Gillies' support for same), led inexorably towards the push for a Scottish insurrection.[27] Collins felt this to be a little premature, writing to O'Brien in March 1921

25 J.J. Lee, 'The challenge of a Collins biography', in Doherty & Keogh (eds), *Collins*, p. 22. For the operation of arms routes in England see work of Birmingham Purchasing Officer, James Cunningham, who had been in the Glasgow IRB in 1918, MAI, BMH, Witness statements, WS/922, statement of James Cunningham.   26 Máirtín Ó Catháin, 'Michael Davitt and Scotland', *Saothar*, 25 (2000), pp 19–28; Peter Lynch, *The SNP: the history of the Scottish National Party* (Cardiff, 2002), pp 28–34; *Glasgow Observer*, 25 May 1907; *Sinn Féin*, 15 Aug. 1908; 21 Nov. 1908; *Sinn Féin Weekly*, 8 July 1911.   27 Erskine of Mar to Art O'Brien, 10 May 1919, NLI, A[irt] Ó B[riain] P[apers], MS. 8427, Folio 1; Art O'Brien to Erskine of Mar, 12 May 1919, AÓBP, MS. 8427, Folio 1; Francis Stewart to Art O'Brien, 23 May 1919, AÓBP, MS. 8427, Folio 1; Art O'Brien to Erskine of Mar, 19 Dec.1919, AÓBP, MS. 8427, Folio 1; James D. Young, *The rousing of the Scottish working class* (London, 1979), pp 194–5, 205–8; and James D. Young, 'The Irish immigrants' contribution to Scottish Socialism, 1880–1926', *Saothar*, 13 (1988), 95–6; Peter Beresford Ellis, *The Celtic revolution* (Talybont, 1985), pp 46–7.

that 'they do not appreciate the particular difficulties they are up against'. He believed that even when the Irish had been at their 'weakest point' (1904–8), they had still be stronger than the Scots. He went on to scotch the idea of issuing a 1916-type proclamation saying it would only raise false hopes and that ultimately (and it serves as a judgement of Collins on the Easter Rising itself), 'failure in this manner would mean much more even to the small group than years of tireless labour and non-recognition'.[28] O'Brien responded that though he doubted Erskine of Mar's estimation of the situation in Scotland and the movement's levels of support, he was 'wont to believe' the same line from Gillies. At this point de Valera got wind of the Scottish nationalist channel, though expressed himself like Collins, doubtful of their use and was clearly somewhat out of the Celtic loop, asking Collins if Gillies was 'the Gaelic Leaguer with the kilt'.[29] Collins concurred, however, with O'Brien on Gillies' value, judging him to be 'a very genuine man', though he brushed off Dev by declaring that it was too long a story to relate about how they engaged with Gillies and he would anyway need to refresh his memory first. His understanding of Scotland, however, showed its limits in his belief, conveyed soon after to O'Brien, that the coal strike of April 1921, might 'have the effect of reviving a spirit of nationality in the Scots generally' and possibly even 'armed conflicts'.[30] Erskine and Gillies continued to make representations to O'Brien and Collins especially with the founding of the Scots National League and Fianna na hAlba as the respective political and military wings of their movement. They clearly felt the time was near to try and emulate the Rising and return reciprocal support thereafter (presumably in an independent Scotland) to the Irish. Counsels of restraint, however, met the ardour of these 1916 groupies rather than weaponry; Collins had been burned already earlier in the year over the Glasgow accounts and no amount of admiration for Gillies was likely to persuade him down another blind Scottish alley. Some Scots left for Ireland anyway to fight and hopefully in some way presage a Scottish war of liberation. Despite their great personal bravery, considerable sacrifice and obscurantist ideology, they were mostly noted with curiosity.[31]

28 Michael Collins to Art O'Brien, 11 Mar. 1921, NAI, DE/2/435; Michael Collins to Art O'Brien, 21 Mar. 1921, NAI, DE/2/435. **29** Art O'Brien to Michael Collins, 29 Mar. 1921, NAI, DE/2/435; Eamonn de Valera to Michael Collins, 2 Apr. 1921, NAI, DE/2/435. **30** Michael Collins to Eamonn de Valera, 5 Apr. 1921, NAI, DE/2/435; Michael Collins to Art O'Brien, 8 Apr. 1921, NAI, DE/2/435. **31** Art O'Brien to Michael Collins, 28 July 1921, NAI, DE/2/435; Michael Collins to Art O'Brien, 29 July 1921, NAI, DE/2/435, Art O'Brien to Michael Collins, 31 Aug. 1921, NAI, DE/2/435; Art O'Brien to Michael Collins, 1 Sept. 1921, NAI, DE/2/435; Art O'Brien probably to Michael Collins ('C'), 22 Oct. 1921, NAI, DE/2/435; Art O'Brien probably to Michael Collins ('C'), 1 Nov. 1921, NAI, DE/2/435; Stephen Coyle to author, 1 July 1991, Private Papers of Stephen Coyle, Glasgow kindly donated by same, letter dated 1 July 1991; *Irish Weekly*, 21 Mar. 1970; *Irish Democrat*, 8 Sept. 2006; Greaves, *Liam Mellows*, p. 231. Support did occasionally go the other way and the acclaimed poet, Pearse Hutchinson's father, who was a leading republican in Glasgow, recalls a number of Sinn Féiners in the city joined the Scottish National Party (probably the Scots National League), but later left because of the anti-Catholicism of some members; see

By early 1921, the very name of Scotland must have raised Collins' hackles. He had recalled Vize in July the previous year appointing him head of purchasing only to lose his trusted comrade within two months in a raid. From his cell in Mountjoy, Vize still managed to provide Collins with information, but Liam Mellows freshly returned from the United States, was appointed Director of Purchases in his place in part through Brugha's influence. Collins tried to hang on with Joe Furlong quietly remaining in place in the background and maintaining some kind of continuity, but the Volunteers were increasingly taking hold especially after a number of key arrests in December followed by Brugha's inquiry into the accounts from January well into March 1921.[32] John Carney was nominally in charge of Scotland, but Furlong kept the engine ticking over for the IRB interest. Eventually, Mellows headed for Glasgow himself, as unsatisfied as Collins was dismayed with things there, but probably for different reasons. Furlong appears to have remained undetected though it is possible the death of his brother Matthew in an explosion around the time of Vize's arrest had also removed a trusted courier and complicated his work. Mellows avoided IRB meetings, however, which may have aided Furlong's attempts to remain unmolested. As able as he may have been to avoid the attentions of Brugha and Mellows, Furlong and his 2nd Battalion coterie in Lanarkshire were less able to avoid the intervention of D.P. Walsh. His position was unclear though he may have been the Volunteers' Scottish Director of Purchases nominee (whether they knew or not of Furlong's work and his local pro-Collins IRB team of Andrew Fagan, Joe Booker, James Byrne and Patrick Mills). When Mellows arrived Walsh was already busy organising a rescue attempt for 'on-the-run' Sligo IRA leader, Frank Carty, who had fled to Glasgow after being sprung from jail in Northern Ireland. The resulting 'Smashing of the Van' mark two ended in two policemen being shot, one of whom was killed in a city centre shoot-out forever embedded in Glasgow mythology, a massive crackdown and round-up of republicans in Glasgow, no release for Carty and an incandescent Minister for Finance back in Dublin.[33] Mellows escaped arrest, as did Walsh and faced instead the ire of Collins on their return, which probably gave the cells of Barlinnie Prison a sudden welcoming air. Collins' anger though was less

MAI, BMH, Witness statements, WS/863, p. 12.   **32** Memorandum from Michael Collins to Joe Vize, 10 July 1920, UCDA, Mulcahy papers, P7/A/11. Joe Vize was asked back by Collins who wished to push him into the Director of Purchases position and not as Patterson wrongly asserts, as a result of the later accounts inquiry, 54–5. See Greaves, *Liam Mellows*, p. 224; Beaslaí, p. 70, 161–3; Hart, 'Operations abroad', 80; Hart, *Mick*, p. 260. **33** John Carney to Cathal Brugha, 7 Dec. 1921, NLI, Seán O'Mahony Papers, MS. 24, 474; MAI, BMH, Witness statements, WS/676, statement of Liam Brady, pp 75–8; WS/846, statement of Dominic Doherty, pp 3–7; WS/776, statement of Booker, pp 3–4; WS/777, statement of Mills, pp 5–6; Greaves, *Liam Mellows*, p. 221, 232; Hart, 'Operations abroad', 84–5; Ó Baoighill, *Óglach na Rosann*, pp 167–71; Cooney, *Irish Republican Brotherhood*, pp 144–54; 'Statement of military activities of Frank Carty, late O/C 4th Brigade, 3rd Western Division (1935)', Private Papers of Stephen Coyle, Glasgow, pp 15–18; Stephen Coyle, 'The smashing of the van', unpublished article; Florence O'Donoghue, *Sworn to be free* (Tralee, 1971), pp 108–15, 122–9.

about the failed rescue than its attempt in the first place which Mellows cautioned in vain against, and also the tightening grip of the authorities in Scotland which ground the arms trade to a virtual halt.

The Truce of July 1921 temporarily put some of Collins' worries about Scotland to rest, and he appeared in even better form (minus the question of the Glasgow legal fees which rumbled on long after his death) after the 'Van' prisoners were all acquitted in August. He missed the chance to accost Lloyd George in his Gairloch idyll, Boland and McGrath going with Scottish Sinn Féin supremo, Jack O'Sheehan as chauffeur and engaging in a mini-Mexican stand-off on a narrow west Highland road where a government car could not pass. He did, however, apparently reach Glasgow finally sometime later that year on his way to the Treaty negotiations in London, though briefly only and probably to try and heal the widening rift in the IRA there over the leftovers of the larger Volunteers–IRB rancour.[34] Eventually, with his mind on more pressing matters than the feuds of the Glasgow Irish, he despatched a liberated Joe Vize to Scotland possibly around or just before December 1921 to put the division to bed and, more importantly, secure supplies for despatch to Ireland through the trusted Purchasing Committee and 2nd Battalion men. The main diffi-culty was the decision of the O/C Scottish Brigade, John Carney, to dismiss every officer of the 2nd Battalion after they failed firstly to attend an inquiry of the dreaded Scottish accounts, and secondly, to attend their consequent court martial. Vize quickly summoned Carney, informed him that for the space of a week he was in command of the Scottish Brigade and promptly re-appointed the 2nd Battalion men, promising an inquiry which never occurred. But this was more than a mere enforced truce, it quickly took on aspects of a putsch against Volunteer control and any possi-bility presumably of Collins' adversaries (or the Scots nationalists and communists) having ready access to a pool of arms and ammunition after the Treaty.[35] This was certainly in keeping with Collins' eye for contingencies, though in this case the cost was high. It is often stated how stentorian and outraged opposition among the Irish in Scotland towards the Treaty was but Collins and Vize were greatly respected and admired, and it is undoubtedly the case that their handling of the 2nd Battalion purge and collectivisation of weaponry for transport (which led to seizure and arrests at Tollcross, Glasgow in December 1921), pushed many into the anti-Treaty camp including, potentially, someone even implicated in Collins' own death.[36]

34 *Sunday Mail*, 9 Dec. 1989; Art O'Brien to Michael Collins, 27 Apr. 1922, NAI, DE/2/435; MAI, S. Dougan document, Account of Mrs Boyle, Glasgow, A/13942; Richard Mulcahy to Major-General Vize, 15 May 1923 and Staff Captain Séamus Fullerton, Director of Purchases, Glasgow to Military Secretary, GHQ, Dublin, 7 Dec. 1922, document RohE/MOS; David Fitzpatrick, *Harry Boland's Irish revolution* (Cork, 2003), pp 232–4; *Glasgow Observer*, 26 Aug. 1922. 35 John Carney to Cathal Brugha, 22 Feb. 1922, NLI, Seán O'Mahony Papers, MS. 24, 474; MAI, BMH, Witness statements, WS/828, statement of Byrne, p. 8. 36 MAI, BMH, Witness statements, WS/863, statement of H. Warren Hutchinson, p. 3; Ó Baoighill, *Óglach na Rosann*, p. 171; Patterson, 'Organisations in Scotland', 58; *Big Issue*, 10–16 July 1997.

Collins' pre-emptive strike in the weeks before the signing of the Treaty paid some dividends in the months after, but the estrangement of Carney and his staff and the re-emergence to prominence of Joseph Robinson and 'A' company of the 1st Battalion, served as a rallying point for those opposed to the Treaty. Visits by Markievicz and de Valera took place before Collins and his colleagues, despite promises to the contrary, managed to take effect. This stole a march on the pro-Treaty side and the continuing propaganda effort (facilitated by the socialist presses in Glasgow) kept P.J. Little and Seán O'Sheehan's publications rolling out. By the end of March there were 33 Sinn Féin clubs and a number of committed activists such as Éamonn Mooney and Joseph Brown traversing substantial parts of the country to evangelize for the republican position. Simultaneously, the IRA was re-organized though in Scotland, with one or two minor exceptions, it was the propaganda war that dominated. This may have been, in part, due to Collins' successes against the Scottish IRA: his men controlled the arms trade, the dumps and the contacts, and he had a solid intelligence network dominated by the former London IRA quartermaster, Seán Golden, who may have known Glasgow well, and whose information eventually secured the 33 Scots deported to Mountjoy in the 1923 swoop on British-based anti-Treatyites.[37]

The manner of Michael Collins' death has had almost as much attention as his life. This JFK-type assassination mania also has its Scottish account focused on the role of his Glasgow-Irish armoured car driver, John 'Jock' McPeake (1896–1974). The theories have been well-documented in both John Feehan and Meda Ryan's books and in considerable detail in a series of *Glasgow Herald* articles published in 1996. Basic conspiracies allege McPeake's complicity based on his later defection to the republican side and comprise everything from his having actually fired the fatal shot to deliberately sabotaging covering fire and/or setting up the original ambush. Most of these theories arise out of the defection and suggest, supported of course by an alternative and largely apocryphal family account, that McPeake was working for the republicans all along.[38] This ignores the fact that McPeake had been arrested in the

37 Joseph Robinson to Eamonn Donnelly, 30 Mar. 1922, Private Papers of Stephen Coyle, Glasgow; Joseph Robinson to Eamonn Donnelly, 24 Apr. 1922, Private Papers of Stephen Coyle, Glasgow; Joseph Robinson to Eamonn Donnelly, 5 May. 1922, Private Papers of Stephen Coyle, Glasgow; Undated statement of Seán Mooney, p. 4, Private Papers of Stephen Coyle, Glasgow; Undated list of Sinn Féin/Cumann Poblacht na hÉireann n-Albain clubs, Private Papers of Stephen Coyle, Glasgow; MAI, BMH, Witness statements, WS/863, statement of Hutchinson, p. 5–11; WS/828, statement of Byrne, p. 8; Hart, 'Operations abroad', 99; Eunan O'Halpin, *Defending Ireland: the Irish state and its enemies since 1922* (Oxford, 1999), pp 20–1; Rex Taylor, *Assassination* (London, 1961), p. 107, 109, 128, 131. Golden may have been related to the Glasgow Fenian and Sinn Féiner, Séamas Golden, who died in November 1908. See National Archives of Scotland (NAS), HH/55/71, '1923–24 Irish disturbances' file for details on anti-Treaty activities in Glasgow. 38 John Feehan, *The shooting of Michael Collins – murder or accident* (Cork, 1981); Meda Ryan, *The day Michael*

Tollcross raid of December 1921, Collins' own tidying up of his Scottish munitions prior to the Treaty, and also that a number of Glasgow IRA men joined the fledgling Free State Army as they did the anti-Treaty IRA. Indeed, famously two members of the 'Smashing of the Van' debacle imprisoned together later faced each other on opposite sides in the civil war resulting in one of them being killed. Neither was defection itself particularly unusual given the earlier case, for example, of Glaswegian British soldier Peter Monahan, who joined the west Cork Brigade of Tom Barry before being killed at Crossbarry in March 1921.[39]

It is a loss to irony if not a pity in some senses that Jock McPeake did not kill Michael Collins. We could then have added to the many other counter-factual narratives surrounding Collins a peculiarly Macbethian end if not an assault on his otherwise punctilious efforts. It remains the case, however, that in several important respects Collins, often in spite of good management and skilled operators like Vize, made serious errors. Much of this is attributable to his disinterest rather than gaps in his knowledge of which there were few. Collins lost the war in Scotland and Scotland almost cost him the war in Ireland so that by the time of his death he was, as Pádraic Colum said of Arthur Griffith, a man who, while not a failure, had failed in certain respects. In contrast it was left to another returned exile, de Valera, who wrote 'of all the children of Irish race in foreign lands, none have been more faithful than you in Scotland. With the same unity and devotion everywhere we cannot fail. In the name of all who stand for the independence of the motherland, I send you greetings'.[40] Politic flattery no doubt, but it was Dev rather than Mick who said it. Both were returned émigrés, but it was de Valera who displayed the keener awareness of the opportunities offered by the closest neighbour Ireland had. Collins' unwillingness to travel out of Dublin certainly put him at a disadvantage in this regard. His desk-bound existence has been sacrificed in most narratives for the on-the-run image but both restricted him to ever-decreasing circles. Others filled the vacuum and Collins, and indeed his associates, were obscured by the very underground they cultivated.

Collins was shot (Dublin, 1989); *Glasgow Herald*, 12, 13 & 14 Sept. 1996; MAI, BMH, Witness statements, WS/776, statement of Booker, p. 4; Pádraic O'Farrell, *Who's who in the Irish war of independence and civil war, 1916–23* (Dublin, 1997), p. 70, 176; *An Phoblacht*, 22 Dec. 1928; 18 May 1929. The 'McPeake Testimonial' indicates the released man got more than the £60 in a Dublin whip-round, as suggested by Coogan, *Collins*, p. 390. **39** Cooney, *Irish Republican Brotherhood*, p. 152; *Rosc*, Mar. 1966. **40** *Poblacht na hÉireann (Scottish edition)*, 18 Nov. 1922.

Notes on contributors

FRANK FERGUSON is a research associate in literature and language at the Institute of Ulster Scots Studies at the University of Ulster. He is the editor of *Ulster-Scots writing: an anthology* (2008).

PETER GRAY took his undergraduate and doctoral degrees at the University of Cambridge before holding research fellowships at the Institute of Irish Studies at Queen's University Belfast, and at Downing College, Cambridge. He taught Irish and British history at the University of Southampton 1996–2005, before returning to Belfast to take up the positions of Professor of Modern Irish History and Director of Research in Irish and British History. In 2004 he was the Burns Library Visiting Professor in Irish Studies at Boston College, Massachusetts. He is chair of the Royal Irish Academy's National Committee for Historical Sciences.

ANDREW HOLMES is a lecturer in modern Irish history at Queen's University Belfast. He is author of *The shaping of Ulster Presbyterian belief and practice, 1770–1840* (2006).

KEVIN J. JAMES is associate professor in the Department of History and Centre for Scottish Studies at the University of Guelph. He is the author of *Handloom weavers in Ulster's linen industry, 1815–1914* (2006); his current research examines the history of tourism in Scotland and Ireland.

S. KARLY KEHOE is a graduate of the University of Glasgow and currently holds a SSHRC postdoctoral fellowship in the Department of History at the University of Guelph. She researches gender, religion, migration and ethnicity in Scotland and Canada.

SUSAN KELLY is a research assistant at the University of Ulster, Centre for the History of Medicine in Ireland (CHOMI). Her PhD research topic was childhood tuberculosis in the north of Ireland. She is currently working on the history of polio in Ireland. Her research interests are history of medicine, history of childhood, and oral history.

PATRICK MAUME is a graduate of University College Cork and Queen's University Belfast; he has taught in history and politics departments and has worked as a researcher for the Dictionary of Irish Biography since 2003. He has published biographies of Daniel Corkery and D.P. Moran and a survey of early twentieth-century Irish nationalist political culture, and has edited several texts for the UCD

Press Classics of Irish History reprint series. He has also worked on Irish newspaper history.

RICHARD B. MCCREADY gained a PhD in history from the University of Dundee for research on the influence of the Irish in nineteenth- and twentieth-century Dundee. Along with teaching politics and history, he has been a parliamentary assistant in Holyrood and Westminster and National Secretary of the Catholic Church's Justice and Peace Commission in Scotland. He is currently an elected member of Dundee City Council. He is an honorary Associate Researcher at the Centre for the Study of Religion and Politics, University of St Andrews.

CLARE M. NORCIO is a doctoral candidate in comparative history at Brandeis University. His thesis examines the relationship between people and landscape in nineteenth-century Ulster.

DR MÁIRTÍN Ó CATHÁIN lectures in modern history at the University of Central Lancashire. His research focuses on the political history of the Irish in Scotland from the mid-nineteenth to the early twentieth century, the history of the Fenian movement in Scotland and internationally, and aspects of labour and radical history.

AMY O'REILLY is a doctoral candidate in history at the University of New Brunswick. Her research involves community identity and cultural expression among Protestant and Catholic Irish immigrants in late eighteenth- and early nineteenth-century Glasgow.

MATTHEW POTTER is an IRCHSS Post-Doctoral Fellow in the History Department of the University of Limerick, where he is working on a project entitled *Urban government and civic cultures in Ireland since 1800*. He is the author of *The government and the people of Limerick: the history of Limerick Corporation/City Council, 1197–2006* (2006) and *First citizens of the Treaty City: the mayors and mayorality of Limerick, 1197–2007* (2007).

Index

Aberdeen, 114
agriculture, 8, 23–34
Alison, William, 105
America, 26, 27, 29, 36, 42, 51, 57, 87, 88,
   135, 160, 172
Anglo-Irish Union, 1800, 62, 65, 93, 108, 110
anglophobia, 8, 10
Anglo-Scottish Union, 1707, 67, 93, 94, 108,
   109, 110, 115, 117
anti-Catholicism, 7, 35, 55, 56, 80, 82, 85, 90,
   157, 158. See also Orange Order
Antrim, County, 9, 23, 24, 26, 27, 31, 32, 33,
   63, 64, 66, 69, 70, 71, 106, 123
apostolic of Finvoy: see Elder, James
Argyll, 142
Ashe, Thomas, 164
Austin, Alfred, 17–18, 22
Australia, 26, 135
Austria, 85, 86

Balfour, Gerald, 15, 19
Belfast, 7, 49, 55, 56, 57, 58, 59, 64, 65, 66, 70,
   72, 76, 77, 78, 82, 87, 91, 92, 106, 122,
   123, 125, 126, 127, 128, 130, 131, 163, 164
Berwick, 109
Bicheno, J.E. 96, 99, 104
Boer War, 141
Boland, Harry, 173
Bonaparte, Charles Louis Napoleon,
   Napoleon III, 65, 85
Branniff, Daniel, 160, 162–164
Breadalbane, 2nd marquess of: see Campbell,
   John
Brice, Revd Edward, 59
British empire, 47, 88
Brown, Revd John, 54
Brugha, Cathal, 167–9, 172, 173
Bryce, R.J., 106
Burns, Robert, 9, 64, 66, 67, 78, 79, 150
Butler, Sr Margaret, 43

Callaghan, Daniel, 101
Campbell, John, 2nd marquess of
   Breadalbane, 82–3
Carmichael, Alexander, 161
Carrigan, Charles, 161

Carty, Frank, 172
Catholic emancipation, 38
Catholicism, 7, 8, 10, 31, 33, 35–41, 44–7, 50,
   52, 56, 60, 61, 77, 80, 83, 85, 86, 88, 89,
   93, 95, 100–4, 111, 113, 116, 117, 134,
   135–9, 141–6, 148, 150, 157, 158, 159,
   161, 166
Chalmers, Revd Thomas, 9, 51, 54, 80, 82,
   84, 93, 95, 96–107, 157–8. See also Free
   Church of Scotland
Charles I, 53, 121
Charles II, 121
Church of Scotland, 50, 51, 55, 60, 79, 80, 81,
   82, 83, 84, 97, 121, 122, 141, 148, 152,
   157
Clapperton, Robert, 136
Coleridge, Samuel Taylor, 66, 69
Collins, Michael, 10, 160–75
constructive unionism, 8, 20–2. See also
   unionism
Cooke, Henry, 10, 55, 76, 77, 80, 81, 85, 91,
   106, 124
Cork, County, 7, 45, 101, 109, 116, 160, 175
covenanters, 53, 58
Crawford, A.G. 59
Crewe, 1st marquess of: see Houghton,
   Robert,
Cromwell, Oliver, 7, 121
Cullen, Paul, archbishop of Dublin
   (Catholic), 52, 89, 130, 137, 143

Dargan, William, 90
Derrick, J. O'Donnell, 141
Derry, 53, 54, 57, 63, 78, 79, 88, 167, 169. See
   also Londonderry
Diamond, Charles, 166
diaspora, Irish, 134, 135, 136, 139, 146, 149,
   157, 160. See also migration
Donegal, County, 15, 16, 17, 19, 26, 63
Douglas, Thomas, 153–4.
Down, County, 23, 63, 164
Doyle, James, bishop of Kildare and
   Leighlin, 95, 96, 98, 99, 100–1, 102, 104
Dromore, bishop of: see Percy, Thomas
Dublin, 8, 14, 22, 39, 49, 87, 101, 102, 103,
   109, 111, 114, 116, 118, 120, 121, 122,

127, 128, 130, 140, 143, 162, 163, 167,
    168, 172, 175; archbishop of (Catholic):
    see Cullen, Paul; archbishop of (Church
    of Ireland): see Whately, Richard
Dublin International Exhibition, 1853, 90
Duffy, Joseph, 162
Dundas, Henry, 1st Viscount Melville, 115
Dundee, 10, 37, 134–46; bishop of: see Smith,
    James
Dunkild, bishop of: see Rigg, George

Easter rising, 1916, 161, 166, 170, 171
Ecclesiastical Titles Act, 1851, 85
Edgar, Revd John, 55, 90
Edinburgh, 29, 37, 41, 56, 72, 87, 105, 114,
    137, 168, 169
Elder, James, apostolic of Finvoy, 79
Episcopalians, 29, 32, 53, 83, 84, 145
Erskine, Ruairidh, 170, 171
Eyre, Charles, archbishop of Glasgow, 44, 136

Fagan, Thomas, 23–4, 167, 172
famine, great, 89, 90, 93, 94, 100, 106, 134, 135
famines, 93, 101
Fenianism, 78, 89, 170, 174
Fermanagh, County, 144, 162, 163
Fleming, Robert, 76, 84, 86
France, 22, 29, 36, 41, 42, 45, 46, 65, 84, 85,
    88, 108, 109, 115
franchise reform, 115
Franciscan Sisters, 36, 37, 39, 40–7
Free Church of Scotland, 51, 82, 84, 141, 157
Frongoch prison camp, 160, 162
Furlong, Joseph, 11, 160, 165, 172

Gaelic language, 54, 64, 89, 148, 170, 171
Galway, County, 16, 87, 110, 111
Garden, Sr Mary, 43–4
Germany, 22, 128, 129
Gillies, William, 170, 171
Glagow, 7, 10, 35–47, 53, 54, 64, 81, 91, 95,
    96, 106, 114, 136, 141, 142, 144, 147–59,
    160–75; archbishop of: see Eyre, Charles
Glorious Revolution, 50, 54, 56, 80, 112
Gray, John, vicar apostolic of the Western
    District, Scotland, 35

Hibernian Society of Glasgow, 10, 147–59
Holder, Joseph, 138
Home Rule, 12, 20, 59, 60, 64, 89, 134, 137,
    139–46, 161
Houghton, Robert, 1st marquess of Crewe,
    14, 15, 16, 19, 20

Hume, Joseph, 93
Humphrey, William, 145. See also Puseyism

Inverness, 40, 42
Irish Folklore Commission, 120
Irish Republican Army (IRA), 10, 162, 164,
    165, 167, 168, 172, 173, 174, 175
Irish Republican Brotherhood (IRB), 69,
    161, 162, 163, 164, 165, 167, 168, 169,
    170, 172, 173, 175. See also Fenianism
Irish Tourist Association, 15, 19, 20, 21
Irish Volunteers, 66, 144, 161–4, 168, 169,
    172, 173

Jacobites, 7, 94
James II, 89
James VI and I, 108
Johnston, William, 56

Kernohan, J.W., 59
Kerrin, Sr Helen, 43
Kildare, County, 26, 101; — and Leighlin,
    bishop of: see Doyle, James
Kilkenny, County, 111
Killen, Revd W.D., 52, 55, 56
Kirk, Robert, 120–2
Knox, John, 49, 50, 52, 56, 57, 58, 79, 80, 81,
    82, 85, 86, 91, 115, 117
Kyle, James, bishop of the Northern District,
    Scotland, 44–5

Lambert, Henry, 101
Land League, 139, 170
Lavelle, Revd Michael, 136, 138
Leitrim, County, 125
Limerick, County, 36, 42, 43, 44, 95, 110, 111,
    114, 116
Lincoln, Abraham, 88
Liverpool, 42, 43, 44, 139, 144, 145, 161, 162
Lloyd George, David, 173
Londonderry, County, 23, 24, 25, 26, 27, 28,
    29, 31, 76, 78, 150
Louth, County, 26, 27, 111
Lynch, James, coadjutor of the Western
    District, Scotland, 35

Madus, Magdalene, 128–9
Maguire, Patrick James, 162
Martin, Robert Montgomery, 101
Mayo, County, 16
McDonnell, Tom, 163, 167
MacEvilley, John, archbishop of Tuam, 138
McGinnes, Revd James

Mac Giolla Íosa, Liam: *see* Gillies, William
McIntosh, Sr Barbie, 45–6
McLeod, Andrew, 83
McMillan, Donald, 60
McNamara, Sr Anne, 43
McNamara, Sr Catherine, 43–4
McNamara, Sr Clare, 43
McNamara, Sr Mary, 43
McComb, William, 9, 55, 76, 77, 78–92
McCormick, Patrick, 161, 163, 164
McPeake, John, 174–5
MacPherson, James, 9, 64, 71
McCrie, Revd Thomas, 58
McSwiney, Sr Hannah, 45–6
McCulloch, J.R. 96
Mellows, Liam, 161, 165, 168, 171–3
Melville, 1st Viscount: *see* Dundas, Henry
migration, 35, 38, 39, 134, 136, 142, 146, 157,
    161, 163, 166, 168, 173
Monaghan, County, 27, 144
Montgomery, Henry, 59–60, 106
Moore, Frankfort, 92
Moore, Sr Anne, 42–3
Moore, Thomas, 42, 44, 78, 79, 92, 161
Municipal Corporations (Ireland) Act, 1840,
    116
Murdoch, John, vicar apostolic of Western
    District, Scotland, 35, 38, 43–5, 141–2

Napoleon III: *see* Bonaparte, Charles Louis
    Napoleon
National Aid and Dependants Fund, 163
National Board of Education (Ireland), 30,
    93
Nicholls, George, 104
Nightingale, Florence, 126
Northern District, Scotland, bishop of the:
    see Kyle, James
Northwest of Ireland Agricultural Society,
    26
Norway, 13

O'Brien, Art, 169, 170, 171, 173
O'Connell, Daniel, 10, 52, 77, 88, 89, 93, 96,
    101, 102, 115, 134, 142–4
O'Dowda, Mary, 18–19, 20
O'Malley, Revd Thaddeus, 104
O'Neill, Denis, 77–8
Orange Order, Loyalism, 7, 10, 134, 140,
    144–9, 157, 158
Ordnance Survey, 8, 23–33
O'Rourke, Hugh, 150, 155
Ossian, 9, 32, 64, 71, 77, 78, 87, 90, 91

Paine, Thomas, 76
Palmerston, 1st Viscount: *see* Temple, Henry
Papacy, 56, 84, 86
Parnell, Charles Stewart, 139
Peel, Robert, 80
Penal Laws, 112
Percy, Thomas, bishop of Dromore, 69, 70,
    71, 72
Phelan, Michael, 137
Plantation, 24, 28, 31, 59, 62,
Poor Law, 23, 24, 29, 36, 54, 81, 94, 101, 103,
    104, 106
Pope Leo XIII, 138, 139
Presbyterianism, 8, 9, 31, 38, 48, 49, 50–66,
    72, 76–92, 95, 106, 111
Prussia, 86, 88
Puseyism, 50, 52, 53, 80, 83, 84, 85

race, 28
Rebellion, 1798, 62, 65, 69, 72, 73, 78, 89.
    See also United Irishmen
Reformation, 9, 35, 41, 49, 53, 54, 56, 57, 58,
    76, 82, 83, 86, 87, 88, 90, 111
Repeal movement, 39, 89, 93
Revival, 1859, 40, 51, 56, 77, 85, 90
Ribbonism, 10, 147, 148, 149
Rigg, George, bishop of Dunkild, 137
Robinson, Joe, 165
Robinson, Séamus, 162, 163, 164,
Rome, 37, 45, 57, 60, 70, 83, 85, 86, 90, 91,
    137, 138, 139
Roxburgh, 109
Russell, T.W., 18
Russia, 85

Sadler, Thomas, 95
Scottish Highlands, 11, 12, 13, 14, 15, 16, 21,
    28, 123
Scott, Sir Walter, 7–8, 14, 19, 22, 35, 38, 52,
    54, 69, 78, 91, 129, 150
Scudamore, Charles, 127
Scullin, Frank, 161
Senior, Nassau, 98, 99, 104
Shand, Alexander Innes, 15, 17–19
Sinn Féin, 163, 166, 170, 171, 173, 174
Sisters of Mercy, 36, 37, 40, 41, 42, 46, 47
Sligo, County, 17, 27, 172
Smith, Alexander, coadjutor vicar apostolic
    of Western District, Scotland, 35, 43–7
Smith, James, 26, 32
Smith, James, bishop of Dundee, 137
Smith O'Brien, William, 104
sodalities, 39

South Africa, 141.
Spring Rice, Thomas, 95–100
St Patrick's day, 10, 40, 134–42, 146
St Vincent de Paul, Society of, 40, 139
Switzerland, 13, 15

Temple, Henry, 1st Viscount Palmerston,
    85
Templemoyle Agricultural Society, 29–30
Tenant-right, 90
Thomson, Samuel, 9, 62, 64, 65, 66, 67, 68,
    69, 71, 72, 73, 140
Tipperary, County, 163
tourism, 11, 12, 15, 17, 18, 19, 20, 21
Trevelyan, Charles, 106
Tuam, archbishop of: see MacEvilley, John
tuberculosis, 10, 119–32
Tyrone, County, 23, 26, 144

Ulster, 8, 9, 23–34, 49–61, 63–7, 76, 81–92,
    94, 106, 113, 116, 119, 122, 123, 124, 144,
    150, 157, 158
Ulster Scots, 8, 9, 25, 26–8, 31, 49, 52, 58, 59,
    67, 157
unionism, 49, 78, 95
United Irishmen, 9, 65–8, 76, 141, 157

Valera, Eamon de, 161, 166, 171, 174, 175
Victoria, Queen, 8, 22, 57, 78, 83, 86, 127, 141
Vize, Joseph, 160–3, 165–9, 172, 173, 175

Wales, 13, 14, 28, 36, 38, 80, 94, 112, 115, 132,
    147
Warwick, Revd James, 56
Waterford, County, 109, 110, 111, 114
Watson, Revd William, 58
Watts, Isaac, 78
Webb, Sidney & Beatrice, 109, 113
Wellesley, Arthur, 1st duke of Wellington, 77,
    95
Western District, Scotland, coadjutors of: see
    Lynch, James *and* Smith, Alexander
Western District, Scotland, vicar apostolic of
    the: see Gray, John *and* Murdoch, John
Wexford, County, 101, 162
Whately, Richard, archbishop of Dublin, 99,
    103–5
Whitlam, William, 130–1
Wicklow, County, 19
Witherow, Thomas, 53, 57, 58
Wordsworth, William, 66, 69

Young Ireland, 104